Black Celebrity, Racial Politics, and the Press

Shifting understandings and ongoing conversations about race, celebrity, and protest in the twenty-first century call for a closer examination of the evolution of dissent by black celebrities and their reception in the public sphere. This book focuses on the way the mainstream and black press have covered cases of controversial political dissent by African American celebrities from Paul Robeson to Kanye West. Jackson considers the following questions: (1) What unique agency is available to celebrities with racialized identities to present critiques of American culture? (2) How have journalists in both the mainstream and black press limited or facilitated this agency through framing? What does this say about the varying role of journalism in American racial politics? (3) How have framing trends regarding these figures shifted from the mid-twentieth century to the twenty-first century? Through a series of case studies that also includes Eartha Kitt, Tommie Smith and John Carlos, Sister Souljah, and Mahmoud Abdul-Rauf, Jackson illustrates the shifting public narratives and historical moments that both limit and enable African American celebrities in the wake of making public politicized statements that critique the accepted racial, economic, and military systems in the United States.

Sarah J. Jackson is an Assistant Professor of Communication Studies at Northeastern University. Her research examines the construction of social identities in national debates about citizenship, inequality, and social change. Jackson's research has appeared in *The International Journal of Press Politics* and *Feminist Media Studies*.

Routledge Transformations in Race and Media

Series Editors: Robin R. Means Coleman
University of Michigan, Ann Arbor

Charlton D. McIlwain *New York University*

1 **Interpreting Tyler Perry**
   Perspectives on Race, Class,
   Gender, and Sexuality
   *Edited by Jamel Santa Cruze Bell
   and Ronald L. Jackson II*

2 **Black Celebrity, Racial Politics, and the Press**
   Framing Dissent
   Sarah J. Jackson

Black Celebrity, Racial Politics, and the Press
Framing Dissent

By Sarah J. Jackson

NEW YORK AND LONDON

First published 2014
by Routledge
711 Third Avenue, New York, NY 10017

and by Routledge
2 Park Square, Milton Park, Abingdon, Oxon OX14 4RN

*Routledge is an imprint of the Taylor & Francis Group,
an informa business*

© 2014 Taylor & Francis

The right of Sarah J. Jackson to be identified as author of this work has been asserted by her in accordance with sections 77 and 78 of the Copyright, Designs and Patents Act 1988.

All rights reserved. No part of this book may be reprinted or reproduced or utilized in any form or by any electronic, mechanical, or other means, now known or hereafter invented, including photocopying and recording, or in any information storage or retrieval system, without permission in writing from the publishers.

Trademark Notice: Product or corporate names may be trademarks or registered trademarks, and are used only for identification and explanation without intent to infringe.

Library of Congress Cataloging-in-Publication Data

Jackson, Sarah J., 1982–
 Black celebrity, racial politics, and the press : framing dissent / Sarah J. Jackson.
   pages cm. — (Routledge transformations in race and media ; 2)
 Includes bibliographical references and index.
 1. African American political activists. 2. African American celebrities. 3. Blacks—Race identity. 4. African Americans—Politics and government. I. Title.
  E185.61.J153 2014
  323.1196'073—dc23
  2014001670

ISBN: 978-0-415-70707-7 (hbk)
ISBN: 978-1-315-88704-3 (ebk)

Typeset in Sabon
by Apex CoVantage, LLC

Printed and bound in the United States of America by Publishers Graphics, LLC on sustainably sourced paper.

Contents

List of Illustrations		vii
List of Tables		ix
Acknowledgements		xi
	Introduction	1
1	Paul Robeson at Peekskill, NY, 1949	20
2	Eartha Kitt, the White House, and Vietnam, 1968	45
3	Tommie Smith and John Carlos at the Mexico City Olympics, 1968	67
4	Sister Souljah, Rodney King, and the Future President, 1992	91
5	Mahmoud Abdul-Rauf and "The Star-Spangled Banner," 1996	116
6	Kanye West and Hurricane Katrina, 2005	140
	Conclusion: Black Celebrity, Racial Politics, and the Press: Going Forward	165
	Appendix	177
	Bibliography	179
	Index	199

Illustrations

1.1 Paul Robeson flanked by volunteer bodyguards and two American flags performs at the second Peekskill concert to benefit the Civil Rights Congress. 24
1.2 Peekskill, NY: An effigy of Paul Robeson hangs from rear of tow truck in Oregon Corners, Peekskill, NY, echoing the sentiments of the town's residents. 29
2.1 Eartha Kitt chats with Lady Bird Johnson and Katherine Peden at the White House in what the *Los Angeles Times* described as "smiles before the outburst." 46
2.2 Anti-Vietnam war protestors outside the White House carrying a sign reading: "Eartha Kitt Speaks for the Women of America." 55
3.1 In a lesser-known image of the Olympians, Tommie Smith triumphantly crosses the two-hundred-meter finish line at the 1968 Mexico City Games. John Carlos came in third after Australia's Peter Norman. Their later demonstration on the medal stand would become an iconic American image. 68
3.2 *Chicago Defender* editorial cartoon, "Flag Raising," October 26, 1968. 84
4.1 Rap artist Sister Souljah speaks at a conference in New York City on June 16, 1992. Souljah made claims that U.S. Presidential candidate Bill Clinton wasn't in touch with the problems of Black-America. Hip-hop star Doug E. Fresh is in the background. 94
5.1 Mahmoud Abdul-Rauf prays during the national anthem at his first game post-suspension. 117
6.1 Kanye West and Mike Meyers appear on NBC's "A Concert for Hurricane Relief." 141

Tables

7.1 Framing Trends and Frequency of Occurrence by Press
and Subject   167
A.1 Sources, Dates, and Number of Stories
Examined by Subject   178

Acknowledgements

Over the years more people than I will remember to thank here have offered insight to this project. Dr. Catherine R. Squires in particular has been an invaluable mentor, critic, and supporter. Her influence on and advocacy for my intellectual work cannot be measured. I would also like to thank Rose M. Brewer, Mark H. Pedelty, Brian G. Southwell, Gilbert B. Rodman, and Kirt H. Wilson, who not only provided immense feedback on this project but also the spaces for me to interrogate black celebrity dissent. Friends and colleagues who have offered support, unique perspectives, and humor to this work include Adrienne Alexander, Carole V. Bell, J. David Cisneros, Greg Goodale, Bethany Iverson, David J. Leonard, R. L'Heureux Lewis-McCoy, Jesica Speed, Suzanna Walters, and Brooke Foucault Welles. My student, Sonia Banaszczyk, played an indispensible role in preparing this volume for publication.

I would also like to acknowledge the members of the University of Michigan Communication Studies Hurricane Katrina research cluster, where my research into black celebrity dissent began. Thank you to Robin Means Coleman and Charlton McIlwain, whose work inspired mine long before I had the privilege to work with them in this series. Thank you also to the staff at Routlege for the work they have contributed herein, especially editor Felisa Salvago-Keyes and editorial assistant Nancy Chen.

And last but very much not least I'd like to thank my mother, Jeanie Shipley, for teaching me that dissent is always the way to go.

Introduction

For a black public person to be both gifted and true to himself is not automatic, or one should say, axiomatic, and it is bound to be subversive by extending the scope and expressive range of black humanity in mainstream culture.[1]

What role have black celebrities played in the shaping of public debates around race, inequality, and nation? How much agency for introducing alternative understandings of politics is available to these celebrities at specific historical moments? What role do journalists in both the historically white mainstream press and the African American press play in constructing discourses about raced public figures and their political interventions? How can answering such questions inform our understanding of the phenomena that is black celebrity in the twenty-first century?

Some answers to these questions can be found by exploring news coverage, from dominant and African American print media, of black athletes and entertainers who inserted themselves into public debates about race and nation at various points in United States history. In this book I focus on journalistic framing at the intersection of national controversy and celebrity while endeavoring to complicate and advance our understanding of how mass media construct political and social dissent by raced figures for the public.

Contrary to popular contemporary narratives that suggest the visibility of black celebrities reflects a period of racial enlightenment in which historical boundaries between racialized groups have broken down, I demonstrate that the presence of black celebrities in mainstream media is neither new nor inherently progressive. Rather, I find that black celebrities are subject to incredibly limited conditions for inclusion and acceptance across time. My work reveals how journalistic narratives have contributed to shaping and reifying these conditions and considers the implications for public understandings of raced public bodies and political dissent. At the same time, I offer an intervention into studies of race and protest that focus solely on how these concepts are framed in dominant cultural narratives by closely considering the ways journalists writing for the black press and for black audiences have contributed to public debates about race and national belonging.

2   Black Celebrity, Racial Politics, and the Press

While across time changes have certainly occurred in both mainstream and black news coverage of black celebrity dissent, I seek here to locate these changes within specific historical moments and national conversations about race and citizenship. Comparing cases across time and news sources, I highlight the ways news discourses reflect cultural anxieties and debates about the citizenship of raced figures. While the dissent of the subjects I examine resulted in significant public attention, investigation of how media makers shaped this attention and how, in doing so, they enabled or constrained the political contributions of African American celebrities have been, until now, largely unexamined topics.

The celebrities I examine include Paul Robeson, Eartha Kitt, Tommie Smith and John Carlos, Sister Souljah, Mahmoud Abdul-Rauf, and Kanye West. While certainly not the only African American celebrities to have engaged in public dissent, I chose these subjects because of their explicit critiques of American inequality and the non-traditional spaces and discourses they used to publicize such critiques. In addition, these subjects allow me to examine how intersectional identities like gender and religion, as well as specific historical conditions and varied celebrity personas, contribute to mediated constructions of black dissent.

NEWS FRAMING AT THE INTERSECTION OF RACE, DISSENT, AND CELEBRITY

I consider in the following chapters how journalists frame moments in which cultural narratives and expectations around race and celebrity are disrupted by political dissent. As Stuart Hall has argued, mass media are primarily ideological sites that create and maintain forms of knowledge, like those about race and nation, which have been defined by the powerful.[2] Journalists therefore, are ideological actors who, as Robert Entman describes, "select some aspects of a perceived reality and make them more salient in a communicating text, in such a way as to promote a particular problem definition, casual interpretation, moral evaluation, and/or treatment recommendation of an issue or event."[3] In other words, framing can be thought of as the embedding by journalists of certain discursive, visual, and thematic devices and the disregard of other such devices (either consciously or unconsciously) within a given news story.[4]

Stephen Reese argues that frames are embedded in a "symbolic environment" that is larger than both media institutions and individual level acts and cognitions—our culture.[5] Frames reflect widespread ideologies and value judgments and in turn can become ideology themselves by strongly limiting and/or binding political debate within specific assumptions. Mainstream media have been found many times over to perpetuate frames that make existing structures of power and oppression in society seem natural.[6] Issues deeply rooted in questions of social power, such as those involving race, protest, and fame, have particularly strong cultural frames given the symbolic power with which such issues are historically and culturally coded.[7]

Media are clearly a powerful force for defining parameters of legitimate discourse and debate over alternative beliefs, values, and worldviews—a force that tends to favor consensus with the status quo. In an investigation of media coverage of protest events, Jackie Smith, John McCarthy, Clark McPhail, and Boguslaw Augustyn found that even when protests that present challenges to the status quo succeed in gaining media attention, the reporting of such protests can undermine social movement agendas because of dominant understandings journalists apply in their descriptions.[8]

Thus, public challenges to the American Dream are often framed as the ramblings of the misguided and/or sinister within dominant media discourse. In particular, when claims of racism and racial inequality are made against elites or elite institutions these claims are often quickly discredited.[9] At the same time, dominant discourses have made racial hierarchies in our society invisible, further allowing accusations of racism to be deemed illegitimate.[10] By promoting these dominant articulations of the social world and discrediting alternatives, the mainstream media not only shape shared understandings but effect individual-level consciousness and action.[11]

Scholarship that considers how media have contributed to defining and redefining race as both ideology and social institution are particularly important to the questions I address in this book. Given that black bodies in the U.S. are constructed through public discourse as sensationalized sites of ideological struggle, I consider the ways such struggles shift depending on the political and social climate of the nation. I argue that black celebrities—with their bodies, personas, and expressive forms—have unique potential to challenge dominant definitions of race and nation even as they are limited by them.

For the purposes of this book I define race as a sociohistorical phenomenon that, as described by Michael Omi and Howard Winant, "signifies and symbolizes social conflicts and interests by referring to different types of human bodies."[12] Importantly then, race is understood here according to a constructivist approach that identifies it as an ideology with real social consequences for which conceptualization has been primarily in the hands of dominant groups and is highly dependent on political, social, and economic contexts.[13]

Given this, media function as a particularly important social structure in the cultural representation of race while being simultaneously subject to these representations and the social and political structures they reinforce. Thus, just as race exists both structurally and ideologically, news media should be understood to play a significant role in constructing, interpreting, reorganizing, and explaining the linkages between racial ideologies and social structures in our society. Importantly, social institutions like media—and the symbols and stereotypes therein that influence social reality—must be considered in their historical contexts given the influence of shifting discursive constructs of race on their practices and organization.[14]

Clearly important to the timeline of my research then are the ways manifestations of racial inequality, and discourses about and around it, have evolved in American culture over time. According to Winant, racial domination in America, characterized by slavery and genocide, morphed after the post-WWII "racial break," which included a drastic shift in racial politics in response to global shifts in economics and power and domestic social protest.[15] Following this period of social upheaval sprung the modern embrace of ideologies like multiculturalism and colorblindness that make claims of equality but often do little at the institutional level to enforce it. This "modern" or "enlightened" racism tends to ignore the deep and lasting legacy of racial oppression while holding up the achievements of a few African Americans as evidence that racial problems have been solved. Implied in such discourse is that the continued marginal position of African Americans is a result of cultural failure and deviance, thus justifying continued racial hierarchy while upholding racist stereotypes about black culture.[16] Plainly, the visibility of black celebrities is inherently intertwined with this phenomenon.

For example, John Hoberman contends that media's insistence on celebrating African American athletes and entertainers, but not black contributors to other sectors of society, feeds essentialist stereotypes and maintains basic assumptions of white racial domination. These assumptions depend on racial ideologies that credit black success in athletics and entertainment to historical articulations of blacks as "essentially physical and thus primitive people" naturally opposed to civility, order, and intellect. Hoberman thus contends that modern representations of black celebrities "probably do more than anything else in our public life to encourage the idea that blacks and whites" are inherent opposites.[17]

Similarly, Ronald Jackson contends that the black body, as represented by popular culture, is the primary site of racialized representation in America whereby ideological discourses are played out on objectified African Americans. Jackson, using a similar concept to that of framing, traces the mass media's "scripting" of the black body with specific political and cultural meanings to histories of racism that, in a contemporary context, implicitly resurrect and reinforce the white supremacist assumptions behind this history.[18] Black bodies in media are therefore contested sites of identity politics that seek to define the Other against normative whiteness.

Jackson equates the social consequences that befall black public figures who behave outside dominant scripts of "normal behavior" to lynching. Because these scripts are hegemonic, defined according to racial power relations that assume the normative gaze, when such figures dare to challenge them they are often discursively "demonized and made spectacular."[19] Further, disciplining discourses commonly pit African American public figures constructed as deviant against other black public figures who are constructed as modeling acceptable social and cultural behavior.[20]

This demonization and disciplining is clear in the familiar case of Muhammad Ali, who I discuss in an upcoming section. Like Ali, the subjects I investigate in this book often faced severe social sanctioning in response to their dissent with journalists playing a leading role. Despite the assumption that the celebrity and economic status of public figures might somehow shield them from such sanctioning, Jennifer Knight, Traci Giuliano, and Monica Sanchez-Ross have demonstrated that while celebrity status functions as an advantage for whites facing public scrutiny, for African Americans celebrity status is often a liability. These scholars suggest that the embedded racial resentments of our society are often heaped upon African American public figures exactly because of their high profile status.[21]

While such findings and critiques of the ways black bodies, and particularly black celebrities, are controlled in mainstream narratives are important to my work, I also argue that the public location and crossover influence of African American celebrities allow them unique access to mainstream debates around race and nation and thus a level of agency to influence such debates rarely allowed or achieved by other African Americans. Further, work on the vulnerability of black figures to dominant resentments and disciplining often robs these figures of their agency. One goal of my work here is to return agency to these figures by recognizing their ability to shape important political and social debates alongside the limitations placed on them through media discourse.

I find it imperative then that discursive media frames be critically deconstructed in order to understand how media texts signify issues of race, celebrity, and nation. Media interrogation that identifies the producers of media texts, the contexts of production, and the historical and contemporary political ideologies and motivations inherent in these texts can contribute to resistive attempts to reframe and reinscript black bodies according to evolving and progressive understandings of race and national culture.[22]

Media discourses examined in this book range from just post-WWII—the point at which Winant places the beginning of a cultural shift from racial domination to racial hegemony—through the culmination of this shift in the 1960s, and into the "enlightened" modern era.[23] Given the media's role in representing what is discussable and real about race to the American public, and given the problems of political agency and action that are inherently intertwined with definitions of race, these historical shifts in constructing race both ideologically and socially are reflected in the news coverage examined herein.

THE PUBLIC SPHERE, THE BLACK PRESS, AND BLACK CELEBRITY

Like other scholars of communication and culture, I identify news media in a modern society as a central public location in which important topics are discussed in order to support democratic decision making. At the same time, I contribute here to critical scholarship that points to the idealized nature of the Habermasian public sphere given the way marginalized people have been excluded from it. My research explores the black press as an example of a counterpublic space, functioning both independently from and in response to normative discourses within the dominant public sphere.

The concept of the public sphere is rooted in the work of Jürgen Habermas, who detailed the value of a public space in which citizens can come together as private persons, debate the activities of the state and act, in turn, in an advisory capacity in democratic societies.[24] In contemporary and increasingly large societies that disallow the practicality and possibility of in-person meeting and debate, forms of mass mediated information dispersal including newspapers and magazines are understood as contributing to an approximation of this ideal public sphere.[25] Like Habermas' public sphere, these information-based media assume an ideal in which access is granted to anyone willing to engage, debate is open and rational, and the topics of debate are those of general interest to the public but with the implicit knowledge that only certain segments of society will engage and make judgments as to the importance of specific ideas.[26]

Habermas' idealized public sphere has fallen subject to critics who recognize that his definition of the "public" was itself subject to class, race, and gender hierarchies. The public sphere was never an egalitarian space but an elite one, accessible only to upper class, educated, white, property-owning men—a critique applicable in many ways to modern mainstream media. In turn, the assumption that issues debated in the public sphere reflect(ed) those of general interest and concern to the "public" is fatally flawed when we recognize that the public has always been highly diversified in "general interest," social understandings, and access to information.[27]

Given this, I build upon scholarship that recognizes that a singular public sphere is not only overly idealistic but also simply infeasible given the variety of publics that actually exist. Specifically, I align my work with the concept of counterpublics as defined by critical scholars who recognize that there exist "parallel discursive arenas where members of subordinated social groups invent and circulate counterdiscourses, which in turn permit them to formulate oppositional interpretations of their identities, interests and needs."[28]

Counterpublic spaces, then, foster the identity-based publicization of oppositional discourses and the introduction of counternarratives into the wider public arena through alternative mediums and spaces. Thus, just as the mainstream press has served in the formation of a dominant public sphere, and in turn dominant ideologies in America, the African American press, with its roots in providing counternarratives to racist discourse and counterrepresentations to racist stereotypes, can be seen as an essential part of a uniquely African American counterpublic space.[29]

I would like to clarify what I mean when referring to the "mainstream" press and "black" press in the context of this project. The mainstream press could be termed, perhaps more accurately, the dominant press in that it includes all mediums of news reportage based in dominant culture.[30] By dominant culture, I refer, in the U.S., to white American culture, the norms of which have controlled and continue to control the primary economic, political, and logistic means of information creation and dispersal.

Like other central institutions in the U.S., the field of journalism has a history of both intentional and unintentional exclusion of and disregard of people of non-European decent.[31] As a result, the acceptance and perpetuation of certain worldviews that ally with whiteness have been the norm in the mainstream press. Additionally, mainstream journalists have understood their audiences to be much like themselves—white, educated, and male—and therefore these journalists have written with certain assumptions about who *is not* consuming the news.[32]

On the other hand, the black press was founded as a response to both the professional and representational exclusion of the African American community from the mainstream press. Catherine Squires considers the black press a "subaltern counterpublic" that has functioned as a safer, separate space for African Americans to discuss their group identity interests without interference or oppression.[33] The first African American newspaper, *Freedom's Journal*, was published in 1827 in New York City and stated: "Too long has the public been deceived by misrepresentations of things which concern us dearly. From the press and the pulpit we have suffered much by being incorrectly represented."[34]

The black press then is not only a place in which its founders and contributors sought to right the wrongs of racism in the mainstream press but also one of the first regularly published ventures into media criticism. Pamela Newkirk argues that as a result the black press was required to have a type of double-consciousness reporting not only on the activities of the black community but also on those of the white community and its press because of the profound effect of dominant understandings on black life.[35]

In fact, early black newsmakers understood the black press to be a supplement to information gathering and hoped its existence would speed the physical and ideological integration of the mainstream press. By all accounts, most black readers of the black press use(d) it to augment their engagement with the mainstream press, therefore gaining exposure to the frames of both, whereas white readers of the mainstream press have not usually engaged the black press.[36] Given this history and what we know about media framing, I focus in this book on examining the material acts of framing that resulted in particular mediated interpretations of black celebrity dissent within both the mainstream and black press, and the links of this framing to culturally specific ideologies.

Considering the differing historical contexts, resources, and power dynamics between the mainstream and the black press, the presence of differing (and similar) frames can be understood as a result of each press' unique location as a sphere for a particular audience and the role producers of each press understand themselves to play in the publicization of narratives and counternarratives.[37] While my discussion of framing details the large amount known about the culturally hegemonic potential of mainstream media frames, less scholarly work has examined the counterhegemonic potential of African American–targeted news. However, Ronald Jacobs has found evidence that black newspapers provide a more historicized and social impact–based critique of particular news items and events, often explicitly recalling histories of racism and poverty and their continued effects on the black community in analysis of racial conflicts.[38]

Accordingly, discursive frames within black-targeted media can be understood to represent both oppositional discourses that present counternarratives to those in the mainstream press and intragroup debates about preferred social understandings that may or may not align themselves with dominant ideologies. Notably, the black press, because of its marginalized position, has sometimes had to temper particular oppositional discourses in light of censorship and intimidation by dominant cultural institutions.[39] The presence of a particular brand of conservatism also exists in the black press that reflects the norms and values of African American elites who, while certainly offering oppositional and negotiated frames to those in the mainstream press, also reveal their own classed and gendered behavioral expectations.[40] In fact, I find in the cases herein that newsmakers in the black press often have explicit generational and ideologically diverse debates about the value of different types of black dissent and the role celebrities should play in politics.

Finally, despite the often ominous tone of research on mainstream media, it too cannot only be seen as a location that constructs an unvarying framework for understanding a particular social issue or event. The dominant news value of "objectivity" (problematic in that it ignores the subjectivity of other news value judgments and the real impact of newsmakers' standpoints) is often the reason, along with the modern embrace of multiculturalism, for attempts at including some differing perspectives in mainstream news.[41] For these reasons it is important to note that despite the hegemonic nature of the mainstream media, publicization of discourses that may, even if rarely, reflect alternatives found in the black public sphere are possible.

Specifically, I argue here that the significance of coverage of African American celebrities by the mainstream media is the possibility it opens up for the consideration and debate of alternative worldviews that reflect those in the black public sphere seeking to radically shift power structures in American society.[42]

Scholars of celebrity note that, like constructions of race, public constructions and understandings of celebrity reflect particular conditions of the social order at specific moments in time. Given this, public discourse, and especially media as representatives of the normative discourses in the public sphere, works as a tribunal for celebrities wherein their value in society is constantly debated, reestablished, and/or denied.[43] Thus, the celebrity status of African Americans is particularly tenuous given the ways it overlaps with racialized discourses that apply simplified notions of good versus bad, deserving versus undeserving, and threatening versus docile blackness in multiple public spheres.

Because celebrity status is marked by instability and spectacle, the influence of celebrities on public debates is based on the attention of public gaze, not concrete institutional power.[44] I suggest this phenomenon is more acute in the case of black celebrities who, by way of their race, are treated as even more spectacular and are further removed from access to institutional power than their white counterparts. Despite these challenges, I recognize black celebrities as agential cultural producers who, given their public status, have the opportunity to introduce unique public discourses and foster dialogic relationships with newsmakers in both the mainstream and African American press.

Given what we know about the limits mainstream discourse places on black cultural expression generally, the work of scholars like Urla Hill, Jane Rhodes, and Herman Gray support that a sole focus on the power—albeit tenuous—of black celebrities to influence and contribute to mainstream discourses of race and nation is inadequate.[45] Inasmuch as black celebrities engage in dissent to advance the state of their particular community and draw attention to marginalized frames and experiences, it is equally important to acknowledge how these figures speak and are spoken to by discourses within the communities whose causes they champion.

Together, the intersection of frames presented by journalists serving different public(s) and larger cultural constructions of celebrity and race at particular historical moments raise profound questions I seek to answer. In assuming certain identity-based expectations from their readership, newspaper producers also assume the appropriateness of certain frames for understanding the social world and in turn contribute to the reification or disintegration of such worldviews in larger culture.

Finally, this work is intended as an answer to the call by scholars like Patricia Hill Collins for the integration of oppositional worldviews into the Eurocentric knowledges of academia.[46] By examining the standpoints of black celebrities and members of the black press alongside those of the mainstream press, I contribute to non-dominant ways of understanding and studying public discourse.

In the remainder of this chapter I offer a familiar case of black celebrity dissent through which to begin to think about the subjects I examine in Chapters 1 through 6. Lastly, I describe the organization of this volume and the methods I used to collect and produce the research herein.

A FAMILIAR CASE

Muhammad Ali (nee Cassius Clay) is, without a doubt, the most remembered non-traditional, black celebrity dissident. Before Cassius Clay beat

Sonny Liston in the 1964 world heavyweight championship, media makers constructed him as a likeable, all-American kid.[47] These representations insisted on constructing Clay's boisterous personality as harmless entertainment and framed the fighter as an underdog who was grateful and patriotic. Such paternalistic framing of Clay in mainstream discourse allowed for the maintenance of dominant ideologies that contended black Americans should be content with their place in society because of the marginal successes of a few.[48]

Importantly, the image of the likable Clay was bound by the boxer remaining silent and good-humored on political issues. When Clay, after defeating Liston, insisted on speaking for himself rather than through white managers to acknowledge his membership in the Nation of Islam (NOI) and announce his initial name change to Cassius X, the tone of media representation of the fighter changed almost immediately.[49] Journalists compared the so-called Black Muslims to the Ku Klux Klan and Adolf Hitler, suggesting that the organization was "a vanguard of a violent revolution against whites."[50] Further, columnists argued, Clay was un-American and ungrateful because of his affiliation with this "racist sect" and was using boxing "as a weapon of wickedness."[51] Often left out of media accounts of the post-fight press conference was Clay's detailed and conscientious attempt to provide reporters with a great deal of information about Islam and its importance both to many Americans and populations worldwide.[52]

The intense and negative shift in mainstream media discourse about Ali following his public affiliation with the NOI demonstrates the tenuous position even the most celebrated African American celebrities inhabit and the ways dominant constructions of these figures depend upon racist (and xenophobic) ideologies. As long as Ali accepted his role as an entertaining but politically silent line-tower, his citizenship remained unquestioned, however his deviation from such dominant understandings of what it meant to be a "good" black American resulted in severe punishment.

Most relevant to the subject at hand is Ali's 1967 refusal to participate in the Vietnam War despite being drafted, his political and religious justifications, and his famous (and historically disputable) proclamation that "No Viet Cong ever called me 'nigger.'"[53] Ali took the proper steps to file for conscientious objector status on the grounds that his religion, Islam, was a peaceful one that did not ally itself with war or the colonization of oppressed people of color (i.e., the Vietnamese). However mainstream media makers were reluctant to acknowledge a link between the Vietnam conflict and American racism and largely constructed Ali as a draft dodger.[54] Ali's complete fall from public grace and subsequent expulsion from participation in the sport on which he depended for his livelihood was directly linked to media discourses that framed the boxer as a national threat.[55]

Even African American publications like *Ebony* magazine published negative coverage of Ali, contending that his beliefs were "a deterrent to the civil rights fight."[56] However, unlike the white press, the black press

Introduction   11

presented a balance of critiques of Ali with George Schulyer, Jackie Robinson, and Leroi Jones publishing columns that contextualized Ali's membership in the NOI. These writers argued Ali had every right to his religious and political opinions and further set a good example for other African Americans through his sincerity and commitment.⁵⁷ Notably, Ali did receive rare sympathetic coverage from several members of the white press including Robert Lipsyte of *The New York Times* who noted that Ali "refused to play the mild and politically uninvolved sports-hero," and Howard Cossell who was labeled a "white Muslim" by some of his colleagues for his apparent friendship with Ali.⁵⁸

The almost engulfing negative mainstream coverage of Ali discussed above is likely unfamiliar to a contemporary audience given the shifts in political consciousness that took place around race and the Vietnam War in the late 1960s and 1970s. As the war dragged on, white and black Americans became more frustrated, and this, along with the assassinations of Dr. Martin Luther King Jr. and Senator Robert Kennedy, began to shift public opinion toward a more sympathetic perspective of Ali's dissent.⁵⁹ Further, many young journalists who allied themselves with the counterculture movements their older colleagues dismissed and denigrated began to print columns constructing Ali as a righteous figure.⁶⁰ Eventually, the very mainstream publications that had demonized Ali became critical of his treatment by the government and boxing establishment.⁶¹

Thus, media coverage of Ali evolved to that familiar to many today; journalists construct him as a man who was ahead of his time, a heroic figure to be celebrated. Importantly, this reembrace of Ali was couched within discourses that insisted on maintaining the superiority of dominant American values while often ignoring oppressive realities. Today journalists often frame Ali as "a symbol of America's capacity to embrace—even if only post-ipso facto—racial, religious, and ideological differences," while ignoring their own institutional role in the social, political, and economic sanctions that had been levied against him.⁶² Rather than contextualizing Ali's original dissent within the experiences of the African American community or larger anti-colonial movements, contemporary discourse also constructs Ali as representative of the spirit of American independence and individualism.⁶³

Scholars like Shaun Powell and Aaron Baker contend that the tone of contemporary media representations of Ali suffer from a historical amnesia that depoliticizes the boxer by ignoring the immense hatred and backlash that was levied against him. At the same time these media representations fail to offer a sustained racial or social critique, instead depending on sanitized and passing narratives of the "tumultuous" 1960s and 1970s.⁶⁴ That contemporary representations of Ali in public discourse fall short of identifying the ironies and failures of America's dominant values illustrates the role media play in constructing and maintaining discourses that reflect the dominant needs of American society. At the same time, the fact that media makers were forced to respond to Ali's dissent, and frame and reframe it within particular historical contexts, demonstrates the influence black celebrities can have on the mainstream public sphere.

I would like to suggest here that Muhammad Ali can work as a cipher through which to understand the other subjects I investigate in this project. Ali's case reveals the impact and limits of African American celebrity dissent on public debates around race and nation, the tangible consequences of this dissent for the celebrity involved, and the ways such dissent is reinterpreted across time. While Ali's relationship with the media and the impact of this relationship on public discourses has been frequently interrogated, I argue that the question of how limited (or not) the power of a black celebrity is to transform national conversations at particular historical moments is best illustrated with additional cases. The cases in this book allow for a larger systematic critique of the role of mainstream and black journalists in facilitating and limiting the agency of raced public figures given shifting cultural and political definitions of race, nation, and celebrity.

Like Ali's embrace of Islam and criticism of the Vietnam war, my subjects' actions and words were deemed radical or controversial in mainstream culture—in part because of their content, in part because of their physical location, and in part because of the particular identities of the celebrities involved. Each figure chose to challenge the existence of the mythic American ethos of equality in ways that fell outside of what was seen as "acceptable" black expression. Each, because of her or his high visibility in American popular culture, was able to bring media attention to a particular social or political perspective that was largely outside those named in the mainstream. Moreover, each levied their claims in locations seen (although technically public) as illegitimate spaces for dissent. Together my cases evidence a long and fraught tradition of black celebrity dissent and media makers'—and their publics'—relationship to it.

ORGANIZATION OF THE BOOK

Each of the following chapters explore how, at different points in time, mainstream and African American print media framed specific moments of dissent by African American celebrities. In organizing my study by these cases, I do not claim complete coverage of every notable moment of political dissent by an African American celebrity, there are in fact far too many for one volume. Rather, my cases represent a diverse sample of black celebrities who reflect various levels of fame, intersectional identities, and particularly hot-button moments of national consciousness around issues of inequality and nation.

I have intentionally not included celebrity dissent that falls into the clearly marked spaces and rituals of the traditionally understood civil rights movement, like marches and rallies. Rather, the moments of dissent I do consider, while surely contributions to the ongoing African American Freedom

Struggle,[65] are subversive often exactly because these celebrities engaged in dissent in spaces not considered acceptable places for protest: international events, White House dinners, Olympic podiums, presidential campaigns, sporting arenas, and televised fundraisers. Examining media coverage of such figures and moments is important given that (1) these subjects have had little scholarship focused on how media makers shaped their contributions to public discourses of race and nation, and (2) such dissent was often deemed seditious and therefore forced to the margins of ongoing struggles for human rights.

I include in this research a chronological case-by-case discussion of the particular historical moment in which each figure's dissent took place in order to contribute sociohistorical context. I discuss the biographies and personas of my celebrities to contribute understandings around their specifically defined brand of fame. Primarily however, I examine how my subjects, like Ali, used their limited agency to present challenges to discourses of race and nation and how media makers in the mainstream and black public spheres made sense of these challenges for their audiences.

In Chapter 1 I consider the case of Paul Robeson, who became a subject of Cold War–era witch hunts because of his public dissent. Robeson's case also highlights a historical moment at which the black press was experiencing higher constraints from dominant institutions than at other moments examined here. My examination of Eartha Kitt in Chapter 2 considers the role of gender and multiracial identity in the construction of black celebrity dissent by newsmakers navigating the national backlash against the Vietnam War and the latter days of the civil rights movement. In Chapter 3 I consider the Olympic dissent of Tommie Smith and John Carlos, which provides unique insight into how journalists made sense of the militancy of young African Americans after the assassination of Martin Luther King Jr.

Chapter 4 examines how journalists both facilitated and responded to dissent by rapper Sister Souljah in the wake of the beating of Rodney King and the acquittal of the Los Angeles police officers who attacked him. Journalistic frames about Souljah reveal the early cultural anxieties that existed around rap music as an unrepentant African American expressive form in a modern era already largely defined by enlightened racism. In Chapter 5 I consider how cultural understandings of Islam intersected with coverage of Mahmoud Abdul-Rauf's dissent regarding "The Star-Spangled Banner." Abdul-Rauf's case also provides a unique opportunity to consider the role of media in inserting celebrities into controversies about race and dissent against their will. My final case carries us into the twenty-first century with a consideration of news media responses to Kanye West's post–Hurricane Katrina dissent. West's celebrity reflects contemporary understandings of hip hop and blackness that reveal both clear shifts in, and the stubborn historical limits on, understandings of black dissent. Finally, in the conclusion I discuss what these cases, taken together, reveal about how black celebrity and racial politics intersect in America and consider new opportunities for the publicization of black celebrity dissent in the Obama Era alongside the ongoing and unique challenges this dissent encounters.

Ultimately, I locate the stakes of these celebrities and their dissent at the center of the contested practices of media discourse and African American agency. The connections between ever-evolving racial politics and the taken-for-granted rules and worldviews of mainstream and black media in covering dissenting raced figures are illuminated. The similarities and/or differences of these rules at different historical moments and concerning different subjects reveal larger trends in the construction and maintenance of racial politics within two of America's most influential public spheres.

A NOTE ON METHOD

This project is critical and comparative, evaluating coverage from mainstream and African American news sources. This entails examinations of some of the most well-known and respected mainstream newspapers including *The New York Times, Chicago Tribune, Los Angeles Times, The Washington Post, Denver Post, Time,* and *Newsweek.* Similarly, in the African American press I examine the *New York Amsterdam News, Chicago Defender, Los Angeles Sentinel, Washington Informer, Pittsburgh Courier, Negro Digest, Jet, Ebony,* and *Essence,* among others.[66] Data was collected from physical, microfilm, and online databases available through university media archives, particularly the University of Minnesota, ProQuest, LexisNexis, and the websites of specific sources.

For each case I used keyword searches to collect all stories published in the two-month period following a celebrity's dissent that in any way covered or referenced that dissent. For example, data was collected from both mainstream and black press sources for Chapter 2 using keywords "Eartha Kitt AND White House," "Eartha Kitt AND Vietnam," and "Eartha Kitt AND luncheon" from January 19, 1968—the day after Eartha Kitt's dissent at the White House—through March 19, 1968. I then analyzed the data for each case via a two-step coding process that included a content analysis and an emergent discourse analysis.

Content analysis is a quantitative process in which the contents or characteristics of a specific media are counted and compared in order to garner a better understanding of how meaning is constructed through language.[67] As part of this process I examined each article, column, editorial, and letter to the editor in each case for the word choices used to describe the celebrity in question and her or his dissenting action. The goal of this content analysis was the discovery of the frequency that words and terms with explicitly understood cultural value attached to them were used by newsmakers to convey underlying assumptions and understandings about black celebrity dissent.

Following this line-by-line coding, emergent discourse analysis was used to discover how journalists included or excluded certain ideas, descriptions, and cultural understandings in order to generate the larger narrative of each story. Discourse analysis, as a qualitative process, insists on interrogating media text not simply for the numerical presence or absence of certain characteristics but for the larger ideological frameworks implicated. During this process, each article was examined holistically for the overall frame presented to readers to make sense of the celebrity and dissent in question. Emergent coding was ideal for this research because it allowed me to approach the texts in question without preestablished expectations that might otherwise limit the story the data was able to tell.

Each text was examined as a part of this emergent process on three dimensions: (1) the characterizations of the particular celebrity in question, (2) the frames applied to the act of the protest/dissent itself, and (3) the overall plot frame that encompasses, connects, and makes relevant the characterizations of these individuals and their actions. Common frames were determined by discursive examination of the words, referents, tone, narrative connections to other people and events, reported meaning of figures and their dissent, and the inclusion and/or exclusion of certain casual interpretations and historical, social, and political contexts.

Together content analysis and discourse analysis allowed for in-depth investigation of the way the news texts examined here reflect the social, cultural, and political norms of their producers and the larger society they claim to reflect. According to Kim Schroder, "an important, if implicit ambition of many discourse and content studies has been to infer from the properties of media texts to . . . their relative contribution to social and cultural processes at large, with specific reference to public opinion or the reproduction of ideology."[68] Given what previous literature has revealed as to the individual and social impact of media frames about race, and my interest in examining how news texts perpetuate certain ideological discourses and counterdiscourses around African American celebrities and racial dissent in the public sphere, these methods were ideal.

I have included editorial content alongside news articles in my analysis. As discussed in great lengths here, the worldviews of journalists, the institutions they work for, and the public they serve unquestionably influence the framing of news article narratives, from the front page to the sports section. This project treats as valid challenges to objectivity in journalism, recognizing that news stories about race, politics, and nation are never written without particular subjectivities in mind. My orientation of viewing news creation as a whole as inherently subjective thus leads to the necessary interrogation of editorial content—which is largely and inaccurately framed to readers as the only opinion-based content in print news sources. While the particular subjectivities and framing strategies used by journalists are sometimes made more explicit in editorial than news content, I find here that they can also be equally implicit. In view of the fact that editors of a given publication have a section where they can, without a byline, offer opinions, critiques, and recommendations about individuals, actions, and social problems; that these same editors employ opinion columnists who they believe will reflect the needs and valued debates of their audience; and that these editors select which of countless letters to the editor to publish based on those same judgments, examining news and editorial content together offers clear insight into how members of each public sphere define their role in news and opinion making for their readers.

Because media texts cannot be removed from the social, cultural, and political conditions in which they are created, my chosen methods enable what cultural theorists like Stuart Hall have called a conjunctural analysis.[69] By grounding the racial and political discourse of both the black and mainstream public spheres in their material conditions—the political and ideological structures of media—and by recognizing and exploring differences in this discourse from a historically specific and comparative perspective, this project illuminates important trends in the framing and reproduction of racial and political ideology to and by various publics.

NOTES

1. Gerald Early, "The Black Intellectual and the Sport of Prizefighting," in *Kenyon Review* 10, no. 3 (1988): 102.
2. Stuart Hall, "Encoding/Decoding," in *Culture, Media, Language*, ed. Stuart Hall, Dorothy Hobson, Andrew Lowe, and Paul Willis (London: Hutchinson & Co. Ltd., 1980): 128–138.
3. Robert Entman, "Framing: Toward Clarification of a Fractured Paradigm," *Journal of Communication* 43, no. 4 (1993): 52.
4. Donald Kinder and Lynn Sanders, *Divided by Color* (Chicago: University of Chicago Press, 1996); Dietram Scheufele, "Framing as a Theory of Media Effects," *Journal of Communication* 49, no. 1 (1999): 103–122, doi: 10.1111/j.1460-2466.
5. Stephen D. Reese, "The Framing Project: A Bridging Model for Media Research Revisited," *Journal of Communication* 57, no. 1 (2007): 148–154.
6. Stuart Hall, *Representation: Cultural Representations and Signifying Practices* (London: Sage Publications, Inc., 1997); Robert M. Entman and Andrew Rojecki, *The Black Image in the White Mind: Media and Race in America* (Chicago: University of Chicago Press, 2000); Catherine Squires, "Rethinking the Black Public Sphere: An Alternative Vocabulary for Multiple Spheres," *Communication Theory* 12, no. 4 (Nov. 2002): 446–468.
7. Hall, "Encoding/Decoding"; Entman and Rojecki, *The Black Image in the White Mind*.
8. Jackie Smith, John McCarthy, Clark McPhail and Boguslaw Augustyn, "From Protest to Agenda Building: Description Bias in Media Coverage of Protest Events in Washington, DC," *Social Forces* 79, no. 4 (2001): 1397–1423.
9. James Druckman, "On the Limits of Framing Effects: Who Can Frame?" *The Journal of Politics* 63, no. 4 (2001): 1041–1066.
10. Roopali Mukherjee, *The Racial Order of Things* (Minneapolis: University of Minnesota Press, 2006); Eduardo Bonilla-Silva, *White Supremacy and Racism in the Post-Civil Rights Era* (Boulder, CO: Lynne Reinner Publishers, Inc., 2001).

Introduction 17

11. Ronald Jackson II, *Scripting the Black Masculine Body: Identity, Discourse, and Racial Politics in Popular Media* (Albany: State University of New York Press, 2006); George Sage, *Power and Ideology in American Sport: A Critical Perspective* (Champaign, IL: Human Kinetics, 1998).
12. Michael Omi and Howard Winant, "Racial Formation," in *Race Critical Theories*, ed. Philomena Essed and David Theo Goldberg (Malden, MA: Wiley-Blackwell, 2001): 123.
13. Gloria A. Marshall, "Racial Classifications: Popular and Scientific," in *The "Racial" Economy of Science: Toward a Democratic Future*, ed. Sandra Harding (Bloomington: Indiana University Press, 1993): 116–125; Cornel West, "A Genealogy of Modern Racism," in *Race Critical Theories*, ed. Philomena Essed and David Theo Goldberg (Malden, MA: Wiley-Blackwell, 2001): 90–112.
14. Thomas Nelson, Rosalee Clawson, and Zoe Oxley, "Media Framing of a Civil Liberties Conflict and Its Effect on Tolerance," *American Political Science Review* 91, no. 3 (Sep. 1997): 567–583; Todd Gitlin, *The Whole World Is Watching: Mass Media in the Making & Unmaking of the New Left* (Berkeley: University of California Press, 1980); Omi and Winant, "Racial Formation."
15. Howard Winant, *The New Politics of Race: Globalism, Difference, Justice* (Minneapolis: University of Minnesota Press, 2004).
16. Komozi Woodard, *A Nation within a Nation: Amiri Baraka (LeRoi Jones) and Black Power Politics* (Chapel-Hill: University of North Carolina Press, 1999); George Lipsitz, *The Possessive Investment in Whiteness: How White People Profit from Identity Politics* (Philadelphia: Temple University Press, 2006); Bonilla-Silva, *White Supremacy and Racism in the Post-Civil Rights Era;* Douglas Hartmann, "Bound by Blackness or Above It?: Michael Jordan and the Paradoxes of Post-Civil Rights American Race Relations," in *Out of the Shadows: A Biographical History of African American Athletes*, ed. David K. Wiggins (Fayetteville: University of Arkansas Press, 2006).
17. John Hoberman, *Darwin's Athletes: How Sport Has Damaged Black America and Preserved the Myth of Race* (New York: Houghton Mifflin Company, 1997): xxiii.
18. Jackson, *Scripting the Black Masculine Body*.
19. Ibid.
20. Hoberman, *Darwin's Athletes*.
21. Jennifer L. Knight, Traci A. Giuliano, and Monica G. Sanchez-Ross, "Famous or Infamous? The Influence of Celebrity Status and Race on Perceptions of Responsibility for Rape," *Basic & Applied Social Psychology* 23, no. 3 (2001): 183–190.
22. Jackson, *Scripting the Black Masculine Body*.
23. Winant, *The New Politics of Race*.
24. Robert Asen and Daniel C. Brouwer, eds., "Reconfigurations of the Public Sphere," in *Counterpublics and the State* (New York: State University of New York Press, 2001): 1–34.
25. Jürgen Habermas, *The Structural Transformation of the Public Sphere: An Inquiry into a Category of Bourgeois Society*, trans. Thomas Burger and Fredrick Lawrence (Cambridge, MA: Massachusetts Institute of Technology Press, 1989); Nancy Fraser, "Rethinking the Public Sphere: A Contribution to the Critique of Actually Existing Democracy," in *Habermas and the Public Sphere*, ed. Craig Calhoun (Cambridge, MA: Massachusetts Institute of Technology Press, 1992); Catherine Squires, "The Black Press and the State: Attracting Unwanted(?) Attention," in *Counterpublics and the State*, ed. Robert Asen and Daniel C. Brouwer (New York: State University of New York Press, 2001): 111–136.
26. Houston A. Baker Jr., "Critical Memory and the Black Public Sphere," *Public Culture* 7, no. 3 (1994): 3–33.

27. Squires, "Rethinking the Black Public Sphere"; Asen and Brouwer, "Reconfigurations of the Public Sphere,."
28. Fraser, "Rethinking the Public Sphere," 67.
29. Baker, "Critical Memory and the Black Public Sphere."
30. Catherine Squires, *Dispatches from the Colorline: The Press and Multiracial America* (New York: State University of New York Press, 2007).
31. Pamela Newkirk, *Within the Veil: Black Journalists, White Media* (New York: New York University Press, 2000).
32. Carole Stabile, *White Victims, Black Villains: Gender, Race and Crime News in US Culture* (New York: Routledge, 2006).
33. Squires, "Rethinking the Black Public Sphere."
34. Quoted in Newkirk, *Within the Veil*.
35. Newkirk, *Within the Veil*.
36. Ronald N. Jacobs, *Race, Media and the Crisis of Civil Society: From Watts to Rodney King* (United Kingdom: University Press Cambridge, 2000).
37. Squires, *Dispatches from the Colorline*.
38. Jacobs, *Race, Media and the Crisis of Civil Society*.
39. Squires, "Rethinking the Black Public Sphere"; Baker, "Critical Memory and the Black Public Sphere."
40. Catherine Squires, "Coloring in the Bubble: Perspectives from Black-Oriented Media on the (Latest) Economic Disaster," *American Quarterly* 64, no. 3, (2012): 543–570; Michael C. Dawson, *Black Visions: The Roots of Contemporary African-American Political Ideologies* (Chicago: University of Chicago Press: 2001).
41. Herbert J. Gans, *Democracy and the News* (New York: Oxford University Press, 2003); Stuart Hall, "The Whites of Their Eyes: Racist Ideologies and the Media," in *Gender, Race, and Class in Media*, ed. Gail Dines and Jean M. Humez (Thousand Oaks: Sage Publications, Inc., 1981): 89–93.
42. Sage, *Power and Ideology in American Sport*; Jackson, *Scripting the Black Masculine Body*.
43. David C. Ogden and Joel Nathan Rosen, *Reconstructing Fame: Sport, Race, and Evolving Reputations* (Jackson: The University Press of Mississippi, 2008).
44. David Meyer and Joshua Gamson, "The Challenge of Cultural Elites: Celebrities and Social Movements," *Sociological Inquiry* 65, no. 2 (1995): 181–206.
45. Urla Hill, "Racing after Smith and Carlos: Revisiting Those Fists Some Forty Years Hence," In *Reconstructing Fame: Sport, Race, and Evolving Reputations*, ed. David C. Ogden and Joel Nathan Rosen (Jackson: University Press of Mississippi, 2008): 102–126; Jane Rhodes, *Framing the Black Panthers: The Spectacular Rise of a Black Power Icon* (New York: New Press, 2007); Herman Gray, *Cultural Moves: African Americans and the Politics of Representation* (Berkeley: University of California Press, 2005).
46. Patricia Hill Collins, *Black Feminist Thought: Knowledge, Consciousness, and the Politics of Empowerment* (New York: Routledge, 2000).
47. David Remnick, *King of the World: Muhammad Ali and the Rise of an American Hero* (New York: Random House, 1998).
48. Donald Spivey, *Sport in America: New Historical Perspectives* (Greenwood Press, 1985).
49. Spivey, *Sport in America*; Remnick, *King of the World*; Grant Farred, *What's My Name?: Black Vernacular Intellectuals* (Minneapolis: University of Minnesota Press, 2003).
50. Spivey, *Sport in America*; Remnick, *King of the World*; Mike Marqusee, *Redemption Song: Muhammad Ali and the Spirit of the Sixties* (New York: Verso, 1999).

51. Ibid.
52. Farred, *What's My Name?*
53. Some accounts contend that Ali's statement was "I ain't got no quarrel with the VietCong," while others report variations of both.
54. Farred, *What's My Name?*
55. Spivey, *Sport in America;* Thomas Hauser, *Muhammad Ali: His Life and Times* (New York: Touchstone, 1999); David W. Zang, *Sports Wars: Athletes in the Age of Aquarius* (Fayetteville: The University of Arkansas Press, 2001); Marqusee, *Redemption Song.*
56. Notably, *Ebony*'s publisher, John H. Johnson, had early on expressed concerns that he would lose white advertisers if he covered racial unrest, critiques of white violence, or black militancy too often. Maren Stange, "Photographs Taken in Everyday Life: *Ebony*'s Photojournalistic Discourse," in *The Black Press: New Literary and Historical Essays*, ed. Todd Vogel (New Brunswick: Rutgers University Press, 2001): 188–206.
57. Marqusee, *Redemption Song.*
58. Robert Lipsyte, "Clay Discusses His Future, Liston and Black Muslims," *The New York Times*, Feb. 27, 1964, quoted in Farred, *What's My Name?*
59. Farred, *What's My Name.*
60. Spivey, *Sport in America.*
61. Zang, *Sports Wars.*
62. Hauser, *Muhammad Ali;* Farred, *What's My Name?*
63. Zang, *Sports Wars.*
64. Shaun Powell, *Souled Out?: How Blacks Are Winning and Losing in Sports* (Champaign, IL: Human Kinetics, 2008); Aaron Baker, *Contesting Identities: Sports in American Film* (Champaign: University of Illinois Press, 2003).
65. From Brian Ward, who defines the African American Freedom Struggle as a post-WWII political, cultural, and artistic move by African Americans to express resistance and publicize the validity of their identities and cultural forms in a variety of ways, of which the civil rights and Black Power movements were only a part. Brian Ward, *Media, Culture, and the Modern African American Freedom Struggle* (Gainesville: University Press of Florida, 2001).
66. For full list of sources included in each chapter see Appendix Table 1.
67. Klaus Bruhn Jensen, ed., *A Handbook of Media and Communication Research: Qualitative and Quantitative Methodologies* (London: Routledge, 2002).
68. Kim C. Schroder, "Discourses of Fact," in *A Handbook of Media and Communication Research: Qualitative and Quantitative Methodologies*, ed. Klaus Bruhn Jensen (London: Routledge, 2002): 116.
69. Stuart Hall and Doreen Massey, "Interpreting the Crisis: Doreen Massey and Stuart Hall Discuss Ways of Understanding the Current Crisis," *Soundings* 44 (2010): 57.

1 Paul Robeson at Peekskill, NY, 1949

Nothing's happened to me. I'm just looking for freedom.[1]

Paul Robeson, the son of an escaped slave, was the first African American to obtain crossover celebrity status and arguably the first modern celebrity of any race in the United States.[2] The Rutgers University football star, law school graduate, and stage and screen actor, was celebrated among Americans for his deep and distinctive baritone and his adeptness with Shakespeare and Negro spirituals alike. Early in his career, Robeson, while supportive of popular civil rights initiatives like anti-lynching laws, was largely silent on more controversial issues, believing his inclusion in white public arenas represented some progress. Initial media discourse about Robeson easily constructed him in line with the stereotypical casting of his early acting career—a primitively strong but comfortably familiar, naturally musical "darkie." Although these roles resulted in some critique from black activists, his mainstream successes and popularity with white audiences led many in the black community to view Robeson as a torch bearer whose success represented a potential communal path toward racial inclusion.[3]

According to Jeffrey C. Stewart, "in the 1920s, and for a good part of the 1930s, Robeson became the site where African American and European American aspirations for the ability to cross over came together."[4] Of course, "crossing over" meant very different things to black and white audiences—for whites the opportunity to consume and appropriate the Other, for blacks the potential to be seen as part of mainstream society. Robeson's celebrity also occurred at a unique historical moment in which entertainment was shifting from a participatory culture to a consumptive one.[5] While on one hand the resulting commodification of Robeson's blackness rendered his presence in white spaces non-threatening, it also became increasingly marked by a new understanding of fame that recognized that roles played by screen stars did not necessarily reflect their real-life personas. In this changing context, Robeson's rise to international fame evolved from a 1920s and early 1930s seamless and safe construction of the star, to a later "inter-textual" representation of Robeson that recognized a conflict between his early roles and his real-life choices and politics. This representational evolution is also testament to Robeson's understanding of the racialized limits placed upon him in the entertainment industry, and his choices to disrupt these limits as his popularity grew.

By the late 1930s, Robeson used his uniquely elevated status to publicly challenge caricatures of blacks in American film, including critiquing many of his past roles, and to turn down roles that he felt catered to the racism of the American South. He spoke publicly about these decisions and became increasingly candid about his frustrations with the lack of racial progress in America. As Robeson consciously represented himself in ways that were not consistent with "safe" black stereotypes, and as his personal life (including affairs with white women and close friendships with radical thinkers) became public, mainstream opinion of the baritone began to shift.[6]

As Robeson articulated his politics internationally in the 1940s—including staunch anti-racist, anti-colonial, and pro-labor perspectives and sympathies with the Soviet Union—he became regarded by many as—at best—tragically misinformed, and—at worst—a threat tarnishing the global reputation of the U.S. Robeson was called to testify in front of the House Un-American Activities Committee (HUAC) as early as 1946 and was the target of politically motivated concert cancellations throughout 1947.[7] Despite this, Robeson's celebrity status meant that he could not be ignored. Even as public understandings of the star became more and more negative, his newsworthiness guaranteed Robeson's alternative articulations of nation, race, and democracy would be re- (and often mis-) articulated to the public by journalists.

In April 1949, the Associated Press reported that Robeson, while attending the Congress of World Partisans for Peace in Paris, had stated, "It is unthinkable that American Negroes would go to war on behalf of those who oppressed us for generations against a country [the Soviet Union] which in one generation has raised our people to the full dignity of mankind."[8] There has been some disagreement as to if this was, in fact, what Robeson said, with some historians suggesting it was a misquote, and many original reports of the speech in international papers quoting him as saying he spoke "on behalf of all American workers," who "shall not make war on the Soviet Union."[9]

Many black leaders and white labor organizations who had previously supported Robeson's political activism disavowed these comments. The Cold War was escalating, anti-Communist sentiment was running high, and McCarthyism was stifling freedom of expression through persecution of Communists, Socialists, and virtually anyone known to support a left agenda.[10] At the same time, race relations in the late 1940s were in a period of flux. Early moves toward desegregating national institutions like the armed forces and baseball took place alongside the increasing influence of segregationist Dixiecrats. African American veterans who had volunteered to fight in World Wars I and II felt a growing discontent at the violation of American democratic principles at their expense at home. And, as Joseph

Dorinson and William Pencak note, prior to the rise of McCarthyism tens of thousands of Americans, black and white, had joined or come to support the Communist Party because it espoused an explicit commitment to racial equality and labor rights.[11]

The intersection of these phenomena meant that as McCarthyism took hold, anti-Communist narratives were often used to silence movements for racial equality and critiques of the U.S. government that went along with them. Civil rights organizations stood on the tenuous ground of attempting to pursue progress and critique national institutions while being forced to shy away from union, grassroots, and more politically radical figures for fear of political persecution.[12] Members of the black press were also well aware of the dangers of the political moment as they had recently experienced governmental censorship and threats of shut down for perceived sedition by the federal government during World Wars I and II.[13] Thus, while Robeson and many other Americans, black and white, journalist, politician, and civilian, held alternative understandings of Communism than that constructed in dominant discourse, the level of public fear generated by the idea that Communism was inherently seditious and threatening made the term a weapon of ideological conformity.[14]

Notably, despite their own vulnerability, many of the most racially and economically diverse left-leaning political organizations (usually headed by black and Jewish leftists and Communists) continued to support Robeson through concert bookings and speaking engagements during these years.[15] On August 27, 1949, Robeson, now labeled a "Communist sympathizer" by mainstream journalists and under the constant surveillance (and harassment) of the CIA, was scheduled to give a concert in Peekskill, New York. As testament to his continuing popularity with both blacks and whites on the left and the active interracial political coalitions that existed at the time, the proceeds of Robeson's concert were to benefit the Harlem chapter of the Civil Rights Congress (CRC).[16]

While Robeson had performed in the area three times in previous years with no difficulty, 1949 was clearly different. Riled up by the editorializing of the local *Peekskill Evening Star,* which labeled the concert "subversive" and the sponsoring organization a "Red Front," a group of Peekskill residents and local veterans associations organized a protest outside the entrance to the grounds where the Robeson concert was to be held.[17] While the veterans publicized the protest as one that would be a peaceful attempt to communicate disapproval of Robeson's politics, there were more nefarious anti-black, anti-Jewish, and anti-labor undertones to the subsequent actions of the protesters. Before Robeson could arrive to perform, the waiting concertgoers were assaulted with loud, often racist jeering—including shouts of "nigger" and "kikes"—and a cross was set ablaze on a nearby hill. Without police intervention, Robeson supporters and fans were assaulted for two hours by the protestors, who set fire to their belongings and hurled rocks as they tried to exit the scene.[18]

Eventually, the slow-to-act police insisted that the rioters disperse. Several days later Robeson gave a speech that was, according to his biographer Martin Duberman "as fierce and telling as he ever delivered," to a Harlem crowd of over three thousand, saying in part:

> It's been a long struggle I've waged, sometimes not very well understood. . . . I will be loyal to the America of true traditions; to the America of abolitionists, of Harriet Tubman, of Thaddeus Stevens, of those who fought for my people's freedom, not for those who tried to enslave them. . . . This means that from now on we take the offensive. We take it! We'll have our meetings and our concerts all over these United States. That's right. And we'll see that our women and our children are not harmed again! We will understand that the surest way to get police protection is to have it very clear that we'll protect ourselves, and good! I'll be back with my friends in Peekskill.[19]

The concert organizers quickly rescheduled the show for the following week and enlisted local union members and black World War II veterans as security for Robeson and the concert grounds. Because of the previous violence, the second Robeson concert became a symbolic protest to both those who were sympathetic to Robeson's politics and long-time fans (Figure 1.1). While those on the left saw the second concert as a move against the "fascism" they felt was reflected by the previous infringements on freedom of speech and assembly, Peekskill's fervently anti-Communist residents and their supporters were determined to again protest the "Russia-loving Negro" and his presumably anti-American fans.[20]

The second concert, attended by twenty thousand fans and supporters and protected by a line of arm-in-arm trade unionists, went on as planned. However, when concertgoers tried to leave the grounds, they were again assaulted by anti-Robeson demonstrators. The second riotous assault lasted five hours and resulted in over a hundred physical injuries and extensive property damage. Many of the pro-Robeson eyewitnesses contended that this time, rather than looking on in apathy, police joined in the assault. Benjamin J. Davis Jr., a former New York City councilman from Harlem, reported shouts of "Hang Robeson niggers with a rope!" and "Get the dirty Jews," and many others in attendance, including folk singer Pete Seeger and novelist Howard Fast, echoed reports of epithets, threats, and intense violence levied against the concertgoers.[21]

In this chapter, I examine news coverage of the Peekskill riots in the mainstream and black press. Across a two-month period, the mainstream press published 102 stories on the riots, with the black press publishing 34.[22] Newspaper coverage of Peekskill can be understood as an early moment in which journalists had to engage in explicit reporting of celebrity-centered political dissent, responses to it, and the entanglement of national understandings of race, nation, and democracy. In the following sections I discuss

Figure 1.1 Paul Robeson flanked by volunteer bodyguards and two American flags performs at the second Peekskill concert to benefit the Civil Rights Congress. (AP Photo)

how Paul Robeson's politics, and the Peekskill riots, were framed and how these frames reflect the social understandings, needs, and histories of the publics each press sought to inform.

OF COMMUNIST LIES AND LYNCH MOBS

White and black press accounts of Robeson at Peekskill exhibited several similarities, including negative constructions of Communism, a concern about the violence at Peekskill aiding Communist propaganda, and the positive valuation of constitutional rights. However, these agreed-upon principles were framed very differently, with the black press contextualizing the riots amid questions of systemic racialized violence and official neglect, and the mainstream press largely ignoring these questions in favor of frames that focused on the ideological and global conflicts created by Communism and Robeson's violations therein. Take, for example, a comparison of editorials run by *The New York Times* and the *New York Amsterdam News*.

A week after the first Peekskill riot, and in anticipation of the violence that would follow the second concert, *The New York Times* editorial board wrote in part:

> Sympathy for Paul Robeson and his followers, after their interrupted concert near Peekskill last Sunday, was not increased by their threat to mobilize "20,000 strong" this Sunday. . . . Mr. Robeson has a right to assemble his followers peaceably, sing and, if he wishes, make a speech. . . . This is the principle of the First Amendment to the Federal Constitution, of Article I of the Constitution of the State of New York and of similar provisions in the constitutions of other states. . . . These facts were recognized by Governor Dewey yesterday when he ordered state police into the Peekskill area to prevent violence as a result of the Robeson meeting. . . . The rights involved, Dewey said, "must be respected, however hateful the views of some of those who abuse them." . . . Mr. Robeson could not hold a meeting or publically sing one note in Russia if his views differed from those of the Moscow bosses. If Mr. Robeson is allowed to hold his meeting in peace today, that very fact will answer the Communist lies more than any words could.[23]

The editorial on Peekskill run by the editors of the *New York Amsterdam News* read in part:

> It might easily be that the two riots occurring within the space of a few days have been the biggest gifts placed in the hands of American Communists since the beginning of WWII. Now they have a clear-cut case of gross and inexcusable violation of constitutional rights because of political belief. Robeson and his left-wing supporters were clearly within their constitutional rights . . . officials had a clear-cut responsibility to protect the Robesonites in exercise of their rights. . . . It was plain that officers responsible for law and order in the Peekskill community were entirely sympathetic to the veterans' plans. That mob at Peekskill was a close blood relation to the lynch mobs of Georgia and Florida. . . . Its members where driven by a blind bigotry in an attempt to deprive American citizens of their constitutional rights. They chose intimidation and violence. . . . Their action was a disgrace to the city of New York and wounded the very democracy which the veterans were supposed to have defended in the recent war.[24]

Clearly, both of these editorials deploy narratives that value the rights seen inherent to American democracy, and both present Communism and violence as forces which undermine this democracy. However, the difference in the application of these values demonstrates how editors serving segregated publics varied in worldview. *The New York Times'* turn of phrase that Dewey had "ordered state police into the Peekskill area to prevent violence *as a result of* the Robeson meeting," places blame on Robeson and his fans for any violence before it even occurred.[25] Dewey's order for state police surely could have been equally reported as an effort to prevent violence as a result of anti-Robeson (or anti-Communist) sentiment by local groups planning to protest, but such constructions, which would have implicated others than Robeson and his fans, never occurred in the mainstream press.

The editors of *The New York Times* also failed to acknowledge the severity of the violence that occurred against Robeson and his followers by describing the first riot as the concert being "interrupted." Further, an assumption is made—despite accounts from the scene of the first—that state police will protect constitutional rights and prevent violence at the second. Robeson's return to Peekskill with his fans after their first assault is quite literally constructed as a "threat" undeserving of "sympathy."[26] These framing choices, along with the fact that *New York Times* editors avoided talking about potential racial motivations for the violence altogether, support Joseph Walwik's observation that when the mainstream press objected to the violence at Peekskill it was not "because of the injuries suffered, or even because of the violation of civil liberties, but because violence played into the hands of Communist propagandists."[27]

Ultimately, the framing of who and what was to blame for the violence at Peekskill—in the mainstream, Robeson and his "meeting," "abuse," and "hateful" views that "result" in "violence" and "Communist lies"; in the black press, the anti-Robeson "mob," their "bigotry," and the officers who facilitated them—differs. The *Amsterdam News'* editors not only place the blame for the riots squarely on the shoulders of the anti-Robeson "mob" and the officers "sympathetic" to their actions, but link their actions to the racism that motivates lynch mobs. Thus, *Amsterdam News* editors make a connection between the democratic constitutional rights that root both editorials and the ongoing violation of African American's rights nationwide as a result of literal and symbolic institutionally sanctioned "lynch mobs."

In the following section, I discuss such framing differences and their implications in more detail.

THE PRO-SOVIET NEGRO INSTIGATOR

Mainstream journalists depended on a set of conventions for reporting on the Peekskill riots that included a reliance on official sources—especially New York state police and government officials at all levels—resulting, perhaps unsurprisingly, in a lack of African American sources or other sources sympathetic with Robeson. The mainstream press also had a tendency to replace "riot" with less-severe terms to describe the violence that took place at Peekskill. "Incident," "battle," "flare-up," "melee," "fist-fight," and "fracas" were popular with white journalists. Some of these terms suggested that the riots were lighthearted and fun; the *Chicago Tribune* called one "the song and slug fest."²⁸ Such language minimizes the violence that took place at Peekskill by suggesting it was engaged in equally by both parties and/or was not very serious. Further, such language undermines the victimhood of concertgoers and the very real threat they, and Robeson, were under.

Along with these discursive similarities, two primary frames for understanding the riots were presented across mainstream sources: (1) that the riots represented an ideological battleground between the values associated with American democracy and enemy Communism, and (2) that Robeson and his fans intentionally planned the concerts for the purpose of instigating physical violence.

Ideological Battleground

This frame, which constructed the riots as solely about an ideological disagreement in which "pro-Communist" forces were pitted against "anti-Communist" forces, was present in just over forty percent of mainstream stories. Characterizations of Robeson described the singer as "pro-Communist," a "Communist sympathizer" or as "pro-Soviet," with the concerts being described as "pro-Communist meeting(s)" being held to intentionally "stir up trouble." This frame obscured the possibility that there were motives beyond disdain for Communism, including racism and anti-Semitism, behind the violence that occurred at Peekskill, while also blaming the victims of this violence and obscuring the complex content of Robeson's critiques.

For example, the *Los Angeles Times* reported on the riots as a "battle" between "anti-communist demonstrators" and "supporters" of "singer Paul Robeson, advocate of Communism."²⁹ *Newsweek* reported on the "ruckus," as "the Peekskill class war games" in which "anti-Communist hotheads" had confronted "Communists, sympathizers and the pro-Communist Negro," making no mention of the possibility of racial motivations for the event.³⁰ Later, in explaining the two riots, an article in *The New York Times* reported that "on the past two week-ends there has been violence in the Peekskill area over the 'Communist issue'" and that "Paul Robson, Negro baritone and outspoken Communist sympathizer" was prevented from singing by "demonstrations by veterans' groups" representing "a mood of growing hostility toward communism and Communists."³¹ Similarly, a *Chicago Tribune* editorial reported that "Paul Robeson, the Negro singer whose Communist propaganda has been vigorously repudiated by members of his own race" was protested by "a patriotic parade" held by "Westchester county veterans."³² In addition to framing the conflict as solely about Communism, this sentiment isolates Robeson and his critiques of American inequality from the larger black community.

Time magazine reported that at a "demonstration protesting the appearance of Communist-tuned Singer Paul Robeson . . . the [Robeson] audience defiantly burst into the chorus of the old radical marching song, We Shall

Not Be Moved," upon which "the veterans charged."[33] While acknowledging that it was in fact the veterans who "charged," labeling Robeson "advocate of Communism" while describing the audience as "defiant" perpetuates a frame that the violence against them was justified by their political attitudes.

Further, *Time*'s choice to label the song "We Shall Not Be Moved" "radical" reveals an explicit linkage of Communism to movements for race and class equality. A song with a history in slave-era, biblically based musical traditions that had been used in social movements for decades was treated as evidence of a radical un-American threat.[34] Without a doubt such discursive linkages illustrate how anti-Communism was used as an implicit cover for anti–civil rights sentiment in dominant discourses during the McCarthy Era. In addition, *Time* ignores the possibility that singing "We Shall Not be Moved" was meaningful to Robeson fans as a protest against what they perceived to be an identity-based attack on themselves and the singer as opposed to an expression of support for a specific political model.

Such early articulations of black civil rights with Communism foreshadow the later labeling of high-profile African American figures as Communist and anti-American. Long before Dr. Martin Luther King Jr. and many other prominent black Americans were called Communists by their opponents, Robeson, a high-profile African American with cross-over appeal who presented challenges to the racial status quo received this (dis)honor.[35]

In a mild critique of the rioters' actions, *Time* also reported "the communist-line Civil Rights Congress quickly denounced the sorry affair as an attempt to 'lynch Robeson.' It was hardly that. But it was an example of misguided patriotism."[36] This statement again marginalizes and undermines the role of racial animus in the events at Peekskill. By labeling the Civil Rights Congress as "communist-line," *Time*, along with mainstream reports on the whole, perpetuated the work of the House Un-American Activities Committee—labeling the CRC subversive undermined the power of its critiques of race, class, and criminal justice inequality.[37]

Time's demonizing of the Civil Rights Congress, and their "it was hardly that," also specifically undermines the claim that the Peekskill mob may have intended to lynch Robeson. Such reporting ignores the validity of this fear given that several effigies of Robeson *had* been lynched in Peekskill leading up to the concerts (a detail that went underreported), and the feeling among many in the crowd that this was the obvious intent (Figure 1.2).[38] Instead, the violence at Peekskill is simply constructed as "misguided patriotism" and no room is made for the possibility that the very nature of such patriotism could result in racial/ethnic and/or religious violence and hostilities. Many Americans at the time had lived through the upswing of lynching following WWI and WWII and likely knew full well that African Americans continued to be lynched for much smaller (but often equally imagined) crimes than being a Communist riot inciter.[39]

Paul Robeson at Peekskill, NY, 1949 29

Figure 1.2 (Original AP caption): Peekskill, NY: An effigy of Paul Robeson hangs from rear of tow truck in Oregon Corners, Peekskill, NY, echoing the sentiments of the town's residents. (Copyright Bettmann/Corbis / AP Images)

In an interesting twist that perfectly illustrates the way motivations of racial bigotry were ignored in the mainstream press, the *Los Angeles Times* reported that the "Imperial Wizard" of the Ku Klux Klan (KKK) had declared "crosses would be burned in a crusade against Communism and to give support to the veterans of Peekskill, N.Y., involved in a riot last Saturday."[40] The article presented no response, opposition, or denunciation of the idea that crosses set ablaze by the Klan were simple expressions of anti-Communist sentiment that supported veterans.

By taking the KKK at its word that its actions following Peekskill would be about patriotism, the *Los Angeles Times* allowed for the association of a terrorist group in the business of committing widespread and vicious racial violence with American values. The fact that the *LA Times* was willing to include, without interrogation or critique, the word of an Imperial Wizard, but not the perspectives of Robeson, his supporters, or anyone else who witnessed and understood the veterans' motivations differently, undermines the value of fairness supposedly at the root of journalistic practice and allows for a disturbingly sympathetic and inaccurate representation of the KKK.

As these examples illustrate, throughout mainstream press coverage of Robeson at Peekskill an ideological binary was created by labeling Robeson, the concertgoers, and most organizations or individuals who spoke out for them as Communist affiliated, while labeling the anti-Robeson forces as "patriotic veterans." According to historical accounts, the anti-Robeson crowd was not only made up of members of veterans' organizations but also civilians of various backgrounds and police from Peekskill and the surrounding areas.[41] Likewise, and equally unreported, is the fact that the pro-Robeson crowd included many black veterans and that these veterans made up a large portion of those who had volunteered to protect Robeson and other concertgoers.[42] Unfortunately the mainstream press' binary construction of "anti-Communist veterans" and "Paul Robeson and his Communist-line followers" disabled complex interpretations of the identities and motivations of the various parties involved.

Each mainstream paper also repeatedly printed an interview with Eleanor Roosevelt in which she stated, "I disagree violently with Paul Robeson," but went on to say that she would be willing to attend one of his concerts if he did not use "his art for political propaganda."[43] The reoccurrence of this report is significant given its basic assumption that a black celebrity living in a country in which members of his ethnic group are not afforded any semblance of equal rights should be apolitical, and, that if such a celebrity chooses to dissent politically, that choice furthers "propaganda." Roosevelt's statement also assumes that artistic expression *can* be apolitical and is at its best that way. Certainly, the wife of a former president labeling Robeson's dissent "propaganda" undermines the validity of any criticism he might levy, while evoking a narrative that suggests Robeson should simply be content in the singular role of an entertainer.

Robeson and His Fans as Violent Instigators

This frame was presented in nearly thirty percent of mainstream stories in two ways: (1) that Communists (including Robeson and/or some of his fans) had intentionally instigated violence at Peekskill as part of a larger campaign to overthrow American values, and (2) that Robeson and/or his fans represented a dangerous physical threat that required physical containment and defeat.

For example, the constant use of the word "provoked" in mainstream coverage of the riots framed Robeson and his fans as the precipitators of the violence while displacing blame from the anti-Robeson crowd. All mainstream sources published quotes from New York Governor Thomas Dewey that "the entire incident was obviously provoked by Communist groups" and that "the meeting was held deliberately to incite disorder."[44] District Attorney George M. Fanelli was reported by *The New York Times* as saying that "the evidence" he had "indicated that the violence was provoked by those who came to hear Mr. Robeson."[45] *The Times* also reported the view of Capt. John A. Gaffney, Superintendent of State Police for New York, that a clash between the two groups had been unavoidable as the Robeson group had come "to provoke" and the veterans were "too willing to be provoked."[46] While this last report placed some responsibility for the violence on the anti-Robeson groups involved in the clash, this responsibility is minimized by the suggestion that ultimately the primary error of the veterans was only in being provoked by a group dead set on causing unrest.

The *Chicago Tribune* reported that "Paul Robeson, controversial Negro singer provoked riots" with his "recent appearance in Peekskill, N.Y."[47] Likewise, the *Tribune* stated that "the situation was precipitated when Robeson and his backers insisted on giving the concert," and a column in the same paper asked, "Why should Mr. Russia, Paul Robeson, be allowed to create riots all over the land?"[48] The alternative possibility that the violence was "precipitated" by the veterans' "insistence" on demonstrating against Robeson, or that it was anti-Communist groups who were being "allowed to create riots," was not made available in mainstream discourse.

While much mainstream discourse constructed Robeson as intentionally perpetuating violence and Communist propaganda, some also constructed him as simply being used as a pawn by unidentified (but threatening) Communist powers in a larger plot. An editorial by the editors of the *Los Angeles Times* noted that "the Commies are taking Robeson on a cross-country tour—on a traveling riot, they hope," suggesting that the violence at Peekskill was but one part of a larger Communist conspiracy to make the U.S. appear to be full of "native fascists."[49] Similarly, articles in the same paper reported, "The recent riots were fomented by Communists and fellow travelers as part of a 'party line program,'" and the (unsubstantiated) contention of veteran organization leaders that "'goon squads of Reds' were sent to Peekskill before the concert to stir up the populace."[50]

Even mainstream coverage that was critical of the veterans' actions perpetuated the theory that ultimately those actions were the natural result of a Communist conspiracy. *The New York Times* reported that "those who participated in the anti-Communist demonstrations fell into a Communist 'bear trap.'"[51] Such conspiracy discourse in the mainstream press allowed for the possibility that, at best, Robeson and his fans were dupes of a larger organized move against American values—at worst, they were active traitors.

Along with the construction of Robeson as instigator or puppet for "Communist causes," many stories in the mainstream press also suggested that Robeson's fans had not only come with the intent of instigating "trouble" but the intent to commit physical violence. Multiple sources reported that at the second concert "Robeson men ... were armed with baseball bats," with few providing the context that Robeson fans might feel legitimate fear for their personal safety given the events of the first riot.[52] The *Chicago Tribune* constructed the concertgoers and the volunteers who were charged with protecting the singer at the second concert as a hostile military force. The *Tribune* reported that the preparation for "the Negro singer's" concert was "in line with the operation of the Russian commissar system" and that "many of the Robesonites were recruited."[53] Not noted by the *Tribune* is that the men who served as protectors of Robeson and the concert grounds during the second concert were organized only after the violence committed against the crowd and the failure of the police to protect them the first time around. Further, the use of sensational and militaristic language by the *Tribune* makes it seem not only natural, but necessary, for an armed force to battle Robeson, as they put it—"the Robesonites had as their opponents in battle, 3,500 veterans."[54]

The mainstream press also constructed the Robeson crowd as being solely composed of adult, able-bodied men when in fact Robeson concertgoers included women, children, and the elderly, some who sustained injuries during the riots.[55] Certainly a large crowd of "armed" and "recruited" "Negro" and "Communist" men could more easily be constructed as a violent threat needing suppression than a multi-racial, pro-equality crowd made up of families.

The pro-Robeson group was further established as a physical threat in the mainstream press through repeated reports of injuries sustained by anti-Robeson war veterans. On the other hand, injuries to Robeson supporters were rarely reported. One *Chicago Tribune* editorial contended that "two of the veterans or 'peaceful pickets,' were hospitalized, one critically stabbed by some music lover."[56] Similarly, the *Los Angeles Times* reported that "one Robeson supporter reportedly attacked a policeman with a baseball bat" and that "the only two hospitalized were war veterans who had participated in a protest parade against the concert."[57] It is unclear where the *LA Times* and the *Tribune* received this information but historians and those present at Peekskill have listed extensively the serious injuries received by members of the Robeson crowd, including those that required stitches, the amputation of a finger, knocked out teeth, and severe head trauma resulting in brain hemorrhaging.[58]

Thus, the general framing of Robeson concertgoers as violent and armed, and veterans as victims of their violence, directly contradicts what investigative and firsthand accounts reveal about the events at Peekskill. In addition to the fact that the charges are unsubstantiated in news reports, historical and contemporary investigations of the events reveal no record of Robeson supporters carrying weapons, suggest that the wounded among the concertgoers included women, and attest that many of the Robeson concertgoers only fought back after attempting to flee for their safety and being prevented from doing so by the anti-Robeson crowd and police barricades. In fact, even in 1949 the only criminal charges filed in the riots' aftermath were against anti-Robeson demonstrators, supporting accounts that the anti-Robeson protestors—not the concertgoers—were solely responsible for instigating the violence.[59]

Together, along with being largely based on hearsay, frames of Robeson and his fans as intentional instigators who preplanned an attack at Peekskill ignored and displaced any responsibility the anti-Robeson crowd had for the riot. Further, framing the mob as solely veterans, veterans as the only victims of the riots, and a disregard for the real injuries that members of the Robeson crowd received, exonerates the anti-Robeson mob, allowing them victim status, while simultaneously implicating Robeson and his fans and denying their victimhood.

Such victim blaming discourse is similar to early-twentieth-century mainstream reports of lynching in which black victims and communities were blamed for violence against them through narratives that implied they stepped out of line or otherwise provoked it.[60] In this case, by focusing on wounded veterans, along with constructing Robeson and/or his concert audience as violent instigators, the mainstream press essentially justified the violence committed at Peekskill while refusing to acknowledge its severity and motivations.

NAVIGATING THE PEEKSKILL DISGRACE

Like the mainstream press, the black press also presented mostly negative characterizations of Robeson, though with less frequency and intensity. Negative characterizations of Robeson were most concentrated in the *Chicago Defender*, whose journalists presented frames much more similar to those of the mainstream press than those writing for other black papers. These findings parallel those in the mainstream press where the *Chicago Tribune* presented more negative coverage than any of its counterparts and suggests that despite the presence of alternative discourses for making sense of the riots, journalists in the black press were not immune to the specific ideological climates of their region.

The negative coverage in the *Defender* primarily focused on denouncing Robeson's politics. An editorial characterized Robeson as "unpatriotic" and stated that "we agree with Jackie Robinson that Paul Robeson sounds 'silly' and we are confident that, save for a small fringe group of screwballs, Mr. Robeson will remain without an army."[61] Similarly, *Defender* columnist A.N. Fields observed that "if not a Communist, he [Robeson] might as well be one," and that he "courts such episodes" by acting "especially obnoxious."[62]

While both of these accounts are undoubtedly negative in tone toward Robeson, two things are important to note. First, while denouncing Communism and Robeson's supposed affinity for it, *Defender* journalists do not construct Robeson as a threat but rather use terms that minimize his politics to immaturity—"silly" and "obnoxious." While accepting the dominant discourse that Robeson is "unpatriotic," this coverage explicitly attempts to convey that Robeson is not a viable threat—he "will remain without an army." Thus newsmakers at the *Defender* walk a line that accepts some dominant understandings of Robeson while challenging the idea that Robeson poses any sort of legitimate threat to America.

Second, *Defender* criticisms of Robeson also included strongly worded denunciations of the Peekskill rioters. For example, the editors also stated that the perpetrators of the violence at Peekskill should be "brought to justice" because using "force to crush unpopular views . . . is the Russian way."[63] Likewise, A.N. Fields labeled the perpetrators of the violence at Peekskill "hoodlums" who in seeking "to silence him [Robeson] by forcible means might as well be Fascists," noting that such action "does the same violence to democratic principles as the crackpot communist."[64] Thus, while denouncing Robeson the *Defender* presents a larger critique of the ideologies that incited the Peekskill riots and contends that these ideologies, and their resulting actions, pose a larger threat to the nation than Robeson—a perspective largely missing from mainstream criticisms of Robeson.

On the other hand, the few explicitly positive characterizations of Robeson published in the black press tended to focus on linking Robeson's popularity and achievements with his political beliefs and actions. Earl Brown's column in the *New York Amsterdam News* listed Robeson as "one of a handful of Negroes" to "have burst the bounds of oppression and succeeded," suggesting that, "Mr. Robeson knows this. And this is probably one reason why he is now saying and doing the things he does."[65] Similarly, in the *Defender*, literary legend Langston Hughes described Robeson as the "world's most exciting singer" in whose "honor" "thousands of Americans braved mob violence." Hughes goes on to acknowledge that while Robeson's opinions are "unpopular" in America they are "held by millions of people in the Soviet Union and China—areas much larger and more populous than the U.S.A., and where race prejudice, poverty, and Anglo-Saxon scorn are booked to go."[66]

Thus, positive coverage in the black press, while infrequent, attempted to celebrate Robeson's achievements while contextualizing his political outlook within a larger assumption of a sincere desire to make a difference for his fans, and particularly African Americans who were subject to "Anglo-Saxon scorn" and had not "burst the bounds of oppression."

Further, Hughes' column in the *Defender* seems to answer many of the critiques of the singer in the same paper that aligned more fully with mainstream discourse. This suggests that even as members of the black press distanced themselves from Robeson's politics, they were more willing than mainstream newsmakers to include a diverse set of ideological standpoints about Robeson and his larger sociopolitical meaning.

Together, black press sources presented overwhelmingly negative representations of anti-Robeson demonstrators, often describing them as "a raging mob." Black journalists had no qualms with describing the events at Peekskill as a "riot" and ubiquitously used this term in their descriptions. At the same time, stories in the black press constructed the violence as intense, dangerous, and one-sided (unlike the minimizing descriptors in the mainstream press).

An editorial in the *New York Amsterdam News* characterized the rioters as an "ignorant and vicious mob," a letter to the editor in the *Los Angeles Sentinel* described the violence as "mayhem," and news articles in the *Chicago Defender* characterized the actions of the veterans as "an attack on the Robeson audience" "waged with such primitive weapons as fence rails, tree limbs, bottles, chairs and sign standards."[67] Unlike reports of the violence in the mainstream press, the black press carried reports of wounded on the anti-Robeson side, often personalizing these reports by listing, along with names, the professions and ages of the wounded.[68] Such characterizations of the anti-Robeson rioters and specifics about Robeson fan injuries construct a clear counterdiscourse that humanizes the pro-Robeson crowd while working to turn stereotypes about black and "radical" incivility on their head.

Overall, the black press presented two primary frames for making sense of the events at Peekskill. Nearly forty-five percent of black press coverage framed the riots as part of a larger climate of racist violence in America. In addition, thirty percent of black press coverage framed the neglect of various local, state, and federal officials who had acted indifferently toward, and sometimes engaged in, the violent persecution of Robeson, his fans, and members of various oppressed cultures as the real story at play in the conflict.

Violence as Part of Larger Racist Climate

African American journalists constructed this frame by discursively connecting the violence at Peekskill to other violent acts committed against blacks throughout the U.S. News articles in the *New York Amsterdam News, Los Angles Sentinel,* and *Chicago Defender* focused on reports of "a fiery cross—emblem of the Ku Klux Klan—burned on a hillside nearby" during the riots and discussed in-depth the "anti-Negro expression shown by the rioters."[69]

Editorials and columns in the black press used especially strong language to contextualize the riots as part of a larger set of racist trends, commonly referring to the anti-Robeson crowd as a "lynch mob." In his column "Violence American Style," the *New York Amsterdam News'* Earl Brown noted that because "Communists are looked upon with about as much scorn and hate as Negroes," the Peekskill "attackers" were provided "with two reasons to attack."[70] Noting that "in the U.S., there is a racial pattern" in which Americans are willing to "continue racial hate and oppression at the expense of democratic institutions," Brown goes on to detail two recent cases of violence against blacks in which one man was unjustly murdered and another kidnapped by whites and forced to work as a "peon on their farm."[71]

Brown contends that in this context, "when the Westchester mob beat up persons who attended Mr. Robeson's concert every colored person was symbolically assaulted."⁷² Another column by Brown argued that the "group of veterans actually provoked the riot and were the aggressors," and thus "slapped democracy down by acting like the Ku Klux Klan."⁷³ A letter to the editor in the *Amsterdam News* further contended that the "war veterans were not against Paul Robeson politically and ideologically one tenth as much as they were racially," and that they had acted like "Klansmen" by attacking Robeson who "symbolizes 13,000,000 comparatively defenseless Negro Americans."⁷⁴ In these cases, it is clear that despite distancing themselves from Robeson's politics at various points in their reporting, African American newsmakers, and their readers, understood Robeson's persecution as reflective of the persecution of their community as a whole.

Similarly, a letter to the editor published by the *Los Angeles Sentinel* noted the continuing racial segregation in veterans' organizations by calling the American Legion a "100 percent American and 99.44 percent Jim Crow organization" and contending that the "cross-burning riots" were motivated by those "who thought a Negro had no right to speak his mind" and thus would "fight anything of benefit to the working man or of the Negro."⁷⁵ Langston Hughes also wrote in his column for the *Chicago Defender* that "nobody in Peekskill or elsewhere threw stones or burned fiery crosses" when other notable, but white, Americans like Ezra Pound criticized their country, "but Robeson is a Negro. It has long been the fashion in this American country of ours to keep Negroes from doing things that other citizens may do with impunity."⁷⁶ By highlighting this double standard regarding the political agency available to white celebrities but not Robeson, Hughes presents as a given the role of race in the persecution of Robeson.

The black press also contained multiple reports of the burning and hanging of effigies of Robeson and the yelling of "racial insults" at concertgoers. These reports directly contradict the mainstream press' tendency to ignore the racist language used by the anti-Robeson mob and downplaying of possible intentions to lynch Robeson.

While this frame focused on critiquing both ideologies and specific acts that supported and reflected anti-black racism within the U.S., it also included denunciations of bigotry targeting other groups. According to a firsthand account of the events at Peekskill by novelist Howard Fast, although the pro-Robeson crowd was mostly white (with a large percentage being Jewish) this did not spare them from being labeled "niggers" by the anti-Robeson crowd. The shouts were simply adapted to include "white" so the slur became "white niggers" for Robeson's Jewish fans.⁷⁷ Fast's account is supported by black press reports from the time.

For example, the *New York Amsterdam News* published a statement from "Mrs. Paul Robeson" that "the battle at Peekskill was a typical example of the violence directed in my country against Negroes, Jews and labor unions."⁷⁸ The presence of anti-Semitic sentiments as a factor in the riots was further noted by black press news reports that "one of the worst features of the riot was the anti-Negro and anti-Jewish remarks heard among the veterans and their supporters."[79] Black papers also reported on accounts of attacks on black and Puerto Rican New Yorkers who were simply passing through the area at the time of the riots and had not attended the concerts.

A strongly worded column by Dean Gordon B. Hancock of the *Los Angeles Sentinel* noted that "the violence attending the appearance of Robeson at Peekskill" was an example of "the pattern of a Nazi state transpiring before our eyes," and argued that "Klanism, whether masked or unmasked, is a symptom of Nazism."[80] By equating the violence at Peekskill with Nazism, Hancock connects the recent memory of World War II anti-Semitism with the persecution of Robeson and his fans. In doing so Hancock also implies that just as the U.S. fought Nazism abroad it should focus its energies to doing so at home.[81]

Hancock goes on to argue, "There was a lynching in Peekskill just as surely as there are lynchings here and there about the south." Hancock then explicitly presents the question at the root of much of the black press' criticism of the violence at Peekskill and mainstream narratives of it—"Why is being a Communist so much more damnable in Negroes than in others? Why a white Communist can sit in the halls of Congress and a Negro Communist cannot sing to an American audience?"[82]

By framing the Peekskill riots as rooted in racial prejudices, the black press both reflected the perspectives of members of the black community and presented a counterdiscourse to those in the mainstream press that refused to acknowledge racism as the motivation of the violence. Given the political climate of the period and the integrationist goals of black journalists, the black press also embraced dominant discourses that demonized Communism as a political ideology and found fault with Robeson for allying closely with it. However, unlike in the mainstream press, these discourses acknowledged the potential of anti-Communist fervor to subsume prejudices against African Americans, Jews, and other groups, and constructed these prejudices as an equal, if not more dangerous, threat to American democracy as Communism.

Complicity of Officials

Black press coverage of the Peekskill riots repeatedly focused on accounts of participation by the police who were supposed to be maintaining order, along with evidence of neglect by local officials who had warning that violence would occur but did not act. Earl Brown reported that "police evidently sided with the hoodlum mob of attackers."[83] A letter to the editor published by the *Sentinel* noted that "policemen gave them [the anti-Robeson crowd] their full cooperation" and several news articles reported that "state and local officials will be sued for failure to protect persons who attended the meeting."[84] Similarly, a man-on-the-street interview by the *Amsterdam News* contended, "The riot seems to have been prearranged. The city officials put the veteran's organization wise."[85] The *Chicago Defender* reported that "some police" "had said frankly that they helped the anti-Robeson group 'whip commie heads.'"[86]

Together, such reporting on the part of the black press calls into question one of the primary mainstream frames—that of Robeson and his fans as instigators—by suggesting that in fact officials had colluded with anti-Robeson rioters to cause violence. At the same time, this framing undermines the credibility of the very officials whose reports and comments on the riots both presses were forced to depend upon, but whom the mainstream press showed no interest in challenging.

An explicit example of this can be seen in an editorial published by the *Amsterdam News* that contended, "District Attorney Fenelli, Sheriff Ruscoe and other county officials had a clear-cut responsibility to protect the Robesonites in exercise of their rights" given that "anyone who was not deaf and blind realized fully the kind of demonstration that the veterans groups was promoting was almost sure to end in disorder."[87] The *Amsterdam News* editors thus recommend "immediate action by Governor Dewey to discipline District Attorney Fenelli and Sheriff Ruscoe and any other public officials whose negligence contributed to the Peekskill disgrace."[88]

The black press also frequently noted in news reports that the very group of officials "investigating" the riots "had been charged with keeping order" and "have themselves been criticized for their handling of the riot situation."[89] The *Chicago Defender* reported that Gov. Dewey's insinuation that "Paul's followers caused the violence is supported by some police who, everyone agrees, failed to do their duty."[90] Under the headline ". . . Police Failed to Prevent Disorder," the *Defender* also reported, "Though plans for the demonstration by the Joint Veterans Council of Westchester County which developed into a full-scale riot were known in advance, no effort was made to prevent it."[91] Such reporting by journalists at the *Defender* allowed them to report on dominant accusations that the riots were the fault of Robeson fans, while simultaneously discrediting these accusations by noting that the plans of the anti-Robeson mob "were known in advance" and officials "failed to do their duty" and "everyone" knew it. Through such framing, *Defender* journalists imply an ulterior motive on the part of Dewey and local police that acknowledges the way blaming Robeson absolves white officials from their responsibility.

The black press also repeatedly emphasized the fact that all six men eventually indicted with rioting charges were members of the anti-Robeson crowd and included at least one veteran as well as "the son of a Peekskill police chief."[92] Noting the participation of the son of the Peekskill police chief and the criminal charges against him served, in very few words, to emphasize the frame that officials were intimately involved in the riots.

Along with these critiques of the official handling of the riots by politicians and police, columnist Earl Brown of the *New York Amsterdam News* presented an explicit acknowledgement of the role mainstream newspapers played in the continuing (mis)handling of the situation. Criticizing the *Los*

Angeles Times and "all such conservative papers" for proving that they are "not for civil rights and other so-called inalienable rights of the people by subtly playing up in its news and editorial columns events in a non-objective way," Brown details the ways in which the *LA Times* in particular had blamed the Peekskill riots on Robeson while failing to critique the rioters as the "hoodlums" and "aggressors" that they were.[93] By contending that the *LA Times* and other mainstream papers "misinformed the public," Brown offers a critique of the official role newspapers are supposed to play as public conveyers of truth and contends that their failure to fulfill this role "encouraged such mobs by never taking a stand for what is right in such cases."[94] Such media criticism places some blame for the violence that occurred at Peekskill, and that which might continue to occur in the future, at the feet of mainstream journalists. This critique of the official role journalism played in constructing meaning around race, nation, and violence is unique to coverage of Peekskill in the black press. The mainstream press neither acknowledged the narratives in the black press nor displayed any self-reflexivity about their own coverage. The black press then not only served as a watchdog of officials involved in Peekskill, but also of the official journalistic record as it was being created.

Together, the black press' focus on the links between racism and the Peekskill riots, and the negligence or collusion of public officials in handling them, presented discourses virtually invisible in the mainstream press. These discourses acknowledged historical and continuing racial violence and oppression against blacks and other groups by pointing out the prominent role of Robeson's race in white constructions and judgments of his politics, the way in which discourses of patriotism and anti-Communism slipped into racism, and the reality of the role official institutions played in such trends.

CONCLUSIONS

Without a doubt, mainstream press coverage of Peekskill contributed to and rearticulated dominant discourses of race and nation that many marginalized American citizens regarded as discourses of persecution. To the mainstream press, Peekskill represented a political battle over Communism instigated by Robeson and his "fellow travelers"; to the black press the violence was political, social, and personal, representing the continued struggle of African Americans to be free from victimization whether for their beliefs, their group identity, or the blackness of their skin.

Unfortunately, the mainstream response to Robeson's attempts at alternative discourse was largely that of vilification, and black journalists, while critical of the bigotry and state collusion at play in Peekskill, had already begun to treat Robeson as a persona non grata. In black press coverage of Peekskill we witness a moment in which the black press, long a defender of Robeson, struggled to navigate this loyalty within the constraints of

McCarthyism. Eventually, like other elite black institutions that engaged in community debates about what type of politics were most productive for goals of integration during the Cold War, the black press would deem Robeson too radical and largely abandoned him.[95]

According to Dorinson and Pencak, "Robeson's international prominence made him a logical target of the zealous anti-communists."[96] The star was eventually blacklisted, ostracized, and legally forbidden to travel internationally. With the revocation of his passport in 1950, the U.S. government symbolically stripped Robeson of his American citizenship and quite literally deprived him of the possibility to make a living. Even with his incredible record of accomplishments, Robeson became, in effect, a non-person, systematically ignored and silenced in dominant spaces. The case of Paul Robeson's rise and fall can be understood as an example of the toll borne by African American celebrities who want to believe in the American Dream while simultaneously finding it morally impossible to sit by in silence as it is denied.[97] His story clearly demonstrates the bind faced by black celebrities in that so long as they fulfill their role as spectacle to be consumed by an audience, their presence in the public sphere is deemed non-threatening; once this role is used to challenge the status quo they are seen as a threat needing to be controlled both discursively and physically.

Robeson faced the institutional denial of basic rights as a result of his open critiques of race and nation, and yet he also fundamentally challenged both mainstream and black newsmakers to engage in debates on these issues. Despite the demonization of Robeson, his loss of career and freedom, historian Manning Marable argued that Robeson was more influential as a cultural and political symbol of resistance than any other figure of the time.[98] Robeson would later reflect that in the days following Peekskill, reporters, yearning for that old Paul Robeson who cheerfully sang Negro spirituals, would ask "Paul what's happened to you?" He'd reply, "Nothing's happened to me. I'm just looking for freedom."[99]

NOTES

1. Martin B. Duberman, *Paul Robeson: A Biography* (New York: Ballantine Books, 1988): 377.
2. Erika Spohrer, "Becoming Extra-Textual: Celebrity Discourse and Paul Robeson's Political Transformation," *Critical Studies in Media Communication* 24, no. 2 (2007): 151–168.
3. Jeffrey C. Stewart, ed., *Paul Robeson: Artist and Citizen* (New Brunswick: Rutgers University Press 1998).
4. Stewart, *Paul Robeson:* 155.
5. Prosper Godonoo, "Paul Robeson: Honor & the Politics of Dignity," in *Sport, Race, and Evolving Reputations*, ed. David C. Ogden and Joel Nathan Rosen (Jackson: University Press of Mississippi, 2008): 48–66; Spohrer, "Becoming Extra-Textual."

6. Spohrer, "Becoming Extra-Textual".
7. Gerald Horne, "Comrades and Friends: The Personal/Political World of Paul Robeson," in *Paul Robeson: Artist and Citizen,* ed. Jeffrey C. Stewart (New Brunswick: Rutgers University Press 1998): 197–215.
8. Quoted in Duberman, *Paul Robeson:* 42.
9. Duberman, *Paul Robeson;* For examples of how Robeson's comments were reported on and received by various organizations and for some contextualization of the comments by Robeson himself, see Philip Sheldon Foner, *Paul Robeson Speaks: Writings, Speeches, Interviews, 1918–1974* (Secaucus, NJ: Citadel Press, 1978): 197–200.
10. Duberman, *Paul Robeson.*
11. Joseph Dorinson and William A. Pencak, eds., *Paul Robeson: Essays on His Life and Legacy* (Jefferson, NC: McFarland & Company, Inc., 2002).
12. Catherine Squires, "The Black Press and the State: Attracting Unwanted(?) Attention," in *Counterpublics and the State,* ed. Robert Asen and Daniel C. Brouwer (New York: State University of New York Press, 2001) 111–136; Philip A. Klinkner, with Rogers M. Smith, *The Unsteady March: The Rise and Decline of Racial Equality in America* (Chicago: The University of Chicago Press, 1999).
13. Squires, "Black Press and the State"; Patrick S. Washburn, *A Question of Sedition: The Federal Government's Investigation of the Black Press During World War II* (New York: Oxford University Press: 1986).
14. Barbara J. Beeching, "Paul Robeson and the Black Press: The 1950 Passport Controversy," *The Journal of African American History* 87 (2002): 339–354.
15. Mark Naison, "Paul Robeson and the American Labor Movement," in *Paul Robeson: Artist and Citizen,* ed. Jeffrey C. Stewart (New Brunswick: Rutgers University Press, 1998): 179–194.
16. The Civil Rights Congress was founded in 1946 as an alternative to the NAACP. It incorporated struggles for black civil rights, labor and immigrant rights, Jewish rights, and civil liberties. It was believed by the U.S. government to be seditious in nature and communist inspired but according to Horne ("Comrades and Friends") was "undoubtedly the most important organization confronting the Red Scare and McCarythism after World War II" (Stewart, *Paul Robeson:* 205).
17. Quoted in Duberman, *Paul Robeson:* 364; Joseph Walwik, "Paul Robeson, Peekskill, and the Red Menace," in *Paul Robeson: Essays on His Life and Legacy,* ed. Joseph Dorinson and William A. Pencak (Jefferson, NC: McFarland & Company, Inc., 2002): 120–129.
18. Horne, "Comrades and Friends": 208; Howard Fast, "Remembering Peekskill USA, 1949," in *Paul Robeson: Essays on His Life and Legacy,* ed. Joseph Dorinson and William A. Pencak (Jefferson, NC: McFarland & Company, Inc., 2002): 130–144.
19. Duberman, *Paul Robeson:* 367.
20. Walwik, "Red Menace."
21. Horne, "Comrades and Friends"; Fast, "Remembering Peekskill."
22. Data was collected for stories appearing between August 27, 1949, the date of the first riot, and October 13, 1949. Sources include *The New York Times, Chicago Tribune, Los Angeles Times, Time,* and *Newsweek* in the mainstream press and the *New York Amsterdam News, Chicago Defender, Los Angeles Sentinel, Negro Digest,* and *Ebony* in the African American press.
23. "The Right to Assemble," *The New York Times,* Sep. 4, 1949: 74.
24. "The Peekskill Riot," *New York Amsterdam News,* Sep. 17, 1949: 18.
25. "Right to Assemble," *The New York Times.*

26. Ibid.
27. Walwik, "Red Menace": 125.
28. "Robeson Forces Well Organized for Outbreaks," *Chicago Daily Tribune (1923–1963)*, Sep. 6, 1949: 27. The *Chicago Daily Tribune* later became the *Chicago Tribune*. I will use both titles throughout the text.
29. "Scores Hurt in Robeson Riot; Battle Halted by State Police," *Los Angeles Times*, Sep. 5, 1949: 1.
30. "Riots: Robeson Ruckus," *Newsweek*, Sep. 12, 1949: 23.
31. "New York," *The New York Times (1923–Current File)*, Sep. 11, 1949.
32. "The Riot That Interests Gov. Dewey," *Chicago Daily Tribune (1923–1963)*, Sep. 3, 1949: 8.
33. "Communists: Picnic at Peekskill," *Time*, Sep. 5, 1949, http://content.time.com/time/magazine/article/0,9171,933865,00.html (accessed Mar. 5, 2010).
34. R. Serge Denisoff, "The Religious Roots of the American Song of Persuasion," *Western Folklore* 29, no. 3 (Jul. 1970): 175–184; R. Serge Denisoff, "Folk Music and the American Left: A Generational Ideological Comparison," *The British Journal of Sociology* 20, no. 4 (Dec. 1969): 427–442; Barry O'Connell, "Whose Land and Music Shall Ours Be? Reflections on the History of Protest in the Southern Mountains," *Appalachian Journal* 12, no. 1 (Fall 1984): 18–30.
35. For more on news constructions of Dr. Martin Luther King Jr., see Richard Lentz, *Symbols, the News Magazines, and Martin Luther King* (Baton Rouge: Louisiana State University Press, 1990).
36. Ibid.
37. Mary L. Dudziak, *Cold War Civil Rights: Race and the Image of American Democracy* (Princeton, NJ: Princeton University Press, 2002).
38. Fast, "Remembering Peekskill."
39. Stewart E. Tolnay and E.M. Beck, *A Festival of Violence: An Analysis of Southern Lynchings, 1882–1930* (Champaign: University of Illinois Press, 1995).
40. "Cross-Burnings Planned by Klan in Red Crusade," *Los Angeles Times*, Sep. 4, 1949: 7.
41. Duberman, *Paul Robeson*; Fast, "Remembering Peekskill."
42. Ibid.
43. For example, "Robeson's Talks—Not Songs—Annoy Eleanor," *Los Angeles Times*, Sep. 1, 1949: 8.
44. See for example, "Dewey Orders Grand Jury Probe of Riot at Robeson Concert." *Chicago Daily Tribune (1923–1963)*, Sep. 15, 1949: A1.
45. Leo Egan, "Dewey Asks Report on Robeson Battle." *The New York Times (1923–Current File)*, Aug. 30, 1949: 1.
46. "State Police Data on Robeson Drawn," *The New York Times (1923–Current File)*, Sep. 11, 1949: 3.
47. "Legion, V.F.W. Urge Members to Ignore Robeson's Concerts," *Chicago Daily Tribune (1923–1963)*, Sep. 14, 1949: 10.
48. "Taxpayers Get the Bill for Robeson's Concert, Plus Riot," *Chicago Daily Tribune (1923–1963)*, Sep. 14, 1949: B13; Hedda Hopper, "Looking at Hollywood," *Chicago Daily Tribune (1923–1963)*, Sep. 8, 1949: N16.
49. "A Travelling Riot?" *Los Angeles Times*, Sep. 13, 1949: A4.
50. "Council Advises Public to Avoid Robeson Show," *Los Angeles Times*, Sep. 20, 1949: 1; "New Group Organizes to Fight Reds," *Los Angeles Times*, Sep. 23, 1949: 2.
51. Leo Egan, "Governor Orders Grand Jury Study of Robeson Rioting," *The New York Times (1923–Current File)*, Sep. 15, 1949: 1.
52. See for example, "Robeson Forces Well Organized for Outbreaks"; and "State Police Data on Robeson Drawn," *The New York Times*.

53. "Robeson Forces Well Organized For Outbreaks," *Chicago Daily Tribune.*
54. Ibid.
55. Horne, "Comrades and Friends."
56. "The Riot That Interests Gov. Dewey," *Chicago Daily Tribune.*
57. "Scores Hurt in Robeson Riot," *Los Angeles Times.* The same article reported later that "one unidentified Negro was reported beaten and thrown over a fence into a nearby cemetery"—apparently this man did not need/receive medical care based on the report. The *Los Angeles Times* also directly contradicted their own prior reporting of the story, which stated, "One man was stabbed, another was beaten severely over the head, and 11 other white and Negro persons were treated for bruises and cuts at a hospital" ("5000 Riot as Veterans Protest Robeson Concert," *Los Angeles Times,* Aug. 28, 1949: 1). Among the sources examined here, there never seemed to be any clear agreement on the number of injuries sustained in the first or second riot with the reported numbers varying from two to "hundred."
58. Horne, "Comrades and Friends."
59. Walwik, "Red Menace"; Fast, "Remembering Peekskill."
60. Tolnay and Beck, *Festival of Violence.*
61. "That Robeson Riot," *Chicago Defender (National Edition) (1921–1967),* Sep. 10, 1949: 6.
62. A. N. Fields, "Akers and Fields See Eye to Eye on Robeson," *Chicago Defender (National Edition) (1921–1967),* Sep. 24, 1949: 7.
63. "That Robeson Riot," *Chicago Daily Defender.*
64. Fields, "Akers and Fields."
65. Earl Brown, "Violence American Style," *New York Amsterdam News (1943–1961),* Sep. 17, 1949: 18.
66. Langston Hughes, "World's Most Exciting Singer Poses Questions of Art, Politics, Race," *Chicago Defender (National Edition) (1921–1967),* Sep. 24, 1949: 6.
67. "The Peekskill Riot," *New York Amsterdam News (1943–1961),* Sep. 17, 1949: 18; Joseph Black, "Letter to the Editor 1—No Title." *Los Angeles Sentinel,* Sep. 15, 1949: A7; "Ask Dewey Quiz of Robeson Riot," *Chicago Defender (National Edition) (1921–1967),* Sep. 3, 1949: 1.
68. For example, "Robeson Launches Boycott," *New York Amsterdam News (1943–1961),* Sep. 3, 1949: 1.
69. See for example, "Truman, Mrs. FDR Hit Robeson Riot," *Chicago Defender (National Edition) (1921–1967),* Sep. 17, 1949: 1; and "Two Vets in Critical Condition Following Paul Robeson Rioting," *Los Angeles Sentinel,* Sep. 8, 1949: A8.
70. Brown, "Violence American Style."
71. Ibid.
72. Ibid.
73. Earl Brown, "Press Propaganda," *New York Amsterdam News (1943–1961),* Sep. 10, 1949: 16.
74. John B. Johnson, "More Comment on Trouble over Robeson in Peekskill," *New York Amsterdam News (1943–1961),* Sep. 10, 1949: 16.
75. Black, "Letter to the Editor 1—No Title."
76. Hughes, "World's Most Exciting Singer Poses Questions of Art, Politics, Race."
77. Fast, "Remembering Peekskill": 66.
78. "Robeson Wife Rips Bias at Mexican Meet." *New York Amsterdam News (1943–1961),* Sep. 17, 1949: 4.
79. "Two Vets in Critical Condition Following Paul Robeson Rioting," *Los Angeles Times.*
80. Dean Gordon B. Hancock, "Between the Lines," *Los Angeles Sentinel,* Sep. 29, 1949: A8.

81. A clear nod to the "Double-V" campaign waged by the black press during WWII, which connected victory against fascism abroad to victory against racism at home.
82. Ibid.
83. Brown, "Violence American Style."
84. Black, "Letter to the Editor 1—No Title"; "Truman, Mrs. FDR Hit Robeson Riot," *Chicago Defender.*
85. "Roundup Interview on the Subject of Peekskill . . ." *New York Amsterdam News (1943–1961),* Sep. 3, 1949: 2.
86. Charley Cherokee, "National Grapevine," *Chicago Defender (National Edition) (1921–1967),* Sep. 24, 1949: 6.
87. "The Peekskill Riot," *New York Amsterdam News.*
88. Ibid.
89. For example, see "Truman, Mrs. FDR Hit Robeson Riot," *Chicago Defender;* "Grand Jury Probes Robeson Riot," *New York Amsterdam News (1943–1961),* Sep. 17, 1949: 1; and "Blame Cops in Riot," *New York Amsterdam News (1943–1961),* Sep. 10, 1949: 1.
90. Cherokee, "National Grapevine."
91. "Ask Dewey Quiz of Robeson Riot," *Chicago Defender.*
92. For example, "Six Indicted in Robeson Rioting," *New York Amsterdam News (1943–1961),* Sep. 24, 1949: 1.
93. Brown, "Press Propaganda."
94. Ibid.
95. Spohrer, "Becoming Extra-Textual"; Beeching, "Passport Controversy."
96. Dorinson and Pencak, *Paul Robeson:* 8.
97. Godonoo, "Honor."
98. Manning Marable, *Black Leadership* (New York: Columbia University Press, 1998).
99. Duberman, *Paul Robeson.*

2 Eartha Kitt, the White House, and Vietnam, 1968

The thing that hurts, that became anger, was when I realized that if you tell the truth—in a country that says you're entitled to tell the truth—you get your face slapped and you get put out of work.[1]

In 1955, the same year a federal judge ruled that the State Department had been within its right to deny Paul Robeson a passport in 1950 because of his suspected ties to Communism, America was introduced to the series of mass civil actions that would come to be known as the civil rights movement. When the sit-in actions and boycotts emerged, many journalists, especially from the North, became increasingly invested in covering the movement. In fact, many historians argue that sympathetic new coverage of the violence faced by civil rights activists in the South played a significant role in moving American public opinion against the racial status quo.[2] However, these "sympathetic" frames of civil rights activism often oversimplified and sanitized the larger movement by representing it as a South-specific struggle between "good" blacks and "bad" openly racist whites.[3] Such frames neglected the movement's larger critiques of systemic and institutional inequality across the United States and globally.

Within a decade, by the late 1960s, a national backlash against the civil rights movement was underway, easily discerned in dominant media discourses that depicted ongoing black activism as dangerous and unnecessary.[4] The legal progress bookended by *Brown v. Board of Education* in 1954 and the 1964 Civil Rights Act led many white Americans to feel that U.S. racial problems were well on their way to being solved. This, in combination with ever-increasing critiques of white racism outside the stigmatized South, led to a swift shift in public support of the movement: by 1966, polls found that most white Americans believed blacks were moving too quickly in their pursuit of racial equality.[5] At the same time the realities of *de facto* racism and lingering *de jure* racism—particularly acute inequalities in housing, employment, health care, and policing—continued to frustrate black activists and politicize younger generations of African Americans. In this context, previously sympathetic media discourses around civil rights campaigns began to shift toward representing black liberation movements as unreasonable, a threat to middle class Northern norms and, by default, larger American society.

It was in this context that in January of 1968 actress and singer Eartha Kitt was invited to attend a luncheon for prominent "women doers" with the First Lady of the United States. The event, billed as a women's problem-solving meeting on youth unrest and delinquency, was one part of President Johnson's larger initiative to solve urban crime—an initiative that sprung up partly in response to increasing racial violence and rioting in America's cities.[6] The luncheon included fifty high-profile women in political, social, and media circles (Figure 2.1). In addition to Kitt, seven other African American women as well as one self-described "Latin American," were present; the other forty-one guests were white. Kitt's invitation to the luncheon was a direct result of both her celebrity status and her ongoing advocacy on behalf of inner city youth organizations in Washington, DC, and the Watts area of California.[7]

The luncheon went largely as planned, with Mrs. Johnson offering opening remarks and three women including Margaret Moore, a journalist from Indianapolis, Martha Cole, a VISTA[8] worker based in Atlanta, and Katherine Peden, the only woman member of the President's Commission on Civil Disorders (commonly known as the Kerner Commission), speaking specifically to their experiences regarding urban unrest and youth crime prevention. Early on, President Johnson stopped by to offer remarks on the challenges of policing from the federal level, noting that the responsibility of

Figure 2.1 Eartha Kitt chats with Lady Bird Johnson and Katherine Peden at the White House in what the *Los Angeles Times* described as "smiles before the outburst." (Copyright Bettmann/Corbis / AP Images)

safety and security in cities was, from his perspective, primarily a state-level issue as well as one of individual-level responsibility. When the President remarked that "there is a great deal we can do to see that our youth do not get into these criminal directions and they are not seduced and are not led off—That is what a mother should do," Eartha Kitt asked him about "parents who have to go to work, for instance, who can't spend time with their children?" Johnson responded that the Social Security Bill helped to fund daycare centers and offered—as he exited the room—"That is a very good question for you to ask yourselves, you women here, and you all tell me what you think."[9]

What is notable both in President Johnson's comments and the tone of the luncheon overall is the way responsibility for the waves of youth and urban unrest washing across the nation was gendered. Neither Mrs. nor President Johnson asked the women at the luncheon to consider institutional-level solutions, but rather framed the conversation as one about what individual women could, and should, do to stem the tide of unrest. As a result, much of the conversation revolved around prescribing individual- and superficial-level solutions. Mrs. Moore, for example, spent a lengthy amount of time detailing how "good housekeeping is a crime deterrent" and speaking on the "moral values that deter crime."[10] Despite this general tone, both Cole and Peden offered systemic critiques in their comments while walking a careful line between recognizing the role of issues like economic exploitation and police brutality on low-income urban communities and individual-level "civil responsibility."[11]

The luncheon ended with Mrs. Johnson telling the luncheon guests, "I do hope that if you have some observations, a story, a suggestion, you will get up and tell us about it,"[12] which prompted a rather lengthy question-and-answer session. Four additional luncheon guests contributed questions and/or comments to the discussion before Eartha Kitt raised her hand and was called upon by the First Lady to speak. In the comments that followed, Kitt, a member of the Women's International League for Peace and Freedom, criticized the Vietnam War—in particular the draft—and linked it to racial and social unrest among youth in America's urban centers. She said in part:

> I have listened to the speeches here today. I feel that somewhere along the line, we have missed out on something. . . . I have lived in the gutters. That's why I know what I am talking about. The youth of America are angry. They are angry because the parents are angry. . . . They are rebelling against something and we all seem to camouflage this something. . . . Why are they so angry today? . . . Because when they get a $4 check per week and this is what the Welfare Department—when it adds up—when you break it all down, they get $4 a week. The other thing is, there are many, many things that are burning the people of this country and mostly the mothers because the mothers feel that if they are going to raise a son . . . they will be snatched away from the

mother and sent off to Vietnam. The mothers don't want it and since the mothers don't want it that emotional feeling goes right down into the children. The boys of this country are doing everything they possibly can to avoid being drafted, and the mothers are helping them do it. This is why the youth of America is crying out today. They also feel that if my education is going to only bring me a diploma, that I will not even have a job waiting for me afterwards, why should I even try to get a diploma? . . . You take the best of the country and send them off to war and they get shot. They don't want that. And particularly since the last world war, when they saw their fathers coming back from war maimed not even being able to get themselves a job. . . . And the way they tell you, they can't come to you and tell you, Mrs. Johnson. They cannot get to President Johnson and tell President Johnson about it. They rebel in the streets.[13]

In one fell swoop Kitt linked nearly every pressing national issue—education, unemployment, youth unrest, and poverty—to the ongoing and increasingly unpopular war in Vietnam. In doing so, she was the only guest at the Women Doers Luncheon to acknowledge there *was* a war going on or that it was even remotely controversial. Her attempt to convey the frustration with the war felt by young people in the communities she most identified with to the President of the United States while in his home and addressing his wife was received with both adulation and ire. Kitt instantly became a hero to many in the anti-war movement and a traitor to those who supported the war and the Johnson administration. In the months after the "Women Doers" luncheon the mainstream press published seventy-two stories on Kitt's dissent at the White House while the black press published twenty-nine.[14] This media frenzy led the Reverend Dr. Martin Luther King Jr. to come to Kitt's defense, reportedly saying that the comments were a "very proper gesture" which "described the feelings of many persons."[15]

However, both King and Kitt were caught in the shift in mainstream media framing of black civil rights action. By 1968 the civil rights movement's most visible and loved leader had begun to fall from public grace as a result of his outspoken critiques of Northern white racism, economic exploitation, and the Vietnam War.[16] In fact, King was being quickly reframed (by mainstream white politicians and journalists) as radical and out of touch, a discursive move that aimed to discredit his continuing critiques.[17] In a fascinating reflection of the disfavor surrounding King in 1968, his words of support for Kitt were reported only twice in mainstream press coverage of the Women Doers Luncheon. Further, one of these mentions, by James Yuenger of the *Chicago Tribune*, described King only as "a leader of the national anti-war movement" without any mention of his civil rights work.[18] Thus in mainstream narratives even King could not leverage enough cultural capital to shield Kitt from vicious backlash. James Earl Ray would assassinate King just two-and-a-half months later. Kitt, who had donated to the Southern Christian Leadership Conference and exchanged multiple letters of support with King over the years, attended his funeral.[19]

This chapter presents press coverage of Eartha Kitt as emblematic of late-1960s framing of black dissent. Like King and Muhammad Ali, Kitt articulated the ways institutional racism and state-sanctioned violence disproportionately harmed people of color at home and abroad. Although such critiques were borne of the same philosophies of non-violence and self-determination that fueled the Southern civil rights movement, Kitt was easily framed in mainstream news as aberrant. She was off-script from the morality play of Southern bigots versus saintly Negroes in an otherwise accommodating America. Moreover, the gendered locale—a "ladies luncheon" with the First Lady—enabled racialized gender expectations that put Kitt, whose celebrity was already inextricably linked to intersecting race and gender stereotypes, at a serious disadvantage. Comparing African American and mainstream reports, I discuss how journalists framed Kitt's dissent for their audiences, the implications of these frames for public debates around race and nation, and the particular role gender played in how journalists came to understand Kitt's agency (or lack thereof).

EMBODYING GENDERED RACIAL ANXIETY

Like Paul Robeson, Eartha Kitt achieved a level of crossover popularity that was unusual for black entertainers of her time. Perhaps best known today for her portrayal of Catwoman in the 1967 *Batman* television series, Kitt began her career as a cabaret performer and was highly accomplished as a singer and dancer as well as an actress. While Kitt was popular with both black and white audiences, she was never fully embraced by either. As a mixed-race African American actress, Kitt's public identity was limited by dominant tropes regarding the sexuality and temperament of the "tragic mulatta."[20] Public knowledge of Kitt's white parentage (which she maintained was the result of her mother being raped) allowed her to be constructed as sophisticated and sexually intriguing to white men, while her blackness ultimately limited her public identity to one of tumultuous moods and animalistic sexuality. Similarly, many of Kitt's stage and screen roles embodied performances of refinement that were usually reserved for white actresses, while at the same time hinging on stereotypes of black female lasciviousness. As Caroline A. Streeter has noted, this specific binary-dependent-yet-blurring construction of gendered identity is often uniquely applied to mixed-race black female celebrities.[21] Such tropes, working in combination with Kitt's casting as Catwoman the year before her invitation to the White House luncheon, led to her being forever described in feline terms.[22]

It is also worth considering how not only Kitt's biracial background but her widely publicized interracial relationships—she married and had a child with white real estate investor John William McDonald after multiple romances with other high-profile white men including a rumored affair with Orson Welles—influenced the way media makers, and the public at large, understood her identity and politics. In particular, these relationships likely reinforced titillating tropes about mixed-race black women as the sexually available racial Other, objectified and exotic, while playing on anxieties about miscegenation. Because Kitt's celebrity was limited to such constructions, her identity, both her blackness and the gendered violence that led to her interracial conception, was largely depoliticized in media discourses and in many ways reinforced a "safe" racial identity: black, but not "too" black; sophisticated like a white woman, but not in terms of her raced sexuality; passionate, but simultaneously easily dismissed as moody and irrational. Thus, Kitt's particular brand of celebrity allowed her distinctive access to elite spaces even as the intersection of her racial background and gender kept her disempowered within the entertainment industry.

These contexts clearly influenced how mainstream journalists in particular covered Kitt's remarks at the White House: Once she explicitly crossed the line of the depoliticized identity that had been constructed around her, Kitt's blackness *and* gender became the dual characteristics through which she was disciplined and denounced. In particular, white journalists overwhelmingly relied on racialized stereotypes that constructed black women as the binary of idealized white womanhood—exemplified by Lady Bird Johnson—to frame Kitt's dissent.

This binary is reflected in the most common frames that emerged in mainstream reports: (1) Kitt's words were a personal attack against the Johnsons—particularly Mrs. Johnson; and (2) Kitt's comments were a breach of proper social behavior given both the setting and the audience. By focusing on a constructed battle between Kitt and the First Lady, and questions of etiquette rather than the substance of Kitt's words, the mainstream press revealed a tendency to gender the event and attempt to domesticate Kitt, a reluctance to address the substance of Kitt's words, and a strong defense of dominant ideologies regarding the speech borders around gender, race, and social status—especially for black women.

Kitt on Attack

In this frame, which occurred in thirty-three percent of mainstream stories and was particularly common in news articles, journalists constructed Kitt as the antagonist against whom the protagonist, Lady Bird Johnson, was forced to battle. Johnson was constructed as sophisticated and vulnerable while Kitt was constructed as a shrewish attacker. This framing of Kitt's interaction with the First Lady not only reinforced gendered racial stereotypes, but also drew focus away from—and in some cases, eliminated— discussion of the substance of her questions about Vietnam and urban youth.

For example, the mainstream press largely failed to report that Kitt's words were part of a larger discussion directed at a group of people, instead framing them as a part of a one-on-one during which the First Lady was confronted without warning. *The Washington Post* ran the headline "Eartha Kitt Confronts the Johnsons: Startled First Lady Responds to Singer's Attack on War."[23] The *Post*'s use of "confronts" and "attack" as descriptors of Kitt's words and the characterizing of Lady Bird Johnson's "startled" response represents Kitt as aggressive and purposefully catching the First Lady unawares. The article goes on to characterize the conversation between Kitt and Johnson as "an impassioned confrontation," and "dramatic confrontation," in which Kitt "pointed a finger to Mrs. Johnson."[24] The *Los Angeles Times* constructed the antagonist/protagonist relationship with even stronger language. One *LA Times* article begins, "Eartha Kitt's Tirade on War Leaves First Lady in Tears," reporting that "Miss Kitt's angry tirade brought tears to the First Lady's eyes" *three* more times before its conclusion.[25] Kitt is described once again as a near-violent attacker—"her eyes flashing in defiance while she puffed on a cigaret (sic) and jabbed a finger at her audience" as she "delivered an emotional tirade."[26]

Descriptors of Kitt in mainstream sources as "angry" and "emotional" and her speech as an "outburst," "blast," and 'tirade" in which she "shouted," "jabbed her finger at a startled Lady Bird Johnson," and "told off the First Lady" were repeated frequently.[27] Such descriptors not only construct Kitt as an attacker but as an uncontrolled and irrational one: an angry instigator. Further descriptors of Johnson as victim—"shocked," "shaken," "stunned," tearful," and "trembling"—were repeated with similar frequency.[28] Despite the heavy reliance on direct quotations from Kitt's White House speech, her message was subsumed by the idea that she personally attacked the beloved figure of Lady Bird Johnson. Poverty, inner city unrest, and the Vietnam War—the topics of Kitt's dissent—became tangential in mainstream news that instead focused on a constructed war of words between an irrational and aggressive black woman and a shaken but controlled and respectable white one.

A day after its initial reporting of the story, *The Washington Post* ran the front-page headline "Mrs. Johnson Chides Eartha Kitt: 'Shrill Voice' Jars First Lady" over an article characterizing Kitt's statements as a "confrontation."[29] This headline again constructs Johnson as a victim "jarred" by the "shrill voice" of Kitt. Further, it allows Johnson the power an adult is commonly understood to have over a misbehaving child—"chides" suggests both that Kitt's actions were childish and irresponsible and that they required denunciation from a reasonable motherly figure (Johnson) who is described in the article as "expressing indignation at Miss Kitt's actions."[30] The use of the gendered term "shrill" to describe Kitt's voice also demonstrates the way outspoken female voices are uniquely denigrated in public discourse.

Notably, *The Post* also explicitly framed the incident as a "women's issue" by publishing over half of its news articles on the subject of Kitt's dissent at the luncheon in the "For and About Women" section of the paper.[31]

This placement of the story assumes a gendered interest in what Kitt had to say (apparently *Post* editors felt men would have little interest) and justifies a focus on the interpersonal relationship between two women. Had *The Post* been more inclined to treat Kitt's dissent as hard news—which, generally, political debate about war and coverage of urban unrest were—the serious domestic and military issues that were at the heart of her statement could have been addressed.

The New York Times also joined in the Kitt versus Johnson storyline, though with less sensational language. Its initial headline, "Eartha Kitt Denounces War Policy to Mrs. Johnson,"[32] reads significantly more even-handed than that delivered by the *Chicago Tribune*—"Eartha's Shouts Stun Lady Bird into Tears."[33] The *Tribune* contended twice more in the same article that Kitt "shouted" her words at Mrs. Johnson although none of the journalists writing for other mainstream newspapers reported that anything was shouted.[34] The *Tribune* also reported that in response to "the confrontation between the Negro singer and the President's wife," Mrs. Johnson considered Kitt "the shrill voice of anger and discord" and that other guests at the luncheon "came to Mrs. Johnson's defense."[35] Notable here is that the explicit recalling of Kitt's race is linked to the construction of Mrs. Johnson requiring defending from a "shrill" and "angry" threat.

Interestingly, the mainstream press also pitted other white women against Kitt in conveying the story. Every mainstream newspaper compared Kitt's words to those of another White House luncheon guest, Mrs. Richard J. Hughes. It was reported that Hughes, the First Lady of New Jersey, "came to Mrs. Johnson's defense" stating that "youth are not rebelling because of the war."[36] These reports also noted Hughes, who had lost her first husband in WWII, had eight sons, none of whom "smoked marijuana" or "wants to go to Vietnam but all will go." Further Hughes is reported as stating that she "will kiss" these sons "good-bye as contribution to my country."[37]

Thus, the white Hughes is constructed as an ideally patriotic wife and mother who properly raised her children to be drug-free and willing to sacrifice for their country despite their reservations. Further, Hughes is constructed as willing to sacrifice not only a husband but also her children for her country. These reports constructed a binary between the idealized womanhood of Hughes and that of Kitt, who is constructed not only as lacking in a specific sort of gendered manners and willingness to sacrifice, but in patriotism. In a further twist, the *Chicago Tribune* made a point to report that Eartha Kitt had only "a 6-year old daughter" in comparison to Hughes' eight military-eligible sons.[38] The implication of the *Tribune*—that compared to Hughes, Kitt has nothing to lose (and nothing to contribute) to the war effort because of her young, female child—seems to take an even harsher ideological dig both at the validity of Kitt's comments (after all, why should she care if she has nothing to lose personally) and her womanhood (one daughter versus eight sons! Clearly someone is the real woman here!).

Together, the various mainstream iterations of the "Kitt on attack" frame worked discursively to silence the actress. Rather than interrogating the content of her statement to Mrs. Johnson's luncheon group, the framing of Kitt's dissent as threatening and irrational justified ignoring the social critiques she raised. At the same time, focus on the First Lady's reportedly rattled state, as well as detailed reports of her defenders, constructed the story along the lines of protagonist versus antagonist with the sympathetically constructed, white, elite women playing the former role and Kitt, a mixed-race African American woman, with little concrete social power, the latter.

Breach of Etiquette

A second frame, occurring in twenty-eight percent of mainstream stories, most commonly in opinion-based pieces but apparent in news articles as well, constructed Kitt's words as a breach of etiquette. This frame depended on dominant social constructions of "polite," "ladylike" behavior and characterized Kitt's "outburst" as both "rude" and threatening to basic concepts of civility. As with the previous frame, this presentation of Kitt's dissent drew from larger dominant social discourses that frame black women as failing to fulfill the requirements of womanhood.[39]

A letter to the editor published by *Newsweek* opined, "You say that there were 50 ladies present at Lady Bird Johnson's White House luncheon.... Judging from Eartha Kitt's behavior and her remarks to the gathering, there were 49 ladies present plus Miss Kitt."[40] This language is fairly explicit in presenting Kitt as not only lacking in basic manners but the qualities that supposedly evidence womanhood. Similarly, nearly seventy percent of the letters to the editor published by the *Chicago Tribune* focused on denouncing Kitt's supposed "breach of etiquet [sic]."[41] These rebuked Kitt's "public display of anger" as "the epiteme [sic] of vulgarity," "bad manners," "discourteous," "shameful," "poor manners" and noted that it is "inexcusable" "to be rude to one's hostess."[42]

One of two opinion pieces published by the *Los Angeles Times*, columnist Joyce Haber characterized Kitt as "an ill-bred lady with a great big chip on her shoulder" in comparison to other African American stars, including Ella Fitzgerald, Sidney Poitier, and Harry Belafonte, whom she listed as "exceptional ladies and gentlemen."[43] This construction draws on a long tradition of discursively reprimanding and marginalizing dissenting black voices by using token examples of successful and seemingly content "good" black Americans to undermine the possibility that there is any just cause for dissent. In this case this move is particularly ironic in retrospect given the activism all three "exceptional" figures engaged in during their lives, especially Harry Belafonte, whose ability to stir controversy through his commitment to radical and grassroots equality movements continues to this day. Further, Haber's use of "ill-bred" to describe Kitt seems a particularly loaded choice of words given Kitt's mixed-race (and violently conceived) background.

This construction also implicitly reveals the way being a "lady" was linked not only to behavior but breeding in a way that already generally excluded women of color.

Editorials in both *The New York Times* and *The Washington Post*—presenting something of a sympathetic take of Kitt's actions—deemed a national dialogue around race, poverty, and the Vietnam War necessary. However, the editors of *The Times* and *The Post* used these same editorials to label Kitt's comments a "rude confrontation" that "disturbed a polite White House luncheon."[44] Thus, even mainstream coverage that supported, at least in small parts, what Kitt had said at the White House found it necessary to frame Kitt as rude and impolite. The idea that Kitt interrupted to make her statement and the constant use of the word "outburst" in the mainstream press is interesting considering the (rarely reported) fact that Kitt had waited for all the other women at the luncheon to speak before she raised her hand and was called upon. The mainstream press' characterizations of Kitt's actions as unexpected not only cue race and gender stereotypes, but are inaccurate and misleading.

It was also frequently reported in mainstream news articles that Lyndon Johnson's pastor, Reverend George R. Davis, had called Kitt's actions "ill-mannered" and that fellow luncheon guest Katherine Peden referred to Kitt's actions as "the rude interruption that shocked the Nation."[45] The reported criticism of Kitt by Davis and Peden (both white) not only gendered but raced Kitt in the mainstream press in a way that constructed her as an (uncivilized) stand-in for all African Americans. In Davis' repeatedly published harsh criticism of Kitt, he apologized to President Johnson for "those Negroes who are ill-mannered, stupid, and arrogant," while Peden was reported as believing that Kitt had done a "disservice" to women's and civil rights.[46] Here we see media coverage of Kitt's dissent dominated by whites, who are presumed valid judges of what is acceptable for black Americans—and particularly black women—to say publicly. This narrative effectively avoids addressing the power held by the individuals to whom Kitt spoke by focusing on the actions and mannerisms of the least powerful among them.

Like the "Kitt on attack" frame, the "'breach of etiquette" frame portrayed Kitt as angry and out of control, acting on impulse and at the whim of her emotions rather than careful thought—uncivilized. A complete reliance on white and elite sources by the mainstream press largely explains the frequency of both of these frames—it is unsurprising that high-status political officials and those with close ties to them (like their wives and religious leaders) found Kitt's criticisms unacceptable. No non-elite citizens, black or white, were consulted about Kitt's actions. Acknowledgement of public support of Kitt by the mainstream press came in the form of several passing reports on a small number of "youth," "some bearded and with long hair," who protested in front of the White House and passed out flyers pointing to the hypocrisy of calling Kitt ill-mannered while "killing innocent civilians and burning little children in Vietnam" (Figure 2.2).[47]

Figure 2.2 Anti-Vietnam war protestors outside the White House carry a sign reading "Eartha Kitt Speaks for the Women of America," January 19, 1968. (Library of Congress)

DEFENDING KITT

The gendering of Kitt was not unique to the mainstream press, but also evidenced itself clearly—although in a different way—in the black press. While highly gendered language existed in mainstream coverage as a tool for denouncing Kitt, there was little explicit sexual objectification of her there. On the other hand, three out of the four black newspapers that covered Kitt's dissent included descriptions of her as "sultry" and a "sex kitten," with one *Pittsburgh Courier* article referring to her as a "tigress" *five* times.[48] The *Pittsburgh Courier* also notably included the sarcastic and sexist statement at the end of its scathing editorial about Kitt dissent: "Who will deny that if you get a group of fifty women together, even in the White House, many things are possible."[49]

Further, a skepticism about Kitt's allegiances to the African American community appeared in the black press that did not appear for any other celebrity I examine in this volume. Considering Kitt's support of the civil rights movement and her public involvement with young people of color in inner cities,[50] it seems likely that this skepticism was at least in part linked to (1) her biraciality/interracial romances, and/or (2) the way her seeming embrace of roles that perpetuated narratives of hyper-sexuality conflicted with the black press' long-standing commitment to the politics of respectability.

Reflecting the sometimes apprehensive relationship between black journalists and their public and the black celebrities whom they perceive as catering to the mainstream, multiple stories published in the black press explicitly noted previous concerns about Kitt's allegiances and praised her for proving through her actions at the White House that she was invested in her community. For example, a letter to the editor in the *Los Angeles Sentinel* noted that Kitt's recent actions were "wonderful" considering that "only a few years ago she seemed reluctant to identify with the masses and, in particular, the Negro masses."[51] However, despite this welcoming of Kitt's apparently newfound activism, several members of the black press remained skeptical about her intentions. These journalists treated Kitt's personal convictions with cultural, political, and racial suspicion given the seemingly conflicting predispositions of Kitt's apolitical celebrity persona. An article by Ethel L. Payne, published by both the *Chicago Defender* and *Courier*, noted that the question remained unanswered as to "why the pussycat [who] had never expressed any views on Vietnam before had turned herself into a tigress and chosen the White House to vent her fury," asking, "Could it have been publicity or was it sheer frustration?"[52]

Overall however, the black press most commonly presented frames for making sense of the Women Doers Luncheon that (1) gauged the political validity—or truth—of Kitt's words, and (2) emphasized the value of freedom of expression.

Truth-telling

It is clear that black journalists felt compelled to respond to critical coverage of Kitt in the mainstream press even as they generated alternative frames for their readers. The most common frame of Eartha Kitt's dissent at the White House, appearing in forty percent of coverage in the black press, was that of truth-telling. The frame that Kitt told the truth was presented most commonly in opinion-based content but also in news articles as a defense to any criticism that might be levied at her. While black press coverage often mentioned the offense Mrs. Johnson reportedly took to Kitt's words and the question of etiquette, this coverage upheld truth-telling as more central than these concerns.

Letters to the editor published by the *New York Amsterdam News* contended that "Miss Eartha Kitt's statement was right to the core," and asked rhetorically in response to criticisms of Kitt, "How can you do harm with the truth?"[53] Similarly, the *Los Angeles Sentinel*'s single published letter to the editor stated, "I see little cause or reason to rise up in indignation over reflective remarks such as those made by Kitt. Surely there was much truth and responsibility in them."[54] Columns in the *Los Angeles Sentinel* contended that Kitt had "fearlessly" "spoken the truth" and noted that one could "always depend on Eartha Kitt to tell it like it is."[55]

Clearly not impervious to the dominant discourses that led to the framing of Eartha Kitt's words at the White House as a personal clash between the actress and Mrs. Johnson, twenty percent of coverage in the black press also presented this idea. However, while this frame occurred with the same negative connotations in the *Chicago Defender* and *Pittsburgh Courier* as in the mainstream press, the *Los Angeles Sentinel* and *New York Amsterdam News* used the personalization of the story as further evidence of the truth-telling frame. Both papers suggested that the reported tears of Mrs. Johnson were actually the result of being "moved" by the truth of Kitt's words rather than fear or offense. The *Sentinel* reported a quote from Kitt herself "that 'because Mrs. Johnson is a mother, as am I, what I said about youth moved her,'" and a letter to the editor in the *Amsterdam News* contended, "Mrs. Johnson was moved to tears knowing how many people are against her husband on account of the war."[56]

The *New York Amsterdam News*' editorial staff noted some "claim that she [Kitt] said words at the wrong time, at the wrong place, and in the wrong way, culminating in bad taste. There are others who think Miss Kitt was the only guest who added *truth* to the luncheon menu. *With this group we align ourselves.*"[57] With this statement the *Amsterdam News* reflects the main difference between framing approaches in each press—most dominant discourse was concerned with *how* Kitt communicated her concerns, while African American discourse was primarily concerned with the *content* of these concerns. Even the *Chicago Daily Defender*, which presented more negative than positive coverage of Kitt in relation to her White House visit, included the truth-telling frame. In its editorial criticizing her for a breach of social etiquette, the truth of Kitt's words was also noted: "Though the logic she advanced as the motivating factor in today's juvenile delinquency may be historically correct, the vehemence with which she said [it] was vexing and irritating."[58]

The *Defender* also quoted several citizens, including a chauffeur and housewife, who felt that Kitt's experiences had "put her in the enviable position of knowing what young people are thinking," and that Kitt "let Mrs. Johnson know how young men who are about to be drafted feel."[59] In both cases, the emphasis of the news report is that Kitt's standpoint reflected a truth in regard to the opinions of "ordinary" members of the African American community.

Significantly, the black press published multiple stories that conveyed the truth-telling framed through the opinions of everyday people rather than elites. In particular, African American women's opinions about Kitt's visit to the White House were reported on. Interviews with "Angeleno women" run by the *Sentinel* contended that Kitt was "courageous" "because she told the truth."[60] While criticism of Kitt's manners appeared in these interviews, the truth-telling frame tempered it: "What she said was the truth, but how she said it was the bad thing."[61] As Bob Lucas of the *Sentinel* reported, "the consensus was that any 'rudeness' that occurred was the unexpected injection of harsh facts of life into a discussion that revolved around 'planting flowers.'"[62] The complete lack of anything but elite sources, and the particular exclusion of black women's voices, excluded this perspective in the mainstream press.

A notable trend appeared within the truth-telling frame in the black press that was similarly altogether absent from mainstream press coverage: the use of Christian discourse and biblical imagery to justify the valuing of truth over social expectations. A letter to the editor in the *New York Amsterdam News* noted of Kitt, "if she is for the right as God is for the right, then whoever is angered by the truth of the matter can cast his lot with the devil, that old Satan."[63] Another *Amsterdam News* letter noted that to suggest "it rude for her [Kitt] to think of the millions of Negroes who are unable to speak for themselves . . . is enough to make God angry and sick."[64] A letter to the *Los Angeles Sentinel* suggested that Johnson's pastor "peruse through his scriptures and read the story of Queen Esther. She also chose a gala affair to embarrass a symbol."[65] And an article in the *Sentinel* quoted a source who felt "Christ Jesus spoke the truth and was crucified. So Eartha Kitt shouldn't feel badly because she is criticized."[66] One *Amsterdam News* reader simply wrote, "Open confession is good for the soul and body. . . . May God Bless you, Miss Kitt."[67]

The truth-telling frame depended on the belief that ultimately telling it "like it is" was a righteous thing no matter if those in power found it distasteful. This focus on truth-telling as righteous reflects the differing understandings journalists in the black press brought to covering Kitt's actions. In this case, her actions were seen as part of a larger, righteous battle to communicate the reality of the feelings and experiences of the black and urban poor to the powers that be in America. That truth is often unpopular but worth ire in pursuit of justice was a theme taken up consistently within the African American Freedom Struggle and is particularly reflected here in the use of religious rhetoric.

Freedom of Expression

A frame that emphasized America's basic commitment to freedom of expression, particularly speech, was also present in black press coverage of Kitt's White House visit. While not as frequent as the truth-telling frame, appearing in twenty percent of stories, this frame also responded to mainstream arguments that Kitt should have edited her comments given her audience and location. This frame predominately occurred in news articles.

Cathy Aldridge of the *Amsterdam News* reported that "Ladies in New York" felt that " 'Miss Kitt, of course, is entitled to her opinion and to the free expression of it.' "[68] Likewise, the *Sentinel* reported that "The effects of the Miss Kitt's [sic] exercising her inalienable right to speak freely in a democratic country at the White House—the citadel of freedom—has caused all kinds of reaction," also reporting the opinions of several women who felt

"[Kitt] has a right to dissent like any other American," and that "everyone has the right to speak their mind in America."[69] While explicitly calling on the basic American value of freedom of expression, this frame also implicitly suggested that Kitt was being subjected to a double standard in the application of this value that the majority (i.e., "other Americans," "everyone") was not.

The *Defender* likewise printed the opinions of several interviewees that "as freedom of speech is an important principle in our country," Kitt as an "American citizen should be able to talk to her [the First Lady] just as she would to anyone else."[70] Unlike the truth-telling frame that focused on the content of Kitt's words at the White House, this frame made the central issue one of basic civil liberties. In this frame an emphasis is placed on the ideal application of the country's founding principles, which as a right of all American citizens, should clearly apply equally to Kitt, an African American woman.

Together black press frames challenged mainstream frames that constructed Kitt as less than American by explicitly evoking the Bill of Rights and undermining mainstream attempts to dismiss Kitt's words by focusing on the validity of their content. While freedom of speech and truth are both rather abstract ideals, the black press' reliance on them was strategic in that—had mainstream journalists attempted to respond—it would have been difficult to justify arguments against these concepts without violating basic American sensibilities.

CONCLUSIONS

According to Joyce Blackwell, Kitt's dissent can be understood as an example of the unique discourse African American women contributed to the anti-war movement in that her criticisms took on an intersectional tone—focusing on the Vietnam War *and* its connections to American racial and economic injustice.[71] The framing of Kitt in the mainstream and black press reflects several trends in how race, gender, and concepts of nation intersected in the construction of narratives by journalists for the publics they serve.

It is clear that journalists in the mainstream press adopted dominant discourses that viewed black challenges to the political status quo—embodied here by Lady Bird Johnson—as both threatening politically and inappropriate socially. While the framing of Kitt as a political threat is unsurprising, her construction as a threat to appropriate social behavior is uniquely linked to her gender. Unlike Muhammad Ali or Paul Robeson—who also presented public critiques that linked American imperialism and American racism during wartime, and who were also framed as threats to an ideal American way of life because of their dissent—Kitt was additionally constructed as lacking in qualities that define the feminine ideal. Questions of rudeness and manners and a focus on interpersonal relationships undermined Kitt's womanhood by locating her outside of normative social hierarchies that expect women to limit their opinions to the private sphere in order to be eligible for the full citizenship.

Understandings of Kitt's biracial background and interracial relationships certainly intersected with mainstream discourses and contributed to constructions of her as a threat to both governmental and gender/race hierarchies. The mainstream press commonly identified Kitt as a "Negro singer" in their coverage of her visit to the White House while failing to identify the race of any of any of the other figures involved in the story. Readers would have been quite familiar with Kitt's racial background without the frequent reminder. All one has to do is imagine how absurd it would sound to constantly refer to Lady Bird Johnson as "the white First Lady" to see how the act of identifying Kitt as a "Negro" constantly Othered her. According to Bambi Haggins, this re-racing is a common mainstream practice when African American women who have otherwise been de-raced in dominant discourses present challenges to understandings of race, class, or gender that appear to contradict the apolitical nature of their public personas.[72] Mainstream press framing thus worked to discipline Kitt socially, culturally, and politically.

On the other hand, black journalists, while not immune to the dominant discourses that framed Kitt negatively, and while expressing some community-level skepticism toward Kitt, attempted to present at least two primary counterdiscourses. The frames of truth-telling and freedom of expression allowed black journalists to respond to dominant criticisms of Kitt by constructing and reinforcing the idea that principles higher than those focused on by the mainstream press existed. While the black press did not spare Kitt criticism (and thus was not necessarily on her side), its journalists successfully presented readers with alternative discourses that allowed Kitt, as a dissenting black woman, to both maintain her citizenship and moral standing in the face of dominant discourses that suggested otherwise. At the same time, African American journalists gave voice to a whole segment of the population largely ignored by the mainstream press—non-elites, particularly black and female ones—and thus were able to construct Kitt as a representative of the thoughts of everyday people.

Notable in this case, despite the differences found between mainstream and black presses, are the differences within each press. First, in the mainstream press, *The Washington Post* presented predominantly neutral coverage of Kitt while all other mainstream sources presented mostly negative coverage of the actress' words. Thus, Americans reading *The Post* had more access to nuanced interpretations of Kitt and her actions even as larger frames limited these interpretations. In fact, a syndicated column published in three black newspapers lauded *The Post* for its coverage of the story and sensitivity toward African American readers: "Credit the dovish *Washington Post* for the most able job of fence straddling in the issue. Geared principally to whites, but sensitive to it enormous Negro readership potential in the District, the *Post*, time and time again faces this dilemma."[73]

Second, in the black press, the *New York Amsterdam News* and *Los Angeles Sentinel* reported on the story without once focusing on solely negative constructions of Kitt, while the *Pittsburgh Courier* was overwhelmingly negative in its coverage in comparison to other black press sources. Differences like those found in *The Washington Post* and the *Courier* reflect the variation in coverage that can occur given the various cultural backgrounds of reporters, the regions in which they are based, and the perceived readership of each press—especially regarding particularly controversial political issues.

On the other hand, an overwhelming common characteristic both within and between mainstream and black press coverage was the representation of Lady Bird Johnson as a likable, sympathetic figure. While mainstream journalists primarily accomplished this by representing the First Lady as a victim of an attack by Kitt, the black press accomplished the same by praising both Eartha Kitt for her truth-telling and Mrs. Johnson for the poise with which she handled the unexpected situation. Given that Lyndon Johnson was the President who presided over the passage of the Civil Rights Act and began the War on Poverty, it is perhaps unsurprising that the tone of black press coverage, along with its more supportive framing of Kitt, reflected a genuine admiration and respect for both the First Lady and President Johnson.

Notably, what all journalistic accounts of the Women Doers Luncheon left out was that while one woman, Mrs. Hughes, felt moved to challenge Kitt's comments through a dominant narrative of patriotism and maternal sacrifice, another guest spoke up almost immediately after the Kitt, Johnson, Hughes interaction to say that, "I have so much sympathy for the experiences that Miss Kitt has had around the country because I have worked with the same kind of people."[74] This validation of Kitt's experiences by another "lady" at the luncheon certainly challenges the media narratives that isolated Kitt's sentiments. Additionally, that multiple women at the luncheon besides Kitt acknowledged the links between youth crime, urban unrest, and educational, economic, housing, and policing inequalities was completely absent from reporting. In effect then, the discursive reprimanding of Kitt's behavior by journalists not only failed to interrogate her critique of the Vietnam War in any substantial way but also silenced the larger and more complex—albeit not unproblematic—conversation about the causes of urban violence at the luncheon.

Ultimately, while journalistic frames limited available interpretations of Kitt's dissent, the extensive news and editorial coverage of it in both presses reflects the impact Kitt had on public discussions around war and urban unrest. While the content of Kitt's words never became the focus of intense debate in the mainstream, and thus her intended impact on policy regarding urban unrest and war were perhaps lost, she did accomplish something unique by using her celebrity access to publicize the worldview of an African American woman from "the gutters" in an elite space that would have otherwise ignored such perspectives. As Cathy W. Aldridge of the *New York Amsterdam News* wrote at the time:

When she confronted the President and Mrs. Johnson with thought provoking questions, usually reserved for more intimate gatherings, she spoke for the ages—daring to place all the hurt felt by Afro-Americans everywhere. . . . This verbal exchange in the hallowed White House broke a barrier for the first time in the mansion's history. There is much to be said for that.[75]

Kitt faced professional sanctions in the U.S. as a result of her dissent but was able to maintain her career in Europe until returning to the American stage nearly a decade later.[76] Like Paul Robeson decades earlier, Kitt was under investigation and surveillance by federal agencies including the FBI, CIA, and NSA long before the dissenting moment investigated here.[77] What is unique about the files kept on Kitt by these agencies is that they reflected a perverse interest in her sexuality and attempts to define her worth based on gendered behavioral conventions. Rather than labeling her activities as threatening or subversive, the men who investigated Kitt labeled her a "nymphomaniac" with "loose morals" who acted like a "crude" "spoiled child" during "escapades overseas."[78] Notably, a week after her 1968 White House dissent at the Women Doers Luncheon, these files were forwarded to President Lyndon Johnson's Secret Service staff.[79]

Forty years later, upon Eartha Kitt's Christmas Day 2008 death, John Nichols, the Washington correspondent for *The Nation* magazine, wrote in the closing of his retrospective of her life and politics:

We remember Kitt as one of those remarkable Americans who was patriotic enough to speak truth to power. And she spoke in such a remarkable voice that it will linger far longer in our memory than those foolish politicians and misguided media moguls who were wrong about Vietnam—and wrong about Kitt.[80]

NOTES

An earlier version of this chapter was published as " 'An Ill-Bred Lady with a Great Big Chip on Her Shoulder': Gender and Race in Mainstream and Black Press Coverage of Eartha Kitt's 1968 White House Dissent," Journal of Interdisciplinary Feminist Thought 5, no. 1, article 4 (2011). Available at http://digitalcommons.salve.edu/jift/vol5/iss1/4

1. From John Nichols, "Eartha Kitt: An Anti-War Patriot," *The Nation*, Dec. 26, 2008, www.thenation.com/blog/eartha-kitt-anti-war-patriot (accessed Mar. 1, 2014), which also appeared in the *Chicago Tribune* with the headline "Eartha Kitt: The Patriot Who Was Right All Along," Dec. 29, 2008, http://articles.chicagotribune.com/2008–12–29/news/0812280062_1_first-lady-eartha-kitt-lady-bird-johnson (acessed Mar 1. 2014).
2. Renee C. Romano and Leigh Raiford, eds., *The Civil Rights Movement in American Memory* (Athens: University of Georgia Press, 2006).
3. Romano and Raiford, *Civil Rights Movement*.

4. Carole Stabile, *White Victims, Black Villains: Gender, Race and Crime News in US Culture* (New York: Routledge, 2006).
5. Philip A. Klinkner, with Rogers M. Smith, *The Unsteady March: The Rise and Decline of Racial Equality in America* (Chicago: The University of Chicago Press, 1999).
6. Janet Mezzack, " 'Without Manners You Are Nothing': Lady Bird Johnson, Eartha Kitt, and the Women Doers' Luncheon of January 18, 1968," *Presidential Studies Quarterly* 20, no. 4 (Fall 1990): 745–760; Klinkner, *The Unsteady March.*
7. Mezzack, "Without Manners."
8. Founded by John F. Kennedy Jr., VISTA is an Americorps volunteer-based anti-poverty program.
9. Liz Carpenter, *First Lady's Luncheon for Women Doers,* White House Social Files, Jan. 18, 1968: 5–6.
10. Liz Carpenter, *First Lady's Luncheon:* 7–10.
11. Ibid., 13–23.
12. Ibid., 23.
13. Ibid., 30–32.
14. Data was collected for stories appearing between January 19, 1968—the day after Kitt's comments to the First Lady—and March 19, 1968. Sources included in this chapter are *The New York Times, New York Amsterdam News, The Washington Post, Pittsburgh Courier, Chicago Tribune, Chicago Defender, Los Angeles Times, Los Angeles Sentinel, Time, Newsweek, Ebony,* and *Negro Digest.*
15. "Eartha Was Right, Dr. King Contends," *Chicago Daily Defender,* Jan. 22, 1968.
16. Edward P. Morgan, "The Good, the Bad, and the Forgotten: Media Culture and Public Memory of the Civil Rights Movement," in *The Civil Rights Movement in American Memory,* ed. Renee C. Romano and Leigh Raiford (Athens, GA: University of Georgia Press, 2006): 137–166.
17. Morgan, "The Good, the Bad."
18. James Yuenger, "Lady Bird Calls Eartha's Blast 'Shrill Discord,' " *Chicago Tribune (1963–Current File),* Jan. 20, 1968: N1.
19. Many of the letters exchanged between Kitt and King can be read online at The King Center archive: www.thekingcenter.org/archive/theme/2790.
20. Sika A. Dagbovie, "Star-Light, Star-Bright, Star Damn Near White: Mixed Race Superstars," *Journal of Popular Culture* 40, no. 2 (2001): 217–237.
21. Caroline A. Streeter, *Tragic No More: Mixed-Race Women and the Nexus of Sex and Celebrity* (Amherst: University of Massachusetts Press, 2012).
22. For example, beyond the cat tropes in the headline of a 1998 *Washington Post* article—"The Nine Lives of Eartha Kitt; At 71, the Singer Is Still Landing on Her Feet,"—Kitt was also described as "slinking," "purring" (twice), "svelte," "climbing," "exotic," "sultry," "growling," "sensual," a "vamp," and a "temptress" (Paula Span, Dec. 31, 1998). My searches for articles on Julie Newmar, the white actress who played the role of Catwoman on the *Batman* series for years prior and much longer than Kitt, reveals no such popularity of language surrounding her.
23. Marie Smith, "Eartha Kitt Confronts the Johnsons: Startled First Lady Responds to Singer's Attack on War," *The Washington Post,* Jan. 19, 1968.
24. Ibid. Note: My reading of the original transcript of the luncheon taken by Lady Bird Johnson's social secretary Liz Carpenter (see n. 9) suggests that Johnson was quite calm in her response to Kitt (and the other luncheon guests with whom she interacted).
25. "At White House Luncheon: Eartha Kitt's Tirade on War Leaves First Lady in Tears," *Los Angeles Times,* Jan. 19, 1968.

26. Ibid.
27. For example, see "Eartha Kitt Denounces War Policy to Mrs. Johnson," *The New York Times (1923–Current File)*, Jan. 19, 1968: 1; Yuenger, "Lady Bird Calls Eartha's Blast 'Shrill Discord.'"
28. Ibid.
29. Carolyn Lewis, "Mrs. Johnson Chides Eartha Kitt: 'Shrill Voice' Jars First Lady," *The Washington Post*, Jan. 20, 1968: A1.
30. Ibid.
31. Though seemingly archaic now, this was a popular practice for newspapers of the time.
32. "Eartha Kitt Denounces War Policy to Mrs. Johnson," *The New York Times*.
33. "Eartha's Shouts Stun Lady Bird into Tears," *Chicago Tribune (1963–Current File)*, Jan. 19, 1968: 1.
34. Ibid. Interestingly, in the black press the *Chicago Defender* also claimed Kitt's words were shouted, but, like the mainstream press, none of the other black press sources reported these supposed shouts.
35. Yuenger, "Lady Bird Calls Eartha's Blast 'Shrill Discord.'"
36. For example, "Eartha Kitt Denounces War Policy to Mrs. Johnson," *The New York Times*.
37. For example, Yuenger, "Lady Bird Calls Eartha's Blast 'Shrill Discord.'"
38. Yuenger, "Lady Bird Calls Eartha's Blast 'Shrill Discord.'"
39. In a contemporary and alternative reading of Kitt's comments, Joyce Blackwell has described them as an example of peace activism "in the traditional sphere of motherhood or womanhood" because of Kitt's explicit attempt to appeal to a female audience and descriptions of her audience and herself as mothers whose concern for their children's safety and futures should result in an anti-war, anti-poverty agenda. Joyce Blackwell, *No Peace without Freedom: Race and the Women's International League for Peace and Freedom, 1915–1975* (Carbondale: Southern Illinois University Press, 2004).
40. "Passion and Politesse," *Newsweek*, Feb. 12, 1968.
41. Hunt T. Dickinson, G.R. McLaughlin, D.A.L., Larry Wanamaker, et al. "White House Luncheon," Voice of the People, *Chicago Tribune (1963–Current File)*, Jan. 24, 1968: 14.
42. Ibid.
43. Joyce Haber, "Los Angeles Fete for Vidal Sassoon," *Los Angeles Times*, Jan. 22, 1968: C21.
44. "From the Heart of Eartha Kitt." *The New York Times (1923–Current File)*, Jan. 20, 1968: 28; "Down to Eartha," *The Washington Post*, Jan. 20, 1968: A10.
45. For example, see "Mrs. Johnson Sorry Furor Obscured Other Ideas," *The New York Times (1923–Current File)*, Jan. 20, 1968: 5; "Johnson's Pastor Sends Apology for Eartha Kitt Tirade," *Los Angeles Tribune*, Jan. 20, 1968; and Elizabeth Shelton, "Miss Peden: 'Outburst a Disgrace,'" *The Washington Post*, Jan. 23, 1968.
46. Ibid.
47. For example, see "Johnson Church Ousts War Foes," *The New York Times*, Jan. 22, 1968: 3; "17 Protestors Back Eartha in LBJ's Church," *Chicago Tribune*, Jan. 22, 1968: 11; Dorothy McCardle, "Mrs. Johnson Cold-Shoulders Heated Protest," *The Washington Post*, Jan. 25, 1968: B1.
48. "'I Didn't Plan to Rap U.S.,'" *Chicago Daily Defender (Daily Edition) (1960–1973)*, Jan. 23, 1968: 7; "50 Women in a Room," *New Pittsburgh Courier (1966–1981)*, Feb. 3, 1968: 6; Ethel L. Payne, "The Inside Story of the 'Pussycat,'" *Chicago Daily Defender (Daily Edition) (1960–1973)*, Jan. 22, 1968: 1.

49. "50 Women in a Room," *New Pittsburgh Courier.*
50. In 1966 she established the Kittsville Youth Foundation, a chartered and non-profit organization for underprivileged youth in the Watts area of Los Angeles. Kitt was also involved with the group Rebels with a Cause in the area of Anacostia in Washington, DC. Kitt supported the group's efforts to clean up the streets and establish recreation areas by testifying with them before the House General Subcommittee on Education of the Committee on Education and Labor (Mezzack, "Without Manners").
51. Father Lewis P. Bohler Jr., "Readers Comment on Issues," *Los Angeles Sentinel,* Jan. 25, 1969: 6A.
52. Payne, "The Inside Story of the 'Pussycat' "; Ethel Payne, "Eartha Kitt Turns it on at D.C. Luncheon," *New Pittsburgh Courier (1966–1981),* Jan. 27, 1968: 1. Notably, John H. Sengstacke, editor of the *Chicago Defender,* had purchased the *Pittsburgh Courier* in 1965. Thus both papers were under similar editorial control ("Newspapers: The Chicago Defender," PBS, www.pbs.org/blackpress/news_bios/defender.html (accessed Sep. 29, 2010).
53. Sylvia Simmons, "Pulse of New York's Public," *New York Amsterdam News,* Feb. 24, 1968: 16; Name Withheld, "Eartha Kitt," *New York Amsterdam News,* Jan. 27, 1968: 14.
54. Father Lewis P. Bohler Jr., "Readers Comment on Issues."
55. Maggie Hathaway, "Tee Time," *Los Angeles Sentinel,* Jan. 25, 1968: B4; Bill Lane, "The Inside Story," *Los Angeles Sentinel,* Jan. 25, 1968: D2.
56. Bob Lucas, "Tempest at a Tea Party," *Los Angeles Sentinel,* Jan. 25, 1968: A1; Elfrida Jordan, "Moved to Write," *New York Amsterdam News (1962–1993),* Feb. 10, 1968: 8.
57. Emphasis added. "Editorials," *New York Amsterdam News (1962–1993),* Jan. 27, 1968: 14.
58. "Eartha Kitt's Outburst," *Chicago Daily Defender,* Jan. 23, 1968: 13.
59. "Inquiring Photographer," *Chicago Daily Defender,* Jan. 31, 1968: 13.
60. Chuck Porter, "What Angeleno Women Think of Eartha Kitt's 'Outburst,' " *Los Angeles Sentinel,* Jan. 25, 1968: 7A.
61. Ibid.
62. Bob Lucas, "Tempest at a Tea Party."
63. Sylvia Simmons, "Pulse of New York's Public," *New York Amsterdam News (1962–1993),* Feb. 24, 1968: 16.
64. Name Withheld, "Eartha Kitt."
65. Father Lewis P. Bohler Jr., "Readers Comment on Issues." According to the book of Esther in the Old Testament, Queen Esther saved the Jews from annihilation when she revealed to her husband, King Ahasuerus, at a banquet that she herself was of Jewish blood and the King's close official, Haman, whom the King had trusted, was plotting to destroy her cousin Mordecai and all Jewish people.
66. Bob Lucas, "Tempest at a Tea Party."
67. Hazel O.B. Rayner, "Eartha Kitt," *New York Amsterdam News (1962–1993),* Mar. 9, 1968.
68. Cathy Aldridge, "The Ladies and Eartha: Pro-Con." *New York Amsterdam News (1962–1993),* Jan. 27, 1968: 1.
69. Chuck Porter, "What Angeleno Women Think of Eartha Kitt's 'Outburst.' "
70. "Inquiring Photographer," *Chicago Daily Defender (Daily Edition) (1960–1973).*
71. Blackwell, *No Peace without Freedom.*
72. Bambi Haggins, *Laughing Mad: The Black Comic Persona in Post-Soul America* (New Brunswick: Rutgers University Press, 2007).

73. Diggs Datrooth, "National Hotline," *Chicago Daily Defender (Big Weekend Edition) (1966–1973)*, Feb. 3, 1968: 6; "National Hotline: Capital Divided on Eartha Kitt Rhubarb," *Los Angeles Sentinel*, Feb. 1 1968: A7.
74. Liz Carpenter, "First Lady's Luncheon": 35. Unfortunately this guest is not identified by name in Carpenter's transcript.
75. Cathy W. Aldridge, "PS," *New York Amsterdam News,* Jan. 27, 1968: 7.
76. Nichols, "Eartha Kitt."
77. Seymour Hersh, "C.I.A. in '68 Gave Secret Service a Report Containing Gossip about Eartha Kitt after White House Incident," *The New York Times (1923–Current File)*, Jan. 3, 1975: 25; Mezzack, "Without Manners."
78. Adam Luck, "Eartha Kitt's Life Was Scarred by Her Failure to Learn the Identity of Her White Father, Says Daughter," *The Observer,* Oct. 19, 2013, www.theguardian.com/music/2013/oct/19/eartha-kitt-suffered-over-identity (accessed Dec. 11, 2013); Hersh, "C.I.A. in '68 Gave Secret Service Gossip"; Mezzack, "Without Manners."
79. Ibid.
80. Nichols, "Eartha Kitt."

3   Tommie Smith and John Carlos at the Mexico City Olympics, 1968

> *It is very discouraging to compete with white athletes. On the track you're Tommie Smith, the fastest man in the world, but off it you are just another nigger.*[1]

Like Eartha Kitt's White House dissent earlier in the year, the 1968 Olympic victory stand demonstration by Tommie Smith and John Carlos can be understood as one of many moments of black unrest that punctuated the 1960s. The black stocking feet, raised fists, and bowed heads of the gold and bronze medal winners have been ascribed a variety of cultural meanings. As one of the mostly widely circulated images of the 1960s, the demonstration has been labeled "sheer expressive genius" and "one of, if not the most, memorable moments in modern American sport history" by scholars.[2] Such retrospective opinions are not limited to academics—in 1996 *TV Guide* ranked the demonstration number thirty-eight on its list of one hundred most memorable television moments, and well into the twenty-first century the image can be regularly found on t-shirts and dorm room posters.[3]

As Tommie Smith's quote reveals, his and Carlos' experiences as black athletes from working-class families on an overwhelmingly white, upper-middle-class campus in the late 1960s significantly informed their understanding of American race relations. Along with their personal experiences, the athletes' activism and racial critiques were influenced by their educational experiences with Dr. Harry Edwards. Edwards, a major player in sport-centered racial protest activities, was one of the few African American professors at San Jose State University at the time, and Smith, along with fellow Olympian Lee Evans, took courses on race relations and black leadership from him. Inspired, Smith, Evans, and later Carlos, would become active in various efforts that focused on confronting racial inequality in higher education and sport through student activism. In the years leading up to the 1968 Olympics, the Olympic Project for Human Rights (OPHR) grew from these efforts.[4]

As Amy Bass notes, "The OPHR attempted to convert the athletic arena into a source of empowerment rather than a forum within which racist interpretations and supposition could continue to run rampant."[5] As part

Figure 3.1 In a lesser-known image of the Olympians, Tommie Smith (right) triumphantly crosses the two-hundred-meter finish line at the 1968 Mexico City Games. John Carlos (center) came in third after Australia's Peter Norman (on an outside lane outside the camera frame). Their later demonstration on the medal stand would become an iconic American image. (Copyright Bettmann/Corbis / AP Images)

of these goals, members of the OPHR, lead by Edwards, initially planned to boycott the Mexico City Games altogether in response to the exploitation and neglect of black athletes globally. In particular, the OPHR listed the stripping of Muhammad Ali's heavy weight title, the inclusion of South Africa and Southern Rhodesia in the Olympics despite their apartheid governments, and the segregation of the United States' Olympic Committee (USOC) administration and coaching staff as grievances.[6]

In the year prior to the Mexico City Olympics, Martin Luther King Jr. and other high-profile black activists had openly supported OPHR's boycott.[7] However, the effort received tremendous pushback from formal sporting institutions, and many black athletes (justifiably) feared that their participation in the boycott would result in permanent persona-non-grata status and the loss of both educational and economic opportunities. When, under immense international pressure, the International Olympic Committee (IOC) voted to suspend South Africa from the games, many OPHR athletes expressed feeling less convinced of the necessity of the boycott.[8]

While a large-scale boycott of the Olympic Games by black athletes failed to gain sufficient support, Smith, Carlos, and Evans, along with other black—and some white—American athletes continued to speak to issues of inequality and publicize the goals of the OPHR in the days leading up to the

Tommie Smith and John Carlos at the Mexico City Olympics, 1968

Games.[9] The sustained activism of these, and other, student athletes—and the press' full awareness of it—is important context for Smith and Carlos' demonstration, especially given that their actions would come to be incorrectly framed as an isolated, unexpected act.[10]

The day after the runners raised their gloved fists on the medal stand and stared solemnly at the ground as "The Star-Spangled Banner" played, Smith explained to famed sports broadcaster Howard Cosell that:

> My raised right hand stood for the power of black America. Carlos's raised left hand stood for the unity of black America. Together they formed an arch of unity and power. The black scarf around my neck stood for black pride. The black socks with no shoes for black poverty in racist America. The totality of our effort was the regaining of black dignity."[11]

While this clearly articulated explanation would be included in later critical and academic examinations of the protest, none of the mainstream publications I have examined here printed it. The consequences of Smith and Carlos' dissent were swift and severe and included a suspension from the American track and field team, revocation of their travel visas, and their expulsion, along with their wives, from the Olympic Village. Each man recounts in his biography the decades-long onslaught of racist hate mail and death threats that resulted alongside the loss of athletic contracts, endorsements, and employment opportunities.[12]

THE END OF AN ERA ON THE INTERNATIONAL STAGE

The dissent of Tommie Smith and John Carlos, and the harsh response to it, should be understood within the increasingly contentious state of national race relations and politics in October of 1968. While Kitt's dissent was certainly immersed in similar debates, especially those regarding Vietnam and urban unrest, the country had, quite literally, become aflame between her January moment at the White House and the Games of the XIX Olympiad. In those short nine months the nation had been rocked by the assassination of Martin Luther King Jr.; the resulting riots in 125 American cities; the passage of the Civil Rights Act of 1968 (which pushed whites to open up their segregated neighborhoods to African Americans and which was met with enormous disapproval); the assassination of Robert F. Kennedy, whose campaign reflected both the civil rights legacy of his brother and a continued commitment to issues of racial and economic justice; and the mass student protests and police violence of the 1968 Democratic National Convention (DNC).

At the moment of Smith and Carlos' dissent, African Americans, and particularly community leaders and journalists, were engaged in an intense struggle to identify successful means for continued racial progress in the wake of the assassination of Dr. King and these other volatile developments. White leaders and journalists simultaneously struggled to control and navigate growing militancy among black activists and an increasing unrest among white youth, who, as evidenced by their support of Robert Kennedy prior to his assassination, increasing anti-Vietnam war protest activities, and targeting of the DNC, were not particularly willing to accept a too-slow-to-evolve status quo either.[13]

While several celebrities discussed in this project offered dissent that called upon discourses of internationalism, Smith and Carlos' dissent uniquely occurred on foreign soil. Considering the political expectations and cultural meanings ascribed to the Olympic Games, Smith and Carlos' dissent can be seen as particularly daring given their explicit attempt to bring international attention to the unrest of African Americans in a space where a national image of cohesiveness was of utmost importance.[14] Further, investigating mediated frames around a single ritualized and highly symbolic event like the Olympics contributes to understanding how such events both enable and limit the introduction of racial dissent into the public sphere.[15]

Unlike previous cases in this volume, Smith and Carlos' celebrity came primarily as a result of their dissent rather than preempting it. While both runners had been interviewed in the sports media in the years leading up to their Olympic appearance, neither had yet been bestowed with the cultural trappings of stardom. Given this, prior to their now famous moment on the medal stand, the runners were more limited in their access to institutional channels of discourse than Robeson, Kitt, and Ali and thus had significantly less control over their images. As a result, constructions of Smith and Carlos' personas in both the black and mainstream public spheres were almost entirely dependent on the simultaneous construction of the meaning of their demonstration. Ultimately, Smith and Carlos were made celebrities (and pariahs) because of a single gesture rather than being understood either individually or as members of a community of athletes and activists.

Taking these contexts into consideration, this chapter highlights frames of Smith and Carlos' dissent presented to the American public by journalists in the mainstream, whose stories on the runners in the following months totaled eighty-four, and the African American press, where stories totaled twenty-six.[16]

BLACK TRACK STARS/WHITE PRESS

Mainstream journalists leaned strongly negative in their coverage of Carlos and Smith's dissent. The runners were regularly referred to as "militants," constructing their politics as an organized threat. The frequency with which this term was used is reminiscent of the use of the term "subversive" in descriptions of Paul Robeson in Chapter One. In both cases, such discursive labeling of African American critics of the status quo served to marginalize and disparage their dissent. Disapproving columnists also referred to Smith and Carlos as "freaks," "racists," and "clowns."[17] The protest was variously described as "an insult to the host country," "discourteous," "rude," "irresponsible," and "immature," and news articles characterized the protest as a threat to the "need to maintain order."[18] While a few mainstream columnists like Robert Lipsyte of *The New York Times* and Charles Maher of the *Los Angeles Times* displayed sympathy for Smith and Carlos and indignation at institutional reactions to them, such instances were outnumbered by highly negative coverage, four to one.[19]

Consistent with findings from the previous two chapters, *The New York Times* was the only mainstream newspaper that did not regularly use the descriptor "Negro" or "Negroes" to describe Smith and Carlos in their coverage.[20] While the use of "Negro" in the rest of the mainstream press is indicative of the common discursive racialization of African American figures not visited upon white public figures, it also reflects an apparent refusal by mainstream journalists to recognize Smith's, Carlos', and many other African Americans' shift toward using the term "black" as a racial descriptor.

Notably, and for the first time in the cases examined here, there appeared to be some evidence of integration of black journalists and sources into the mainstream press. The *Los Angeles Times* ran a column contrary to all its others by NAACP leader Roy Wilkins, the *Chicago Tribune* ran several interviews with black track coach Stan Wright, and all three mainstream sources ran quotes from other black athletes on the subject of Smith and Carlos' dissent.[21] However, this material step toward integration did not translate into anything near balanced coverage or the treatment of alternative ideological interpretations as valid. Quotes from black athletes were largely used by mainstream journalists to highlight disapproval of Smith and Carlos' actions, and, in an apparent show of regret for their attempt at inclusion, the *Tribune*'s editors went so far as to follow up its interviews with Wright, in which he made claims of racial bias in athletics and sympathized with Smith and Carlos, with a scathing response that not only discredited these claims but questioned Wright's abilities to offer valid commentary on the subject.[22]

Overall the mainstream press relied heavily on frames that (1) constructed sport as naturally apolitical, and therefore "insertions" of politics, controversy, or dissent into the Olympics as a violation; and (2) Smith and Carlos as having intentionally "insulted" the U.S., and lacking in patriotism, appreciation, and respect for the "American way."

The Incompatibility of Sport and Politics

In nearly forty-five percent of mainstream coverage of the Olympic demonstration, journalists presented their audience with the frame that athletic competition was naturally incompatible with political debate. This was accomplished through two primary discursive constructions: First, mainstream stories explicitly stated the incompatibility of the two and the idea that sport represented a pure institution that politics (particularly racial politics) could only muddy; second, the mainstream press perpetuated the idea that any insertion of politics into an athletic competition represented an unwelcome intrusion and evidence of disrespect toward sport. This frame in particular aligns with Douglas Hartmann's findings of the way public discourse in general, and especially popular magazines like *Life,* sport magazines like *Amateur Athlete,* and various U.S. newspapers constructed "sport as special" in their objections to OPHR's initial intention to boycott the Olympics.[23]

In reporting on the protest, *The New York Times, Chicago Tribune,* and *Los Angeles Times* all depended heavily upon official statements from the IOC that "Smith and Carlos deliberately violated a universally accepted Olympic principle by using the occasion to advertise domestic political views," and from the U.S. Olympic Committee that Smith and Carlos' dissent was a "violation of the basic standards of sportsmanship."[24] The news articles that reported such statements treated them as common sense without providing alternative views, thereby immobilizing the possibility of alternative interpretations of Smith and Carlos' dissent.

Associated Press reports published by mainstream newspapers liberally quoted the official apology offered by the USOC to the IOC, which stated: "One of the basic principles of the Olympic Games is that politics play no part whatsoever in them. This principle has always been accepted with enthusiasm by all, of course, including the competitors," and that Smith and Carlos showed "discourtesy by departing from tradition."[25] Mainstream papers also frequently quoted Jesse Owens' opinion that Smith and Carlos had chosen the "wrong battlefield" by protesting at the Olympics.[26] While constructing Owens' competition in the "Nazi Olympics" as a good example for young black athletes to follow, journalists did a poor job offering context to the 1936 Olympic Games—an event that was not only inherently political but explicitly racialized and clearly dependent on symbolic demonstrations of politics and power.

By glossing over the history of racial/ethnic politics in the Olympic games, while invoking the disapproval of a well-known black athlete like Jesse Owens, mainstream journalists provided a comparison of a "good," supposedly appropriately apolitical, African American to embrace, while simultaneously marginalizing any who aligned themselves with Smith and Carlos.

In reference to the viewpoint of other Olympic athletes, sportswriter Arthur Daley of *The New York Times* reported, "Some thought it was legitimate to drag a protest movement onto the global stage, but a majority condemned it as disgraceful, insulting, and embarrassing."[27] Daley's colleague,

Neil Amdur, reported that some "American black athletes" at the Games "resent the mixing of sport and politics, especially at this crucial point in their lives."[28] And one of the *Chicago Tribune* interviews with Stan Wright reported that although he felt Smith and Carlos' action took "courage" they protested in the wrong place because "I have talked to Jesse Owens and Ralph Metcalfe and as many people as I could who've competed in the games and they all assured me that the Olympics have always been based entirely on merit."[29]

The *Los Angeles Times* published interviews with white Olympians Sue Gossick and Bill Toomey, who disapproved of Smith and Carlos' actions and variously contended that at the Olympics, "it's people, not politics, that is important," and that "the Olympics are strictly for competition."[30] Thus, the two primary groups with whom Smith and Carlos were identified, blacks and athletes, were called upon frequently to reaffirm discourses that suggested their dissent was inappropriate and that sport exists naturally free from racial politics. Almost entirely ignored in mainstream coverage of the demonstration and athletes' responses to it was the support of white Australian silver medal winner Peter Norman, who was present for the planning of the demonstration and, in solidarity, wore an Olympic Project for Human Rights pin on his uniform during the ceremony. Mainstream sources failed altogether to note that in the aftermath of the demonstration Norman refused to disavow or critique Smith and Carlos despite pressures from his home country.[31]

Through such inclusions and exclusions, this frame constructed the protest by Smith and Carlos as both inappropriate given the athletic context and as an isolated incident. The *Los Angeles Times* called their dissent the "one discordant note during the Games."[32] Such discourse ignores that the 1968 Olympics were plagued with political "discord" long before they started, including contentious international debate about the inclusion or exclusion of apartheid-ruled South Africa, the massacre of countless student and civilian protesters by the Mexican government in the days leading up to the Games, and the highly political nature of Cold War discourses about athletic competition with communist governments including the Soviet Union and Cuba.[33] Further, it blatantly ignores that other athletes, including Lee Evans and Bob Beamon, performed symbolic protests in support of Smith and Carlos and the OPHR.[34]

Discourse in the two mainstream newsmagazines also successfully framed the protest as a singular and inappropriate interruption of the otherwise jubilant and achievement-filled games. *Time* magazine's editors wrote that Smith and Carlos' "display of petulance" "turned the high drama of the games into the theater of the absurd," and that "the saddest thing about the ruckus raised by Tommie Smith and John Carlos was that it dulled the luster of a superlative track and field meet."[35] In their more in-depth coverage, *Newsweek's* editors—who described Smith and Carlos as wearing "pimp socks" for their preliminary heat—wrote that the "controversy" that resulted from their dissent "almost over-shadowed all the brilliant performances and personal dramas of the XIX Olympiad," and that "the furor interrupted a week of some of the most brilliant Olympic feats in the history of the Games."[36] Such language notably presents the runners' dissent as uncontrolled and violent ("ruckus," "furor"), with the reference to "pimp socks" apparently a not-so-covert nod to stereotypes of deviant black masculinity.

Smith and Carlos' dissent was not only constructed as inappropriate given its "intrusion" on sport according to institutional elites, fellow blacks, and athletes in general, but in general public opinion. Published letters to the editor argued that, "to stain the purity of the Olympics with mere politics is unthinkable," and that the Olympics represented the "rare atmosphere where sportsmanship and good manners exhibit the dignity of all men" but "Tommie Smith and John Carlos used the Olympic games as a political arena" and thus showed "flagrant disrespect for the competition," and that "politics belong in the United Nations. Sports belong in the Olympics. It is not racist to enforce that simple rule."[37]

Similarly, *Los Angeles Times* sports columnist Jim Murray contended that Smith and Carlos "have mistaken the International Olympic movement for the hierarchy of the state of Mississippi" and that their protest violated "the purpose of the Olympics to foster international goodwill and fellowship among men."[38] Murray's fellow *LA Times* columnist Charles Maher was more sympathetic to Smith and Carlos but also noted that the protest was wrong "not on the grounds that it was in itself offensive but that the occasion was inappropriate," and that "it is clearly understood by everyone that the Olympics are not supposed to be used for political purposes."[39] In his scathing critique of the runners, *New York Times* columnist Arthur Daley stated that "Smith and Carlos brought their other world smack into the Olympic Games, where it did not belong, and created a shattering situation that shook this international sports carnival to its very core."[40]

Together the frames presented by mainstream journalists constructed sport, and the Olympics in particular, as naturally void of political sentiment and somehow purer than other institutions in its ability to provide opportunities to all people. This mainstream mythological discourse of sport as a bastion of equality has, as evidenced here and elsewhere, long played a powerful role in dominant public understandings of race, often being called upon to undermine claims that society remains unequal. Further, the idea that the natural state of athletic competition is apolitical ignores its roots in nationalistic, militaristic, and religious ideologies.[41]

"An Act Contemptuous of the United States"

In just over forty percent of coverage, mainstream journalists also framed Smith and Carlos' actions as a direct threat to basic American values. This frame depended upon constructions that suggested Smith and Carlos' behavior reflected a lack of respect and appreciation for their country and that any political philosophy that supported them was similarly un-American. While discourses of patriotism were the primary means of constructing this frame in the mainstream press, it was also enabled through discourse that explicitly linked the politics of Smith and Carlos to Nazism and other threatening political ideologies. Published editorials and letters to the editor in the mainstream press also tended to construct the runners as ungrateful and unpatriotic.

An Associated Press report run by the *Los Angeles Times* described Smith and Carlos' downcast eyes on the medal stand as a "refusal to look at the American flag" and explained that "Smith thrust his gloved right hand and Carlos his black-sheathed left toward the sky in a Nazi-like salute."[42] Similarly, after discussing the financial costs of the Olympics for the "American people," *Los Angeles Times* columnist Jim Murray noted that "they could have gotten someone to insult the flag cheaper than that," and that if the Olympic victory stand was a place "where a man is his own judge, jury, and law . . . we may get our next Hitler out of Lane 4."[43] A letter to the editor published by the *Chicago Tribune* noted that Smith and Carlos' expulsion from the games was right because "if a white athlete raised a George Wallace sign he would justifiably be given a ticket home."[44]

The false analogy of non-violent African American critique of the status quo with Hitler and the Ku Klux Klan here is disturbing. Such discourse marginalizes struggles for racial and economic justice and self-empowerment by presenting raced figures like Smith and Carlos as both outside mainstream American values and agents of racial violence. Affiliating Smith and Carlos with such violence justifies their disciplining within mainstream discourse and presents a familiar and early version of the "reverse racism" frame that would become a popular method for demonizing black dissent in the later part of the twentieth century.[45]

Sportswriter Jim Murray presented what was perhaps the most off-the-mark explanation of the motivation of the runners when he reported that John Carlos' "outlook on white people was doubtless colored by the fact he got beat by one of them. Peter Norman treated him like a third-place runner."[46] Not only does Murray seem completely oblivious to the fact of Norman's support of Smith and Carlos, he implies that the runners' dissent is purely based in spontaneous, egotistical resentment about losing to whites (which also fails to explain Smith's reasoning for his actions). Such individualistic attributions of dissent like Smith and Carlos' to sudden and unexpected feelings of personal discontent minimize the mass and organized nature of black activism.

Further, in what Urla Hill has called an "unsophisticated association" that continues to this day, mainstream journalists commonly described Smith and Carlos' upraised fists as a "Black Power" "salute" or "sign," and the event itself as a "Black Power protest."[47] Notably, as the rising tide of black liberation movements in the late 1960s gained momentum, the

Black Panther Party had become the face of the Black Power movement and had been branded in mainstream discourse as a dangerous and violent threat. While the politics and performances of the Black Panthers have been investigated elsewhere (see Rhodes 2007; Jones 1998), the association of Smith and Carlos with this group, and the inability of newsmakers generally to understand concepts of black power and solidarity, allowed their intended messages about poverty, inequality, and black uplift to become forever linked with a constructed violent social threat.[48] Occasional mainstream narratives also implied a link between Smith and Carlos' dissent and the threat of communism.[49]

Discourse in the *Chicago Tribune* in particular constructed Smith and Carlos' protest as a dangerous and deliberate attempt to undermine American values. David Condon called Smith and Carlos "exhibitionists who sought to bring discredit to the United States," and an editorial contended that the athletes "deliberately waited for the award presentation to put on an act contemptuous of the United States."[50] "Unfortunately," *Tribune* editors wrote, "when these renegades come home, they will probably be greeted as heroes by fellow extremists."[51] The labeling of Smith and Carlos as "renegades" and "extremists" paints them as violent figures while the assumption that their intent was based in "contempt" and a desire to "discredit" the U.S. completely ignores the motivations of the protest as articulated by the men who performed it.

Again mimicking discourses of the "good" versus "bad" Negro, Smith and Carlos' patriotism (or lack thereof) was consistently compared to that of others, particularly other black athletes. *Los Angeles Times* columnist John Hall dedicated a column to comparing Smith and Carlos to a young George Foreman, who after his Olympic victory "pulled a little American flag from his glove and waved it proudly" as a symbol of "American power."[52] Hall used this column to compare Forman's actions to those "rooted only in hatred and bitterness" by Smith and Carlos, and further described the protest as "black racism" and "bigotry," noting that fortunately "Foreman's stand" "is really the majority stand." Through such constructions, Hall links a false anti-racist discourse with jingoism to denigrate the dissent of Smith and Carlos while constructing them as deviant from "proud" blacks.[53]

Similarly, *New York Times* columnist Arthur Daley described Smith and Carlos' action as a "defiant refusal to look at the American flag while it was being raised" and compared this to black runner Lee Evans who "stood with chin held high during the flag-raising ceremony."[54] This point of comparison is particularly misinformed given that Evans was not only completely sympathetic with Smith and Carlos but was equally involved in the Olympic Project for Human Rights and that he (and the two other black Americans who ran with him) wore a black beret (also emblematic of a "militant" black philosophy) and raised his fist on the medal stand. However, according to Daley's account, Smith and Carlos were the solely "defiant" black athletes at the games.

Again, the comparison of Smith and Carlos to other black athletes—while complimenting these figures for their patriotism—reflects an early iteration of the "modern racism" that would become common within public discourse in the later twentieth century.[55] It facilitated a denial of claims of racial inequality and unrest by suggesting that Smith and Carlos represented a political or social fringe within an otherwise content black community. It also allows the white authors of such pieces to avoid being called bigots for their demonization of black dissent by demonstrating affection for African Americans they regarded as appropriately patriotic. Or, as *Los Angeles Sentinel* writer Clint Wilson Jr. would note in his critique of John Hall's *LA Times* framing of the runners, "You know the bit: 'Some of my best friends are Negro super-athletes.'"[56]

Several mainstream stories explicitly suggested that if Smith and Carlos felt the need to criticize the American status quo there was no place for them in American society. The *Los Angeles Times* ran a quote from John Carlos in which he stated that he was "not concerned about the national anthem" because "it was written for white people."[57] Assuming Carlos said this, reporters covering it had the unique opportunity to directly address the white supremacist history of America that only allowed white males full citizenship. After all, the anthem was written in 1814 long before African Americans (or a whole cadre of other groups) were considered human beings, least of all citizens. Instead, the comment from Carlos was framed in the context of discourse that constructed America as infallible alongside a quote from black Olympian Bob Seagren's that "if they [Smith and Carlos] don't like the United States, they can always leave."[58] Thus, the mainstream press summarily dismissed Carlos' critique of the national anthem while disciplining him with threatened expulsion from the nation as articulated by one of his own.

Mainstream discourse also constructed the U.S. as having provided plenty of opportunity to African Americans and thus deserving of their uncritical love. The editors at the *Los Angeles Times* contended that as a result of "a tremendous barrage of anti-white, anti-United States nonsense by their senior black indoctrinators," Smith and Carlos "used the victor's stand as a propaganda platform to denigrate their homeland" and that "one wonders where else in the world their chances would be any better."[59] A letter to the editor in the *Chicago Tribune* called their action "a betrayal of the very system which allowed them to pursue their studies and develop into great athletes. . . . The system that is the envy of every person in every country of the world" and suggested that "those who are not happy here leave our shores for a place more to their liking. Most of us like it the way it is."[60]

In addition to discourse that framed Smith and Carlos as not deserving of American citizenship as a result of their supposed lack of patriotism, multiple stories in the mainstream press also suggested that no matter their athletic ability they were also undeserving of the opportunity to compete athletically. A letter to the editor in the *Los Angeles Times* argued that "we should make it totally impossible for them to participate in any way whatever unless they have enough patriotic decency to refrain from such degrading demonstrations" against "the great and wonderful United States of America."[61] And a letter to the editor published by *The New York Times* noted that the author was ashamed "of any American who cannot look at the flag as it is being raised. I would rather not have these men represent my country."[62] *Chicago Tribune* columnist William Carsley, who affectionately referred to Smith and Carlos as "a pair of boorish refugees from a motorcycle gang," stated that the runners "obviously achieved no satisfaction from competing for their country" and "occupied places on the United States team that could have gone to athletes who cared."[63] The possibility that Smith and Carlos protested exactly because they cared was clearly excluded from such interpretations.

Together, the two most common mainstream press frames of Smith and Carlos' dissent set the groundwork for contemporary discourses that according to Hill "effectively trivialize, dilute, or even erase altogether" the deeper social meaning of the demonstration.[64] The use of loaded discourse, and the construction of Smith and Carlos as individual actors whose sentiments existed at the margins of society, displaced and disallowed mainstream news coverage that presented a more complex and sympathetic context for their actions. Mainstream journalists like Robert Lipsyte, who acknowledged ongoing racial inequalities in the U.S. and an understanding of sport culture as inherently political, were essentially shouted down by their peers.

BLACK TRACK STARS/BLACK PRESS

In a trend found throughout the cases I examine in this volume, black press journalists offered scathing criticism of mainstream coverage of Smith and Carlos' dissent. Clint Wilson Jr. of the *Los Angeles Sentinel* wrote that the paper's staff was "quite distressed over the reaction of some of our local White Press."[65] A front-page *Sentinel* article quoted an observer who likened mainstream reporters at the Olympics to "coyotes and vultures" and chastised them for targeting black athletes with "explosive and volatile questions, viciously tied together to produce a damaging answer."[66] Columnist Booker Griffin contended that mainstream reporting was "shallow, petty and self-centered," while "contorting and ignoring" the truths behind the demonstration.[67] Several columns were dedicated to directly critiquing *Los Angeles Times* columnist John Hall, who Wilson wrote could "neither comprehend nor empathize with a sincere black gesture," "exemplified the very attitudes they [Smith and Carlos] were protesting," and was not "the only local journalist to express an unenlightened disapproval of the incident."[68]

While engaging in such critiques of mainstream journalists, the black press did present negative coverage of the athletes' dissent, notably at almost twice the ratio (twenty-three percent) of which any positive coverage (twelve percent) appeared in the mainstream press. It is likely that some elder members of the black press, who would have also enjoyed the most editorial control, genuinely disagreed with Smith and Carlos' approach to addressing issues of racial inequality. This disagreement likely stemmed from intense debates within the African American community regarding the appropriate means of achieving progress. The rift between the traditional and older proponents of integrationist civil rights and the younger proponents of black liberation appeared clearly in the editorial pages of the black press, where each newspaper's editorial at times denounced the action by the runners alongside other editorials that sang their praises. Further, the presence of negative coverage in the black press generally reflects the ideological limitations of African American newsmakers given their dependence on white institutions of publishing and advertising and, seemingly, a genuine willingness by these newsmakers to present their audience with a diverse set of interpretations.

Positive characterizations of Smith and Carlos in the black press described the "sincere gesture" as "courageous," "noble," "profound," and an attempt to assert their "manhood." Most black press coverage, however, did not apply any explicit value-ridden characterizations to Smith, Carlos, and the protest but rather focused on contextualizing it within two frames. The first frame focused on locating Smith and Carlos' actions within a larger movement for black solidarity and uplift. The second frame constructed the expression of dissent by the runners as a moment of truth-telling that, like Eartha Kitt's previous moment of blunt discourse, was valid because of its reflection of authentic experiences and sentiments in the black community.

"Smith and Carlos' Actions Were for You"

Sixty-five percent of black press coverage of the 1968 Olympic victory stand dissent framed it within concepts of unity and uplift in the black community. Journalists presented this frame through discussions of (1) the demonstration as representative of the sentiments of the black masses who were otherwise voiceless, (2) larger trends of black achievement and protest, and (3) community debates around the most productive means for achieving equality for people of African descent. Thus, while reporting on the raised fists of Smith and Carlos, the black press presented its readers with a larger call to action for black pride and against all forms of racial and economic apartheid.

Los Angles Sentinel columnist Clint Wilson Jr. contended that "Smith and Carlos' actions were for YOU; the humble Negro clerks, custodians, gardeners, laborers and unemployed who are 'trying to make it' because YOU can't run 200 meters in 19.8," and that Smith and Carlos evidenced "black men have the dignity to show the world that they possess more than world-class athletic ability but also a love for their people that transcends politics and fear for their future careers in a white dominated society."[69]

Similarly *Sentinel* columnist Jack Tenner, who was white, wrote that in an "identification with the unskilled, the uneducated and the untrained. They [Smith and Carlos] spoke for and to millions of black people who identified with them. It was perhaps incidental that white people were able to witness this relationship."[70]

John G. Griffin of the *Chicago Defender* explicitly stated that Smith and Carlos had made the "gesture" to "show blacks are united," and *Ebony* explained that "they were saying that they were black Americans who had performed to their best of their ability and that they protested the way their black brothers have been treated in the very country they represented."[71] This discussion of Smith and Carlos from *Ebony* came only after describing in detail the various athletic achievements of male and female, black and white, athletes at the Olympics with a specific focus on the world records set by Bob Beamon and Wyomia Tyus. Thus *Ebony* couched their rare foray into covering controversial black dissent within a larger context of black success that acknowledged the popularity of Smith and Carlos' actions with other high-achieving black athletes.

Similarly, nearly every black press article that covered the demonstration did so in a context that focused on the athletic achievements of Smith and Carlos alongside those of other black athletes, male, female, American, and international. The *New York Amsterdam News* ran the now famous photograph of Smith and Carlos on the victory stand on its front page alongside two other photos of African American athletes protesting at the 1968 Olympics. The caption notes that Lee Evans, Larry James, and Ron Freeman "who finished 1-2-3 for the U.S. in the 400 meter in world record time" also raised their fists on the medal podium and that Bob Beamon and Ralph Boston subsequently protested the "expulsion of Smith and Carlos" by ascending the medal stand "in bare feet."[72]

Through this side-by-side display of black political expression, the *Amsterdam News* presents its opening coverage of Smith and Carlos' dissent as part of a larger movement in which other black athletes are in explicit solidarity. Every black newspaper also noted the political discourse of other black athletes, including Jim Hine and Charlie Greene, who had expressed dismay at the possibility of having their medals presented to them by Avery Brundage, "the man who fought for the admission of [apartheid-ruled] South Africa to the 19th Olympiad" and thus according to one Jamaican athlete "should live in South Africa" rather than "the free world."[73]

In addition to discourse that focused on the support Smith and Carlos had from other black American athletes, the frame of black solidarity and achievement was also constructed through the recognition of achievement by, and sympathy from, African athletes and the use of "black is beautiful" discourse.[74] Griffin reported that "many black athletes . . . were ready to pack and pull out" in support of Smith and Carlos and that "the Jamaicans, Nigerians, French and other teams were ready to follow." In the same "Olympic Exclusive," Griffin reported, "Black is truly beautiful to the

Mexico City natives. The brown brothers on the other side of the border roll out the red carpet for American blacks."[75]

White *New York Amsterdam News* columnist Gertrude Wilson wrote that she could not understand why anyone would "flip their lids" just because Smith and Carlos wore black gloves on their "beautiful brown skins."[76] *Sentinel* sports editor Brad Pye Jr. described the raised-fist gesture given by Smith and Carlos as "the black power or black is beautiful sign," noting that "there were other black demonstrators too. And all their demonstrations were black and beautiful."[77] Constructing the dissent of Smith, Carlos, and other black athletes as beautiful is perhaps the most radical of alternative narratives presented in the black press. The idea that black masculine bodies in an internationally visible act of defiance embody beauty runs simultaneously counter to mainstream narratives of acceptable behavior in raced/gendered athletic performance, Eurocentric norms of beauty, and taken-for-granted ideologies of national image.

Pye also contended that "the first real true black demonstrators were the three black men who swept the 10,000, an event black people aren't supposed to win.... But with Kenya's Neftali Temu, Ethiopia's Mamo Wolde and Tunisia's Mohammed Gamoudi running one, two, three, this myth was destroyed." In detailing the success of African athletes at the Olympics, Pye wrote, "As these black men from the black countries of the planet paraded ... they seemed to echo the words of James Brown's No. 1 hit: 'Say It Loud! Say It Clear! I'm Black and I'm Proud!'"[78] By linking the success of African athletes with an American song rooted in the black American cultural shift toward self-empowerment and Smith and Carlos' dissent, Pye acknowledges a larger diasporic movement for solidarity around black identity and experience.[79]

An internal community debate about the best ways to achieve uplift for African Americans was also a significant theme within this frame. John H. Sengstacke, editor of the *Chicago Defender,* wrote that the Olympic protest by Smith and Carlos was "tragic" not for any of the reasons presented by the mainstream press but because of reports that John Carlos had rejected the active involvement of white Olympic athletes who reportedly "feel deeply about the treatment of black men in the United States and want to help."[80] Rather than suggesting that the political goals, intentions, or location of Smith and Carlos' protest were inappropriate or threatening, the *Defender* editor levied his criticism of the runners on the contention that more could have been accomplished if black and white U.S. athletes had dissented in a more "integrated fraternal force."

Like the *Defender* editorial, the *Los Angeles Sentinel* also ran an editorial critical of Smith and Carlos but not in disagreement with their sentiments; it stated, "We are all in favor of racial pride," but suggested that Smith and Carlos were not best equipped to be leaders of "our cause." Rather, the editors state, "We firmly believe it is far past time for American Negroes to place more emphasis on basic, nitty-gritty issues ... and we are in dire need of truly-great, dedicated, hard-working leaders who can bring to us, activate, and maintain the basic programs through which we can achieve our goal of full equality in our country."[81]

Despite such critiques of the runners, these publications also sought to undermine the legitimacy of African Americans who appeared too willing to tow the mainstream media's line. For example, in his column "Take Ten," John A. Helem of the *Chicago Defender* condemned "these Negroes who criticize every effort of black Americans to carve out an identity of their own" by "constantly striving to say what he thinks the 'great white leaders' will have him say." Noting that such "Negroes'" "cries . . . have rung out loud and long, this past week against the action taken by Olympic champions, Tommie Smith and John Carlos." Helem goes on to argue that "what they [Smith and Carlos] did took more courage than all the do-nothing Negroes will do toward the salvation of the black man the rest of their lives. May God give us more Tommie Smiths and John Carloses. . . . AMEN!"[82]

Here, Helem specifically calls out black Americans with accommodationist politics as being counterproductive to "the salvation of the black man," and calls for more rallying around Smith and Carlos and the performance of actions like theirs. In a candid example of the way dominant racial discourses are rearticulated by the African American community to highlight internal community debates, the author notably only uses the mainstream term "Negro" to refer to those African Americans "who criticize every effort of *black Americans*."[83]

Together, discourse that constructed Smith and Carlos' dissent as being based in a desire to speak for the disenfranchised black community, and as having the support of other athletes of African descent, allowed for a frame that acknowledged the larger movement and sentiments that inspired the demonstration—something altogether absent from mainstream coverage. At the same time, couching this discourse in calls of "black is beautiful" and for community consensus around efforts for equality "for all black people," resulted in a frame that further located the protest in diasporic efforts toward black solidarity and uplift.

"The Disillusioning Truth"

In a frame that mimicked the earlier representation of Eartha Kitt's dissent by the black press, sixty-five percent of stories framed Smith and Carlos' actions on the medal podium as a form of truth-telling, and thus criticisms of it as illogical. This frame focused on presenting evidence of social inequality, and at times specific inequality in athletics, as context for the general mood of unrest within the black community. Through this frame, the black press acknowledged to its readers the profound need of African Americans to communicate the realities of their lived experiences.

For example, a book review in the *New York Amsterdam News* for "The Black Athlete: A Shameful Story," detailed the "dehumanized, exploited and discarded" experiences of African American athletes who were reportedly treated by white coaches as "watermelon eating idiots." The article concludes that "the disillusioning truths concerning the treatment of the Negro in both College and professional sport . . . is expected to help the American public understand the troubled mood of the black community, the manifestations of which have included a threatened boycott of this month's Olympic Games by the nation's most talented Negro amateur athletes."[84]

Similarly, *Ebony* noted that "U.S. officials" "seemed bent on tarnishing the names of black athletes," and thus the ruling institutions of sport "must make sure that black amateurs are treated as fairly as white amateurs. If this is done then the 1972 Olympics might be contested with no demonstrations of any kind."[85] *Chicago Defender* columnist John A. Helem wrote that Smith and Carlos' "courageous action said to the world, 'Even though we can win international championships and prove to be the best in the world, at home we are not accepted on an equal basis, or judged strictly on how well we perform as human beings.'"[86] These constructions in the black press specifically contradicted the mainstream idea that sport represented a platform in which all people competed on equal terms and without bias.

The black press also published stories on Smith and Carlos that focused on general racial inequality as the subject of their truth-telling. An October 26, 1968 editorial cartoon in the *Defender* titled "Flag Raising" depicted Smith and Carlos' raised, gloved-fists lifting the American flag to unveil the word "racism" in huge, block letters imposed on a partial map of the U.S. and a building resembling the U.S. Capitol (Figure 3.2). This image profoundly represents Smith and Carlos' dissent as a moment of truth-revealing in which the cover of patriotism was lifted to reveal the omnipresence of racism in American society.

The *New York Amsterdam News*' Gertrude Wilson constructed the truth-telling frame in similar terms in a column extremely critical of the negative reaction to Smith and Carlos' dissent. Wilson wrote that Smith, Carlos, and other black athletes demonstrated at the Olympics "to symbolize their problems . . . and proclaim that they were black Americans bringing honor to their country . . . a country which spits on their blackness."[87] Through this discourse, Smith and Carlos were constructed as heroic figures who competed for their country in spite of the "humiliation" they faced and wished only to express the reality that "we are Americans who are brown skinned, who are rejected even when we carry the flag of our country to triumph."[88]

The black press also evoked histories of truth-telling within the African American community in framing Smith and Carlos. Tenner directly quoted from the first issue of *Freedom's Journal,* when he wrote that Smith and Carlos "spoke eloquently" to the fact that they "feel themselves sorely aggrieved under the existing state of things" and that at the Olympics "they plead their own cause."[89] *New York Amsterdam News* editors evoked the tradition of Christian-based protest and truth-telling within the African American community by running the headline "Spreading the U.S. Gospel

84 *Black Celebrity, Racial Politics, and the Press*

Figure 3.2   *Chicago Defender* editorial cartoon, "Flag Raising," October 26, 1968.

Elsewhere" above the image of the protesting athletes. Given that the Gospel is understood as the word of Christ and its spreaders his disciples, labeling the Olympic dissent of Smith, Carlos, and other black athletes as "the U.S. Gospel" clearly defines it as infallible truth.

Together, this truth-telling frame worked alongside the community uplift frame (and overlapped with it frequently) to present black press readers with alternative interpretations of Smith and Carlos' actions from those presented in mainstream discourse. In particular, these frames acknowledged both the reality of inequality in the U.S. and the need for cohesive community action in response to it. Notably, while some black journalists took issue with the nature of Smith and Carlos' dissent, they did not undermine the legitimacy of the athletes' experiences nor the need for social change.

CONCLUSIONS

Both presses contributed to a public sphere that at specific moments in covering Smith and Carlos' dissent appeared more, but more often less, ideologically integrated. The two primary points of disagreement revealed by the presses framing of the demonstration were (1) how successfully the U.S. was (or wasn't) fulfilling its promises of liberty and justice for all, and (2) what Smith and Carlos' personal intentions had been. Newsmakers in the black press took as fact that equality was being actively obstructed, that overcoming this obstruction would take a relentless and united community effort, and that Smith and Carlos acted in the spirit of this effort.

On the other hand, mainstream newsmakers primarily constructed the U.S. as successfully working toward fulfilling the promise of equality and not requiring any extra push to get there, especially not from "militants." Further, a striking finding in mainstream coverage of Smith and Carlos' dissent is the appearance of discourses that suggested the runners' dissent made them bigots and racists and thus represented a threat to egalitarian America values. Such discourse, alongside that highlighting non-controversial African Americans as evidence that white racism was all but dead, is usually identified as having evolved in the post-civil-rights era—particularly in the 1980s—but this research illustrates its presence while Jim Crow was being dismantled.

Despite the limitations placed on their dissent by mainstream journalists, it is clear Smith and Carlos succeeded in drawing marginalized discourses into the mainstream, if only because their action forced these meaning makers to acknowledge them and respond. At the same time, black journalists were compelled to offer alternative discourses that reflected the growing frustration and debates of a community constantly being told to wait for full inclusion in the nation as they watched their leaders murdered and communities burned.

While clear differences in framing black celebrity dissent existed between journalists in each press, it would be inaccurate to assume these frames reflect a simple binary. Rather, similarities in meaning making did exist. Both presses commonly described the gesture by Smith and Carlos as representing "black power" but did so in largely different contexts that in one presented the concept as a threat, and in the other as a form of racial identification and unity. Newsmakers in both presses also constructed the International Olympic Committee and U.S. Olympic Committee as having overreacted in their expulsion of Smith and Carlos from the Olympic Village and the revocation of their travel visas. However, while the black press saw this overreaction as an example of the "double-standard" with which African Americans who breached orthodoxy were treated by the powers that be, mainstream journalists saw the overreaction as problematic because of the sympathy it generated for Smith and Carlos and the extra tension it created among athletes at the games.

Further, both presses evidenced the beginnings of newsroom integration. The mainstream press included black sources in their coverage of the demonstration and published pieces authored by Roy Wilkins and Stan Wright. Despite this inclusion, the sentiments of blacks that supported Smith and Carlos and/or levied criticism of dominant institutions were overshadowed or directly undermined. The black press, which importantly was never a deliberately segregated space, also included editorial content by whites; the *Los Angles Sentinel* printed the transcript of a radio broadcast by KABC's Allin Slate and a column by Jack Tenner, while the *New York Amsterdam News* printed (in what would become a regular column titled "White-On-White") the sentiments of Gertrude Wilson.[90] Unlike the inclusion of black writers in the mainstream press, who attempted to carefully challenge mainstream discourses, the editorial content of white-authored pieces published in the black press tended not only to be in line with the discourse of the black public sphere but presented some of the most supportive coverage of Smith and Carlos.

Finally, according to David C. Ogden and Joel Nathan Rosen, the nation has still not fully come to terms with Smith and Carlos' demonstration.[91] While true in many respects, I would argue that the immensely reproduced image of their dissenting bodies, even in commodified forms, continually requires some level of critical engagement with race and history by both the media and the public. While mainstream newsmakers limited the availability of alternative frames for understanding the runners in 1968, over time some of the frames made available by the black press seem to have seeped into contemporary public understandings. In 2005 San Jose State University unveiled a twenty-four-foot interactive statue of the pair, and in 2008 they received the Arthur Ashe Courage Award from ESPN at the ESPYs. Undoubtedly, as in the case of Ali, contemporary mainstream celebration of Smith and Carlos reflects the safety and sanitization that comes with locating a highly political moment squarely in the past and memorializing individual acts rather than long-standing networks of black resistance. Despite these limitations, I believe the continued visibility of Smith and Carlos in American culture also reflects a national acknowledgement that they, and not their mainstream critics, were on the right side of history.

NOTES

1. Tommie Smith quoted in "Boston Gets into the Act Again," *The Modesto Bee and News-Herald*, Sep. 26, 1967: A15.
2. Douglas Hartmann, *Race, Culture, and the Revolt of the Black Athlete: The 1968 Olympic Protests and Their Aftermath* (Chicago: The University of Chicago Press, 2003); Urla Hill, "Racing after Smith and Carlos: Revisiting Those Fists Some Forty Years Hence," in *Reconstructing Fame: Sport, Race, and Evolving Reputations*, ed. David C. Ogden and Joel Nathan Rosen (Jackson: University Press of Mississippi, 2008): 102–126.
3. "100 Most Memorable Moments in TV History," *TV Guide*, Jun. 29, 1996.
4. Hill, "Racing after Smith and Carlos"; Hartmann, *Race, Culture, and the Revolt of the Black Athlete*.
5. Amy Bass, *Not the Triumph but the Struggle: The 1968 Olympics and the Making of the Black Athlete* (Minneapolis: University of Minnesota Press, 2002): 82.

6. Richard Hoffer, *Something in the Air: American Passion and Defiance in the 1968 Mexico City Olympics* (New York: Free Press, 2009); Bass, *Not the Triumph*.
7. Bass, *Not the Triumph*; Hartmann, *Race, Culture, and the Revolt of the Black Athlete*.
8. Ibid.
9. In particular, members of the white Harvard crew team released a statement in August of 1968 offering their full support of any action OPHR members might take at the Olympics because of a "moral commitment to support our black teammates" (Robert Lipsyte, "The Spirit of the Olympics," *The New York Times*, Aug. 1, 1968).
10. My background research shows that in the three years leading up to the Olympics, mainstream newspapers carried multiple reports about the activities of Harry Edwards, the OPHR, and Tommie Smith particularly, in regard to a potential Olympic boycott.
11. Harry Edwards, *The Revolt of the Black Athlete* (New York: Free Press 1969); Bass, *Not the Triumph*; Hartmann, *Race, Culture, and the Revolt of the Black Athlete*; Tommie Smith and David Steele, *Silent Gesture: The Autobiography of Tommie Smith* (Philadelphia: Temple University Press, 2007).
12. Smith and Steele, *Silent Gesture*; John Carlos and Dave Zirin, *The John Carlos Story: The Sports Moment That Changed the World* (Chicago: Haymarket Books, 2011).
13. According to Pew, among voters under thirty years of age Robert F. Kennedy led in a potential three-way race for the Democratic nomination with thirty-seven percent of the vote. Seth Motel, "Polling Flashback: Remembering RFK," Pew Research Center, Jun. 5, 2013, http://www.pewresearch.org/fact-tank/2013/06/05/polling-flashback-remembering-rfk (accessed Nov. 12, 2013).
14. Alan Tomlinson and Christopher Young, *National Identity and Global Sport Event: Culture, Politics and Spectacle in the Olympics and the Football World Cup* (New York: State University of New York Press, 2006).
15. David I. Kertzer, *Ritual, Politics, & Power* (New Haven: Yale University Press, 1988).
16. Stories examined in this chapter were published between October 16, 1968—the day of the demonstration—and December 16, 1968. Sources I examine include *The New York Times, Chicago Tribune, Los Angeles Times, Time,* and *Newsweek* in the mainstream press and the *New York Amsterdam News, Chicago Defender, Los Angeles Sentinel, Negro Digest,* and *Ebony* in the African American press.
17. For example, John Hall, "Foreman's Fan Club," *Los Angeles Times*, Nov. 6, 1968: H3.
18. For example, see "The Natural Right of Being a Slob," *Chicago Tribune*, Oct. 19 1968: A10; "Confusion, Shock Grip U.S. Squad after Pair Ousted," *Los Angeles Times*, Oct. 19, 1968: A1; Joseph M. Sheehan, "2 Black Power Advocates Ousted from Olympics," *The New York Times*, Oct. 19, 1968: 1.
19. See for example, Robert Lipsyte, "The Morning After," *The New York Times*, Nov. 2, 1968: 47; and Charles Maher, "Smith Case (Continued)," *Los Angeles Times*, Nov. 7, 1968: C2.
20. Only twelve percent of *New York Times* stories did this. Notably, *The Times* also presented a significantly smaller percentage of negative constructions of Smith and Carlos than its mainstream counterparts—presenting mostly neutral coverage of the protest and an equal amount of positive and negative constructions.

21. Stan Wilkins, "The Big Olympic Mistake," *Los Angeles Times*, Nov. 4, 1968: B7; Robert Markus, "Sports Trail: WIU Track Coach Man of Principle," *Chicago Tribune*, Nov. 13, 1968: C3; Robert Markus, "Sports Trail: Future of Olympics Worries Wright," *Chicago Tribune*, Nov. 14, 1968: C3.
22. See Neil Amdur, "Davenport Gains Seventh Track Gold Medal for U.S. in Winning Hurdles" (*The New York Times*, Oct. 18, 1968: 54) for an example of mainstream interpretation of quotes from black athletes. See also Markus, "Future of Olympics"; and "Double Standard?" *Chicago Tribune (1963–Current File)*, Nov. 15, 1968: 24.
23. Hartmann, *Race, Culture, and the Revolt of the Black Athlete*.
24. For example, see Sheehan, "2 Black Power Advocates Ousted From Olympics;" Tribune Wire Service, "Suspend 2 Negro Olympians," *Chicago Tribune*, Oct. 19, 1968: 1; and "U.S. Apologizes for Athletes 'Discourtesy,'" *Los Angeles Times*, Oct. 18, 1968: D1.
25. Ibid.
26. For example, see "Keino Faints at Jubilant Nairobi Fete," *Los Angeles Times*, Oct. 31, 1968: B10.
27. Arthur Daley, "The Incident," *The New York Times (1923–Current File)*, Oct. 20, 1968: S2.
28. Amdur, "Davenport Gains Seventh Track Gold Medal for U.S. in Winning Hurdles."
29. Markus,"WIU Track Coach."
30. William Estes, "U.S. Olympic Star Tardy but Get's Hero's Welcome," *Los Angeles Times*, Nov. 5, 1968: 10B; Associated Press, "Black-Fist Display Gets Varied Reaction in Olympic Village," *Los Angeles Times*, Oct.18, 1968: D1.
31. The bond between Norman and Smith and Carlos would last a lifetime. In 1996 the gold and bronze medal winners served as pallbearers at the Australian silver medal winner's funeral. Smith and Steele, *Silent Gesture*.
32. Associated Press, "80,000 Watch Olympics End on Happy Note," *Los Angeles Times*, Oct. 28, 1968: E10.
33. Hartmann, *Race, Culture, and the Revolt of the Black Athlete*.
34. "Spreading the U.S. Gospel Elsewhere," *New York Amsterdam News (1962–1993)*, Oct. 26, 1968: 1.
35. "The Olympics: Black Complaint," *Time*, Oct. 25, 1968, http://content.time.com/time/magazine/article/0,9171,900397,00.html (accessed Apr. 15, 2010); "Sport: Records All Around," *Time*, Oct. 25, 1968, http://content.time.com/time/magazine/article/0,9171,900399,00.html (accessed Apr. 15, 2010).
36. "The Olympics' Extra Heat," *Newsweek*, Oct. 28, 1968: 74–80.
37. Scott Tinsman Johnson Jr., "Indomitable John Akhwari Cited as Symbol of Sports' True Purpose," *Los Angeles Times*, Oct. 28, 1968; "'Silent Protest' at Olympics." *Chicago Tribune (1963–Current File)*, Oct. 23, 1968: 20.
38. Jim Murray, "The Olympic Games—No Place for a Sportswriter," *Los Angeles Times*, Oct. 20, 1968: H1; Jim Murray, "Excuse My Glove," *Los Angeles Times*, Oct. 18, 1968: D1.
39. Maher, "Smith Case (Continued)"; Charles Maher, "Tommie to the Rams?" *Los Angeles Times*, Oct. 31, 1968: H2.
40. Daley, "The Incident."
41. John Sugden and Alan Tomlinson, eds., *Power Games: A Critical Sociology of Sport* (New York: Routledge, 2002); Robert J. Higgs and Michael C. Braswell, *An Unholy Alliance: The Sacred and Modern Sports* (Macon, GA: Mercer University Press, 2004); Robert Higgs, *God in the Stadium: Sports and Religion in America* (Lexington, KY: The University Press of Kentucky, 1995); John Hargreaves, "Globalisation Theory, Global Sport, and Nations

and Nationalism," in *Power Games*, ed. John Sugden and Alan Tomlinson (New York: Routldge, 2002): 25–43.
42. Associated Press, "Black-Fist Display Gets Varied Reaction in Olympic Village."
43. Murray, "The Olympic Games—No Place for a Sportswriter."
44. Daniel J. Sobieski, " 'Silent Protest' at Olympics," *Chicago Tribune (1963–Current File)*, Oct. 23, 1968: 20.
45. I discuss this phenomenon in detail in the next chapter.
46. Murray, "The Olympic Games—No Place for a Sportswriter."
47. Hill, "Racing after Smith and Carlos."
48. Jane Rhodes, *Framing the Black Panthers: The Spectacular Rise of a Black Power Icon* (New York: New Press, 2007); Charles E. Jones, *The Black Panther Party (Reconsidered)* (Baltimore: Black Classic Press, 1998). At the time, and to this day, Smith, Harry Edwards, and others have insisted that the OPHR was exactly that, a project for "human rights" and categorically "not the Black Power movement." Smith and Steele, *Silent Gesture*; Hill, "Racing after Smith and Carlos."
49. See, for example, Thomas J. Dunne, " 'Silent Protest' at Olympics," *Chicago Tribune (1963–Current File)*, Oc.t 23, 1968: 20; "U.S. Women Dedicate Victory to Smith, Carlos." *The New York Times (1923–Current File)*, Oct. 21, 1968: 60; and "Olympic Show—Press Interview." *Chicago Tribune (1963–Current File)*, Oct. 23, 1968: C2.
50. "In the Wake of the News," *Chicago Tribune*, Oct. 28, 1968; "The Natural Right of Being a Slob," *Chicago Tribune*.
51. "The Natural Right of Being a Slob," *Chicago Tribune*.
52. John Hall, "Foreman's Fan Club," *Los Angeles Times*, Nov. 6, 1968: H3.
53. Ibid.
54. Daley, "The Incident."
55. Robert Entman, "Modern Racism and the Images of Blacks in Local Television News," *Critical Studies in Media Communication* 7, no. 4 (1990): 332–345; Sut Jhally and Justin Lewis, *Enlightened Racism: The Cosby Show, Audiences and the Myth of the American Dream* (Boulder, CO: Westview Press, Inc., 1992).
56. Clint Wilson Jr., "Olympic Games' Events Most Disturbing," *Los Angeles Sentinel*, Oct. 24, 1968: 4B.
57. "Smith, Carlos in Flight from 'Mean' Reporters," *Los Angeles Times*, Oct. 22, 1968: E6.
58. Ibid.
59. "Racial Display at the Olympics," *Los Angeles Times*, Oct. 24, 1968: C6.
60. A.H. " 'Silent Protest' at Olympics," *Chicago Tribune (1963–Current File)*, Oct. 23, 1968: 20.
61. Donald McDonald, "Smith, Carlos Receive Praise and Blame for Stance at Olympic Fete," *Los Angeles Times*, Oct. 24, 1968: C6.
62. Helen L. Busby, "Seagren Example Cited," *The New York Times*, Oct. 27, 1968: S2.
63. William E. Carsley, "Athletes Who Care and Those Who Don't," *Chicago Tribune (1963–Current File)*, Oct. 25, 1968: 20.
64. Hill, "Racing after Smith and Carlos"; Hartmann, *Race, Culture, and the Revolt of the Black Athlete*.
65. Wilson Jr., "Olympic Games' Events."
66. "Mills Proud of Carlos and Smith," *Los Angeles Sentinel*, Oct. 24, 1968: A1.
67. Booker Griffin, "Olympic Exclusive: Some Untold Tales of Mexico City," *Los Angeles Sentinel*, Oct. 24, 1968: B5.

68. Wilson Jr., "Olympic Games' Events"; Clint Wilson Jr., "No Title," *Los Angeles Sentinel,* Oct. 31, 1968: B4.
69. Wilson Jr., "Olympic Games' Events."
70. Jack Tenner, "Let's Take a Look . . . at Quotes and Questions," *Los Angeles Sentinel,* Oct. 24, 1968: A6. Upon Tenner's death in 2008, white supremacist neo-Nazi website Stormfront described him as a "Jew puppet master for Negros," a ringing endorsement if ever there was one.
71. John G. Griffin, "Black Power Bows at the Olympics," *Chicago Daily Defender (Big Weekend Edition) (1966–1973),* Oct. 19, 1968: 1; "Photo-Editorial: Olympic Retrospective," *Ebony* (Dec. 1968): 160–161.
72. "Spreading the U.S. Gospel Elsewhere," *New York Amsterdam News (1962–1993).*
73. Brad Pye, Jr., "Quiet and Loud Protests," *Los Angeles Times,* Oct. 24, 1968: B1.
74. While this construction was absent in mainstream press coverage of Smith and Carlos' dissent, it would become a common chant of the black cultural revolution of the 1970s.
75. Griffin, "Olympic Exclusive": B5.
76. Gertrude Wilson, "UFT Egos—and Black Athletes," *New York Amsterdam News (1962–1993),* Nov. 2, 1968: 19.
77. Brad Pye Jr., "A Beautiful Black Demonstration," *Los Angeles Sentinel,* Oct. 24, 1968.
78. Pye Jr. "Quiet and Loud Protests."
79. Unfortunately Pye also genders this movement by only mentioning "black men" despite the accomplishments and involvement of African American women in the Olympics and Olympic protest movement. While the marginalization of women in the Olympic protest movement and larger movements toward racial equality is well documented (see Hartmann, *Race, Culture, and the Revolt of the Black Athlete;* and Bass, *Not the Triumph*), Pye's ignoring of female athletes seems particularly callous considering that the photo accompanying his article, "A Beautiful Black Demonstration," was of female medal winners Barbara Ferrell and Wyomia Tyus.
80. John H. Sengstacke, "Olympic Blacks' Nonsense," *Chicago Daily Defender (Big Weekend Edition) (1966–1973),* Oct. 26, 1968: 10.
81. "Life on Roller Coaster," *Los Angeles Sentinel,* Oct. 24, 1968: A6.
82. John A. Helem, "Take Ten," *Chicago Daily Defender (Big Weekend Edition) (1966–1973),* Oct. 26, 1968: 19.
83. Ibid. Emphasis added.
84. "'Black Athlete—' A Book," *New York Amsterdam News (1962–1993),* Oct. 26, 1968.
85. "Photo-Editorial: Olympic Retrospective," *Ebony.*
86. Helem, "Take Ten."
87. Wilson, "UFT Egos."
88. Ibid.
89. Jack Tenner, "Let's Take a Look . . . at Quotes and Questions."
90. "KABC's Allin Slate: White Man Backs Smith and Carlos," *Los Angeles Sentinel,* Nov. 7, 1968.
91. David C. Ogden and Joel Nathan Rosen, eds., *Reconstructing Fame: Sport, Race, and Evolving Reputations* (Jackson: The University Press of Mississippi, 2008).

4 Sister Souljah, Rodney King, and the Future President, 1992

*If my world's black and yours is white
How the hell could we think alike?*[1]

Nearly twenty-five years after Eartha Kitt, Tommie Smith, and John Carlos attempted to influence public understandings of America's (failed) promises of equality, a black celebrity again found herself at the center of a fiery debate about race and nation. In 1992, the racial contradictions of what Mark Anthony Neal and Nelson George have described as a "post-soul" America were everywhere.[2] Many Americans had come of age in a country that, while appearing fully integrated and celebratory of African Americans, was simultaneously scaling back *de jure* efforts toward equality established during the civil rights era. According to Manning Marable, the 1990s represented "the culmination of a thirty-year ideological and political war against the logic of the reforms of the 1960s."[3]

While *The Cosby Show,* featuring an all-black cast, was the most popular program among Americans of all races, Reaganism had brought about the raced "War on Drugs" and curtailing of affirmative action programs.[4] President George H.W. Bush's now infamous Willie Horton ad had defined crime in America through stereotypes of African American men as violent, uncontrollable rapists of white women, and the news media responded to the controversy surrounding the ad by re-airing it ad nauseam. The Billboard charts were dominated by African American artists, and the success of these musicians, along with black athletes like Michael Jordan, were widely hailed as evidence of racial progress.[5] The era of what scholars have variously labeled "modern racism," "enlightened racism," and "colorblind racism" was in full swing.[6]

While, by 1992, countless moderate reforms had been made to appease the demands that rose from the cultural politics of the 1960s and 1970s, more radical antiracist movements had been systematically dismantled and suppressed.[7] Howard Winant has detailed the ideological contradictions of this era noting that as the new period of racial hegemony "touted 'color blindness' and claimed largely to have achieved racial equality, the United States racial state had hardly transformed the fundamental social structures of race and racism. It was simply managing white supremacy in a significantly updated and revised fashion."[8]

It was within this ideological landscape that, on April 29, 1992, news of the acquittal of the four white Los Angeles Police Department (LAPD) officers who had been tried for the brutal beating of unarmed black motorist Rodney King reached the nation. The rage of the African American community was tangible; Los Angeles erupted into the worst urban unrest since 1964, and newsmakers across the nation faced the challenge of making sense of it all to their readers.

Notably, while the injustices surrounding Rodney King's beating and the acquittal of his victimizers were everyday experiences for many living in urban communities, mainstream news coverage of the story treated these events, and the rage that followed the acquittal, as extraordinary and momentary.[9] Further, Ronald Jacobs has argued that the not-guilty verdicts returned in the trial of the LAPD officers were a "reality check" to many mainstream journalists whose "liberal-progressive belief in the power of news publicity" had led them to assume coverage of the beating would lead to justice being served.[10] Others have argued that the same news values that lead mainstream newsmakers to air the video of King being brutally beaten later justified a fixation on the most sensational scenes of urban violence during the post-verdict uprising, displacing conversations about police brutality and black victimhood with ones that justified the draconian control of urban populations.[11] Finally, for journalists in the black press, the verdicts and mainstream responses to the Los Angeles uprising reinforced intense cynicism about the possibilities for productive conversations and interventions about race in the public sphere.[12]

SISTER SOULJAH, HIP HOP, AND THE CULTURE WARS

Two weeks after the not-guilty verdicts, rapper Sister Souljah sat down for an interview with *Washington Post* reporter David Mills. Mills asked Souljah to explain the mindset of "rioters" in Los Angeles, who he described as "rampaging on the streets," "shooting at firemen," and "perpetrating violence." He asked Souljah, in reference to a widely aired video of white motorist Reginald Denny being attacked during these riots, what "America" was supposed to think when they saw "white men being dragged from their vehicles and beaten."[13] Souljah gave a lengthy answer in an attempt to explain what she saw as the hypocrisy of such questions, and of politicians and newsmakers who became invested in inner city violence when white interests seemed in peril but appeared otherwise oblivious to black life and death. She stated in part:

> Black people from the underclass and so-called lower class do not respect the institutions of white America. . . . You don't care about their

lives, haven't added anything to the quality of their lives, haven't effectuated anything for the quality of their lives, and then expect them to respond to your opinions? Why would they? ... I mean, if black people kill black people every day, why not have a week and kill white people? You understand what I'm saying? In other words, white people, this government, and that mayor were well aware that black people were dying every day in Los Angeles under gang violence. So if you're a gang member and you would normally be killing somebody, why not kill a white person? Do you think that somebody thinks that white people are better, or above and beyond dying, when they would kill their own kind? ... It's rebellion, it's revenge. ... That's what they believe. And I see why. I don't understand why anyone would even ask me that question. In the real world, black people die on a daily basis. Always rooted in the hands of white supremacy. That's what I know.[14]

These remarks, when originally published, received marginal attention. However, a month later presidential hopeful Bill Clinton gave a speech at a meeting of Jesse Jackson's Rainbow Coalition in which he criticized what he characterized as Souljah's "racial hatred." Clinton said of Souljah's interview, "If you took the words 'white' and 'black' and reversed them, you might think that [Ku Klux Klan leader] David Duke is giving that speech."[15] Suddenly Souljah was thrust into the media spotlight.

The sentence, "If black people kill black people every day, why not have a week and kill white people?" became, on its own and without the context of Mills' larger interview, the focus of intense media scrutiny.[16] The possibility that Souljah's statement was entirely rhetorical in nature was lost on mainstream newsmakers, who treated it as a literal suggestion. This decontextualization of Souljah's words ignored the line of questioning to which she was responding—she was *asked* to speak from the perspective of someone set on committing violence—as well as her use of hyperbole to convey the intense frustration and anger felt by many young African Americans.[17]

As the controversy spread, Souljah held a press conference in an attempt to put her comments in their proper context (Figure 4.1). According to the *New York Amsterdam News:*

She said her statement was taken out of context ... she said she made reference to the mindset of gang members. She described them as people accustomed to a hostile lifestyle. They murder at random she explained. In that mindset where gang violence accounts for the daily death of children, grandmothers, and women, she asked why would it be inconceivable for those same gang members to murder Whites. Her point, she said, is that in America black lives are valueless and it is only when the threat of death to Whites is voiced that politicians act responsibly.[18]

Figure 4.1 (Original AP caption): Rap artist Sister Souljah speaks at a conference in New York City on June 16, 1992. Souljah made claims that U.S. Presidential candidate Bill Clinton wasn't in touch with the problems of Black-America. Hip-hop star Doug E. Fresh is in the background. (AP Photo / Alex Brandon)

Despite this attempted at clarification, mainstream journalists continued to report Souljah's words according to Clinton's interpretation. In this case, the acceptance of Clinton as a more viable interpreter of black expression than Souljah herself reflects both the way white subjectivities are assumed by newsmakers to represent objective knowledge and a profound misunderstanding of the rhetorical dissent of the hip hop generation.

In fact, the rising popularity of rap among young people was the subject of great concern in the early-1990s culture wars; white elites had defined the music and its artists as threats long before Souljah sat down for her interview.[19] It is likely that at least some of the motivation behind the *Post*'s choice to interview Souljah—whose celebrity status was limited largely to citizens familiar with political hip hop—grew from this larger climate. Unless *Washington Post* readers were fans of Public Enemy or Paris, with whom Souljah had collaborated, it is unlikely they had ever heard of her.

Given the unrepentant political rhetoric of her music however, David Mills and his *Post* editors must have been aware they would receive passionate, and likely controversial, anti-establishment discourse from the rapper.

Notably, in his original reporting of the interview with Souljah, Mills made a clear, albeit not unproblematic, attempt to validate the political relevance of hip hop. He wrote, "The King verdict and its backlash have shown America the power of hip-hop music as a political medium. Television coverage of the crisis confirmed, as never before, the status of hard-edged rappers as spokesmen for the black lower class, delegates of America's angry youth. Opinion-makers. Leaders."[20]

Yet once Clinton made Souljah's words a talking point, Mills' mainstream colleagues expressed an open disdain for rap music (and black youth culture more generally). Columnist Eve Zibart of *The Washington Post* characterized rap music as "separatist" and "antisocial." Courtland Milloy, also of the *Post,* wrote that, "rappers were incapable of making a point without profanity, or a move without holding their crotches."[21] Through such discourse Souljah became a convenient flash point to sustain cultural debates that devalued hip hop and implied deviance and pathology in black urban culture.[22]

In an incredibly insensitive use of rhetoric for someone criticizing the "imbecilic images" of "unfocused and semi-literate" rappers, *Los Angeles Times* columnist Greg Braxton used the controversy that exploded around Souljah's words to report that some "would like to put a noose around the neck of rap music."[23] Braxton's own use of hyperbole, via a lynching metaphor, to critique the "offensive" content on rap music and supposedly racist discourse of Souljah seems both disturbingly and comically unaware. Braxton's column of course ignored histories of lynching in America and the ways younger generations of African Americans might view ongoing acts of institutionalized white violence against black bodies—like the beating of Rodney King—with understandable rage given this history.[24]

While such coverage of rap music in the mainstream public sphere reveals the ways it was delegitimized and treated as threatening by white elites in the early 1990s, it was not particularly popular among black cultural elites either. Neal and Boyd argue that the shifting generational experience of being black in America in the late twentieth century created a rift between the civil rights generation and the hip hop generation.[25] Of particular contestation were understandings of how public representations of blackness might impact racial equality efforts, with older generations and black elites remaining attached to the politics of respectability and members of the hip hop generation rejecting the binary of "good" versus "bad" forms of self-presentation.

Such debates about rap music in the black community exemplify the ideological diversity that exists within counterpublics where the expression of new and alternative discourse is allowed long before being accepted (and commodified) in mainstream audiences.[26] Hip hop artists became important contributors to the black public sphere by finding new ways to reflect the continued veiled position of African Americans—and the particular challenges of urban black and brown youth. Thus, discourses offered by rappers like Souljah can be understood as a form of black cultural expression that served, in a so-called colorblind modern society, to introduce the frustrations of marginalized youth into both alternative and mainstream discourse.

Given these contexts, the way journalists in the mainstream and African American press framed Souljah reveals how an especially unapologetic form of celebrity dissent, intended to call out the unequal valuing of raced life, was constructed for American audiences.[27]

COVERING SISTER SOULJAH

Mainstream coverage of the Sister Souljah controversy, totaling 143 stories, outnumbered that of every other case examined here. Mainstream coverage of Souljah was also the most negative in tone of any in this volume (followed closely by coverage of Smith and Carlos). The amount of coverage of Souljah in the black press, 29 stories, equaled that of Kitt, only outnumbered by coverage of Paul Robeson. This significant amount of coverage in both the mainstream and black press suggests that Souljah's dissent, despite her limited celebrity, was deemed especially newsworthy. In the mainstream press this newsworthiness was clearly a result of the high-profile figures involved—Bill Clinton and Jesse Jackson in particular—and the dominance of ideologies that labeled black anger especially threatening to the status quo. The frequency of coverage of Souljah in the black press is remarkable given the sharp decline of black newspapers between 1968 and 1992 and suggests that in addition to the newsworthiness of the figures involved, black newsmakers felt a particular need to contribute alternative understandings of the story to their audience.[28]

WHITE PRESS/BLACK RAGE

The heavy dependence by mainstream journalists on Bill Clinton and other elite figures' interpretations resulted in characterizations of Souljah's dissent as an "incitement to murder," "inflammatory," "pointless hatred," and Souljah as "divisive," "racist," and "angry." In complete disregard of her educational background and work as a political organizer, Richard Cohen of *The Washington Post* described Souljah as "having the political sophistication of a ficus tree." Jon Pareles of *The New York Times* labeled her a "lonely crank," and his colleague Anna Quindlen wrote that the "woman who thinks with her mouth" had "already gotten more attention than her talents as a rap artist or a social commentator merit."[29]

Letters to the editor published by *The New York Times* labeled Sister Souljah a "hard-core hater" "poison[ing] all efforts toward interracial reapproachment." Other letters published by mainstream sources characterized Souljah as "incoherent," "ignorant," "sick" and "cowardly."[30] A column by Colman McCarthy of *The Washington Post* contended that Souljah the "motor mouth" was "pushing violence and hate as solutions to conflict" and thus "worsen[ing] the lives that this hot-blooded rapper pretends to care about."[31]

Together, the overwhelmingly white, male, mainstream journalists agreed that Souljah should not have a public platform (an irony given that it was a mainstream journalist like them who gave her the largest audience), and should, as Richard Cohen suggested, "Just shut up!"[32] This level of negativity and rearticulation of raced access to the public sphere reflects the intense reaction Souljah's particular brand of commentary evoked in mainstream journalists. While the presence of drama and extremes on the part of dissenters should not preclude journalists from incorporating discussions of the underlying social tensions that motivate such dissent, white-authored opinion pieces on Souljah made no attempt to understand the black perspective on racism or interrogate oppressive white power structures.[33]

Of the 143 mainstream stories examined here, less than one percent—a single story by Jack Nelson of the *Los Angeles Times*—reported Clinton's remark nearly a month after initially criticizing Souljah that he "understands the anger behind the songs of rap singer Sister Souljah. 'She obviously believes that the system values white people's lives over blacks. . . . I think that's the point she was trying to make.'"[34] The insistence of mainstream newsmakers in reprinting Clinton's original demonizing interpretation of Souljah's dissent but paucity of coverage of this later, more sympathetic interpretation is startling. Thus even when their original elite source, a promising white, male, presidential candidate, offered a more realistic and nuanced interpretation of Souljah's words, the mainstream press omitted it from their reporting.

Overall, mainstream journalists framed Souljah's dissent as an example of "black racism" and framed the stakes of the controversy that followed as the potential resolution of a political power struggle between Bill Clinton and Jesse Jackson.

"I Doubt Even Mr. Duke Has Been That Vile"

The existence of "reverse racism" and its parity to white racism was assumed in the forty-three percent of stories in the mainstream press that framed Sister Souljah as a racist. The terms "black racism" and "reverse racism" were used alongside the terms "incendiary" and "inflammatory" in reports on Souljah's dissent in every mainstream source. The authors of these stories discursively constructed Souljah as having incited racial violence against whites, and/or constructed her as a hypocrite for using "racist" language and violence to criticize the same.

The editors of *The New York Times* described Sister Souljah as "a careless voice for violence." *The Times* columnists called Souljah's words "the language of hate and murder," described Souljah as having an "open hatred for whites," and argued that Souljah presented an "apocalyptic vision of interracial relations" and "oratory extolling bloodshed" that was the equivalent of "throwing around kerosene when your house is on fire."[35] Jack White of *Time* magazine contended that Souljah's "eye-for-an-eye message is unmistakable," and writers for the *Los Angeles Times* and *The Washington Post* contended that Souljah was "fueling racial tensions" and made an "incendiary call to kill."[36] Every mainstream newspaper published without question Clinton's quote that Souljah had "advocated racial violence."

The New York Times reported "some critics" of Souljah "characterized [her] as racist and anti-feminist," and explained to readers that Souljah was "suggesting that whites should be killed in proportion to blacks," and "blacks would be justified in killing whites."[37] The *Los Angeles Times* reported that the controversy was the result of "rapper Sister Souljah urging blacks to kill whites instead of each other" and Eve Zibart reported that Souljah "professes to find the murder or economic ruin of whites rational and even righteous redress for the historical exploitation of blacks."[38] None of these interpretations reflected words Souljah actually said or attempted to interrogate Souljah's critique about the cultural value of black lives.

The *Los Angeles Times* and *The Washington Post*, apparently oblivious to the irony, reported that West Virginia Senator Robert Byrd (former Klan member and outspoken segregationist), "took the Senate floor to commend Clinton for his rebuke of such blatantly inflammatory rhetoric and for reminding the country that no race has a monopoly on racist provocation and demagoguery."[39] Similarly Richard Cohen argued that "racism is not a white monopoly" and that Souljah's words were "bigotry pure and simple."[40]

The incongruity of presenting the words of a black woman with virtually no social power as a racist threat to the social structure seemed lost on most journalists. Further, the lack of criticism of racist acts by other relevant figures (like Byrd, whose anti-black record speaks for itself; Clinton, who had recently played golf at a whites-only country club in Arkansas; or even the police who got away with nearly killing Rodney King) is blaring and demonstrates the way challenges to white hierarchy are, as George Lipsitz notes, treated "much more seriously than the millions of directly racist actions by public and private actors in society every day."[41]

To this point, *The Washington Post* published an article that included a quote from a white citizen who felt that "the KKK is for terrorizing black people. She's [Souljah] doing the same thing on the other side." Likewise *New York Times* columnist A. M. Rosenthal opined, "I doubt even Mr. Duke has been that vile in public."[42] Constructing Souljah's words as not only equivalent to but worse than the actions of the Ku Klux Klan requires both a very kind representation of that organization and its adherents and assumes

Souljah and her statements have the potential to do the same sort of damage that extreme violence at the hands of (oft-state sanctioned) racist militias have done to black communities for generations. Such discourse, which both echoes and amplifies the false equivalences made between Tommie Smith and John Carlos' dissent and the Klan, downplays the actions of such groups by conflating their organized terrorist activities—including actual violence and murder—with supposedly "racist" speech acts. Further, such narratives imply that Sister Souljah had the power to lead (or spark) a willing and ready mass rebellion of black people in the torturing and murder of white people, an idea that (needless to say) severely misconstrues the African American community as a single-minded, violent, vengeful, and easily swayed mass.

Further, the oft-reported contention by Clinton and members of his campaign that by criticizing Souljah he demonstrated a commitment to anti-racist ideology that required condemning all acts of "racism" equally exemplifies the problematic nature of colorblind rhetoric.[43] The idea that Souljah's words should be attacked alongside instances of institutional white racism in the name of "equality" conflated people of color's responses to racism with racism, ignored the reality of who the primary victims of individual and institutional racism are, and reinforced the idea that dissenting black cultural forms produce deviant ideologies rather than politically viable ones.[44] Not only does this type of colorblind rhetoric distract from identifying and addressing actual structures of oppression in society, it in many ways justifies them.

Further, discourse of an (imagined) incitement of black-on-white crime is rooted in ideologies that have traditionally been used to justify racial retribution against blacks as a pre-emptive measure. Such fantasies of an inherent violent black threat against the larger white populous can be seen historically in popular cultural narratives that justified lynching (e.g., films like *Birth of a Nation*). Similarly, constructing Souljah as a dangerous reverse racist allowed mainstream discourses to justify sanctions against her (and by association hip hop and young black people in urban centers) while claiming an anti-racist mantle.

For example, the editors of *The Washington Post* praised Clinton for taking issue with "the rapper who uses the rhetoric of race war to defend the Los Angles rioters," contending that Souljah's "angry and hate-filled thought" "is a form of racism and deserves to be publicly criticized."[45] And a letter to the editor published by the *Los Angeles Times* suggested "they should stop debating Sister Souljah and simply put her in jail for inciting felonies and genocide."[46] This sanctioning of Souljah missed the nuanced point behind her dissent, made any support of her (or alternative interpretation of her words) seem morally indefensible, and, perhaps most importantly, overshadowed the fact of the real recent and historical violence committed by whites against blacks (rather than the other way around).

As a seeming reassurance to those concerned about "race war," Jeffrey Schmalz of *The New York Times* reported that, "many blacks said they have no real sympathy for the rap performer" and did not believe that "anybody should kill whites."[47] The fact that a journalist felt it necessary to clarify that "many" black people (what about the rest?) did not support killing white people is not only incredible, but reflects how rhetoric deemed threatening from a black celebrity is assumed to reflect upon the entire black community. In the midst of all the literal interpretations of Souljah's statements, only one mainstream journalist, Tim Rutten of the *Los Angeles Times*, took the time to report that, "of course, no white people were killed" in the Los Angeles uprising.[48] Given the way newsmakers treated Souljah's statements as a real threat that could actually result in white death, mainstream readers might have easily missed this fact.

Likewise, only 1 of the 143 stories run by the mainstream press included the argument that "black racism" was not a real problem in American society and, according to one political scientist, could not significantly impact society, if it existed at all, given the lack of institutional power available to African Americans. This account, reported by Sam Fulwood III of the *Los Angeles Times*, was included in an article in which various other figures labeled Souljah's words unquestionably racist.[49]

Ultimately, by defining racism as the problem of an individual, and a black individual at that, mainstream journalists discursively absolved the larger political and social establishment from its responsibility for the oppressive circumstances surrounding the Rodney King beating and various responses to it. The blinding hypocrisy of a status quo in which the justice system acquitted those who actually committed race-based violence, but publically persecuted Souljah for her words, is apparent in this framing.

(Racial) Politics as Usual

Sister Souljah was framed as a pawn in a politics-as-usual game within the Democratic Party in nearly thirty percent of mainstream coverage. These stories (1) constructed Clinton's criticism of Sister Souljah as a political move to show his "independence" from "special interests" and, (2) constructed Jesse Jackson's pushback against Clinton for his criticism of Souljah as a move to try to levy influence in the election. Like all mainstream coverage of the controversy, Sister Souljah was rendered entirely voiceless in this frame. Instead, any mention of her relevance was relegated to the "cards" Clinton and Jackson were presumably using to play a game of political goaltending.

Mainstream journalists frequently reported that Clinton had criticized Souljah to "woo" "middle-of-the-road and conservative white voters" who might otherwise be turned off by the perception that he had a friendly relationship with the African American community.[50] While much has been said about how such constructions pit black and white voters against one another in campaign coverage, it is notable that this frame assumed large subsections of white voters felt disdain for Jesse Jackson particularly and black concerns and frustrations generally.[51]

Further, mainstream journalists used laudatory language to construct Clinton's inclusion of Souljah in the campaign even while identifying it as a form of political manipulation. Russell Baker of *The New York Times*, for example, wrote, "By deliberately embarrassing Reverend Jackson, Mr. Clinton was declaring independence."[52] Other articles contended that "both Walter S. Mondale in 1984 and Michael S. Dukakis in 1988" had to "placate" Jackson but "Mr. Clinton has served notice that he does not intend to do so," and that "Gov. Bill Clinton, reaching for a symbol that would demonstrate his desire not to be held captive by special interests, used a conference sponsored by the multiracial Rainbow Coalition to attack statements made by a popular rap artist."[53]

According to *Washington Post* columnist Mary McGrory, "Clinton gave politicians in the Democratic Party important reassurance" in criticizing Souljah by "suggesting that Jackson is not infallible."[54] Thomas B. Edsall reported for *The Post*, "Clinton campaign officials had been looking for a way to break the candidate's image among voters as a loyal supporter of Democratic orthodoxy, and a number of his key strategists argued that a confrontation with Jackson was the best mechanism to achieve this goal."[55] McGrory and Edsall's colleagues reported that by criticizing Souljah at the Rainbow Coalition meeting, Clinton had demonstrated "that he was willing to tell important groups what they don't want to hear."[56] Such reports not only sidelined Souljah's dissent and rewarded Clinton for his critique of her but also denigrated Jesse Jackson and encouraged the idea that he needed to be put in a less powerful (literal and symbolic) place within Democratic politics.

When Jackson attempted to defend both Souljah and himself from such narratives, his actions were treated as an overwhelmingly negative force. Gwen Ifill of *The New York Times* wrote that Jackson "made plaguing Democratic nominees something of an art form," and that his disagreement with Clinton over Souljah "has continued just long enough to risk becoming a long-term liability that could outweigh the short-term benefit Clinton strategists had hoped to gain."[57] David Lauter of the *Los Angeles Times* stated that the Souljah controversy allowed Jackson to "keep alive his feud" with Clinton.[58] David S. Broder, also of *The Washington Post* reported that Jackson's had a history of "hijacking attention" in the Democratic Party.[59] And his colleague Dan Balz reported, "The escalating feud between Clinton and Jackson has simmered for many months. If Jackson attempts to use Sister Souljah to keep it alive, the controversy could disrupt next month's Democratic National Convention."[60] Such assertions dismissed Jackson's very legitimate concerns about the way Clinton's actions regarding Souljah might reflect larger misunderstanding of the needs of black citizens.

Further, both *Newsweek* and *Time* published lengthy articles arguing outright that Jackson did not actually care about the black community but was taking issue with Clinton's characterizations of Souljah's dissent in his own self-interest. Joe Klein of *Newsweek* wrote that Jackson was using the incident as "a weapon of ongoing struggle" but "that this isn't *really* about high-minded ideas and downtrodden masses. It's mostly about the ego and needs of Jesse Louis Jackson."⁶¹ Michael Kramer of *Time* called Jackson a "megalomaniac" who "denounced Clinton's courage" in a "move" to control Clinton and further his own political power.⁶²

Likewise Richard Cohen wrote that "the Sister Souljah flap has become, to no one's surprise, all about Jesse Jackson." Cohen described Jackson as "menacing," "turbulent" and "petulant" while contending to readers that Jackson's initial refusal to endorse Clinton was not so much about "the residents of America's inner cities" but "Jesse Jackson's pride."⁶³ That the blame for the "feud" that threatened the Democratic Party was displaced from Clinton to Jackson reveals the way political disagreement over raced controversies are blamed on black politicians who, in turn, are treated as threats to political order, a trend well documented to influence how voters perceive black leaders.⁶⁴ Most obviously, however, none of this mainstream discourse attempted to address the concerns Souljah laid out in her dissent.

While characterizations of Clinton that suggested he was using Sister Souljah to further his political career were largely positive, several members of the mainstream press offered a cynical view of the political process or levied critiques of the candidate through this frame. In comparing Clinton's criticism of Souljah to Dan Quayle's criticism of rapper Ice-T for example, *New York Times* columnist Jon Pareles astutely snarked, "Both candidates clearly believe that the contrast between a politician in a suit and a rapper in street clothes works to their advantage."⁶⁵ Dorothy Gilliam of *The Washington Post* and Alexander Cockburn of the *Los Angeles Times* also offered notably more cynical narratives about Clinton than their colleagues.⁶⁶

Overall, Sister Souljah's marginalization in this politics as usual frame is clear; she is named often, but only in passing and only in relation to how she is being used for gain by others. Rather than being constructed as agential, she is a pawn—and her words, when quoted, are regarded simply as one of many semi-relevant issues being used by two men, one white and one black, one a rising star and one a perceived problem, in a game of political one-upmanship. Any discussion of the meaning of Souljah's dissent in relation to the Rodney King beating, the Los Angeles uprising, or police brutality and race relations more generally was lost by this marginalization.

BLACK PRESS/WHITE BETRAYAL

Only ten percent of black press coverage of Souljah's dissent was negative, and some of this aligned with mainstream discourse, however black press journalists used far less sensational language in critiques of Souljah. For example, Abiola Sinclair of the *New York Amsterdam News* editorialized, "As for Sister Souljah, I'm not going to defend her rap. I guess I know what she meant, but it seemed rather awkwardly put. In any event, it's been said before."[67] Here the criticism levied against Souljah is one that, while taking issue with how she communicated her dissent, does not suggest that the sentiment behind it was wrong. Rather, Sinclair acknowledges that the disparate valuation of black and white lives in American society is old news in the black community.[68]

Unlike the mainstream press, where it was clear many journalists were unfamiliar with Souljah, black press reports tended to highlight her achievements and community work alongside reporting on the controversy around her dissent. The *New York Amsterdam News* variously described her as a "rising star," "intelligent," articulate," "fearless," and a "learned, organized and confident young woman" who was "not at all the typical rapper" in their coverage of the controversy.[69] The *Washington Informer* described her as "a strong African American woman with a strong message," and the *Los Angeles Sentinel* contended that Sister Souljah's "outspoken stance against racism and oppression . . . made her a hero to young Blacks."[70]

As in other cases examined in this volume, the black press offered its readers criticism of mainstream news discourses. Esther Walker of the *Amsterdam News* reported, "More than 3,000 people converged on Harlem's famed Abyssinian Baptist Church last Sunday in support of and to pay tribute to Sister Souljah for the unkind and unfair treatment accorded her by the print media and television."[71] Abiola Sinclair wrote that "the media is involved in this whole Clinton-Souljah business in a very insidious way," and Lillian Wiggins of the *Washington Informer* noted that the "major media" barely reacted to racist utterances by white public figures but "seized upon the opportunity to make a national issue" of Souljah's comments.[72] Black press journalists also freely and frequently reported that the truncated Souljah quote popular with mainstream journalists had been "misunderstood" or taken "out of context," and cast doubt on Clinton's version of the quote by reporting it was something Souljah was only "alleged" to have said.[73]

Significantly, the interpretations of Souljah's quote offered by members of the black press aligned quite pointedly with her stated intent. The *Los Angles Sentinel* reported that "Sister Souljah poignantly pointed out the double standard involved in White America being appalled at the attacks of Black gang members on Whites in L.A., while accepting the daily reality of Blacks [sic] gangs killing Blacks as routine and normal."[74] Vinette Pryce of the *New York Amsterdam News* reported, "Her point . . . is that in America Black lives are valueless and it is only when the threat of death to Whites is voiced that politicians act responsibly," and an *Amsterdam News* letter to the editor noted "for we audience, we understood very well that her remark did not imply that we should go out and kill White people."[75]

Together journalists in the black press framed Souljah's dissent through discourses that held Clinton accountable for the controversy that erupted and questioned his respect for and understanding of the black community. These journalists framed the stakes of the controversy in questions of raced political neglect and its consequences to the everyday lives of Americans.

Bill Clinton the Betrayer

A large majority—sixty-two percent—of stories on Sister Souljah's dissent in the black press stated or implied that Bill Clinton's criticism of her at the Rainbow Coalition meeting represented an attack on the black community and its political agenda. Unlike the mainstream press' general use of the term "criticizing" to described Clinton's comments while constructing Souljah as the violent force, journalists in the black press commonly framed Clinton as an aggressor having "attacked," "lambasted," "insulted," and "dropped a bomb on" Souljah, Jesse Jackson and the Rainbow Coalition, and the black community as a whole.[76] Within this frame, Souljah, and especially Jackson, were constructed as symbolic representatives of the black community.

Notably, Clinton's relationship with the black press had been strained when, just a day before his appearance at the Rainbow Coalition meeting, he pulled out of a confirmed engagement to speak with the National Newspaper Publishers Association.[77] The combination of this slight and his critique of Souljah were received with clear displeasure from many black press journalists.

Alvin Peabody of the *Washington Informer*, for example, reported that as a result of his recent criticism of Souljah and "refusal" to address the National Newspaper Publishers Association, "Bill Clinton and the nation's Black voters are squaring off." While running the quote from Clinton in which he labeled Souljah's dissent "hatred," Peabody goes on to explain that, "Clinton was referring to Souljah's earlier comments in which she made headlines for denouncing 'White racism.'" The author further details that "the candidate's criticisms of the rap singer immediately drew uproar from several quarters of the Black community across America," and that an attendee at the Rainbow Coalition luncheon disagreed "with him going someplace where he had been invited to embarrass the host like he did."[78]

Here, Souljah's words are explained as a direct denunciation of racism (rather than as racism as they were described by the mainstream press) and Clinton's criticism is framed as both uproar-worthy to "the Black community" generally, and insulting to his "host" Jesse Jackson specifically. Similarly, Vinette Pryce reported on Clinton's comments on Souljah as a "diatribe" through which Clinton "usurped the hospitality extended" by Jesse Jackson and "acted like an unruly guest" in an effort to "appease White conservatives." In the same article Pryce included Souljah's voice by quoting and summarizing her press conference both in terms of her controversial comments and her contentions that Clinton was "unfamiliar with inner-city youth and rappers" and showed "distain for women."[79]

Other news articles in the *Amsterdam News* noted that the "verdict by a number of African American leaders" was that Clinton "put his foot in his mouth when he rebuked rapper Sister Souljah."[80] Labor leader Dennis Rivera was quoted by the *Amsterdam News* as feeling that "he [Clinton] insulted Rev. Jackson and the Rainbow . . . he is playing with the politics of suicide by attacking his own political base among Blacks and labor," with others describing Clinton's words to the Rainbow Coalition about Souljah as a "cold calculation," a "dumb move," and "outrageous."[81]

It is perhaps not surprising that the *Los Angeles Sentinel,* the black newspaper closest to the events and community about which Souljah spoke in her dissent, offered some of the most searing condemnation of Clinton. *Sentinel* editors ran an editorial and byline-less column that contended that Clinton's criticism of Souljah "was not only a blatant attack against Sister Souljah, it was an 'in your face' insult to Rev. Jesse Jackson at his own convention. Beyond that it was an affront to Black people and progressives," and that "Clinton has disrespected too many black people along the campaign trail" including "trying to belittle the significance of the Rev. Jesse Jackson" in "his broadside attack of Sister Souljah."[82] Unlike the mainstream journalists who were at times congratulatory in their descriptions of Clinton's "insult" to Jackson, the *Sentinel* framed this action as a reflection of Clinton's "arrogant attitude."[83]

These *Sentinel* pieces also argued that "Bill Clinton should know that reaction to racism is not the same as racism," and that the "attack on Sister Souljah" was just one example of the fact that "Bill Clinton is bad news for Black people, minorities workers [sic] and poor and working people." This statement was followed by a recounting of Clinton's "failure" to pass a civil rights bill in Arkansas, his support of the death penalty, and his golfing at a segregated country club, in addition to his failure to appear at the National Newspaper Publishers Association meeting, as evidence of his "pathetic stance on issues of importance to Blacks."[84]

Journalists in the black press also focused on the importance of the black vote to Democratic presidential candidates and the ways mainstream politics pitted black and white voters against one another in their criticisms of Clinton. Calvin Rolark wrote that "Bill Clinton chose to embarrass Jesse Jackson" because he "feels entirely confident that he will get overwhelming support from Black voters with or without Jackson's help." Further, Rolark argued, Clinton had "been having trouble attracting press attention" and thus felt it necessary to speak to "blue-collar White Democrats who supported Ronald Reagan and George Bush because of their misguided belief that the Democratic Party has been directing its attention more to issues of concern to Blacks."[85] The *Los Angeles Sentinel* noted that "Clinton should not bite the hand that is helping to feed him" and that his criticism of Souljah at the Rainbow Coalition meeting was "grandstanding" "to appeal to Whites and anger Jackson."[86] *Jet* found Clinton's actions "shocking" and a letter to the editor published by the *Amsterdam News* contended, "Clinton's intentions are in demeaning Rev. Jesse Jackson, the Rainbow Coalition and Black people."[87]

Many of the articles and opinion pieces published by the black press in this frame noted a sense of political fatigue and frustration about black voters being treated as pawns by white politicians. A letter to the editor published by the *Los Angeles Sentinel* stated, "If Bill Clinton's move on Sister Souljah was intended to distance himself from Black voters in the eyes of white voters, he succeeded because I no longer intend to vote for him. I am completely fed up with black people being used as scapegoats and targets whenever the need arises for some politician to boost his standing in the polls."[88]

The editors of the *Los Angeles Sentinel* expressed this exasperation perhaps most clearly in stating that "Black people are tired of being lied to by politicians," and that "the African-American community is tired of being treated as the whipping boy to appease white ethnics and southerners."[89] Likewise, *Amsterdam News* columnist Abiola Sinclair noted that "it's regrettable that Governor Bill Clinton took the opportunity to thrash rap artist Sister Souljah at the Rainbow Coalition Convention" given that previously "most Blacks were generally of the opinion that Clinton . . . was the lesser of assorted evils."[90]

Together, journalists at African American publications framed the story of the controversy over Souljah's dissent as one about the neglect, abuse, and betrayal of the African American community within mainstream politics. While Bill Clinton was named in the majority of the coverage as bearing a particularly large amount of guilt because of his claims of friendship and touting of supposedly antiracist goals, this frame levied a larger critique against the American political system for ignoring the needs of black voters while simultaneously using racial ploys to rack up votes from segments of the white population that traditionally exhibited anti-black attitudes.

"The Hard Issues of Survival"

Forty-five percent of stories in the black press framed the Souljah controversy as a distraction from more important political and social issues. Both the *New York Amsterdam News* and *Los Angeles Sentinel* described Clinton's criticism of Souljah and the resulting media frenzy as a "smokescreen." Black press sources either explicitly used the term "diversion," or implied as much by contextualizing the debate about the Souljah/Clinton controversy as insignificant compared to larger questions of racism and political efficacy.

Amsterdam News journalists noted, "There are serious problems Clinton could have addressed" but that "instead of addressing" the "vital subject" of Jesse Jackson's "$500 billion plan for revitalizing the inner-cities," "Clinton did the Souljah moonwalk away from the issues on the table. Jesse was pissed and rightly so."[91] Other black press sources reported that Jackson was "baffled by the diversion" from the "critical issues being discussed" including "how to get Americans back to work."[92] Columnist David R. Jones of the *Amsterdam News* opined that "instead of dealing patiently and thoughtfully with the hard issues of survival facing millions" the presidential "hopeful" had instead "attacked rapper Sister Souljah."[93]

In a front-page story, the *Amsterdam News* also reported that according to "one delegate" present at the Rainbow Coalition meeting where Clinton spoke, "there was this reporter next to me, and he was dictating this story and it was completely about Sister Souljah, not one word about the program we've been here talking about for three days." "One effect of Clinton's bombshell address," the article explained, was that "the summit's 'Rebuild America' urban development program would get short shrift in the major media."[94]

Focusing on race-based problems facing the country, the *Los Angeles Sentinel* reprinted on its front page a letter to the editor originally printed in the *Los Angeles Times* that noted that amid all the criticism of Souljah (and Ice-T) the community was "still waiting to hear one word of concern of [sic] any of those individuals [Clinton, Dan Quayle, and city councilwoman Joan Milke Flores] of the actual killings of blacks and Latinos by police."[95] The article following this letter detailed the recent killing of a(nother) black motorist by a white police officer.[96] The *Amsterdam News* also published a letter to the editor arguing that Clinton's criticism of Sister Souljah was evidence of "how ignorant the so-called peace advocates are of the political problems and plight of Black people everywhere in this nation."[97]

Likewise, the *Washington Informer*'s Lillian Wiggins contextualized the Souljah/Clinton "misunderstanding" amid a story detailing the neglect of African American members of the armed services and noting that "there are many stories of this kind" that might "educate those Whites in our society who ask repeatedly, 'What does the Black man want?'"[98] In the wake of events like the uprising in Los Angeles and controversies like that around Souljah the answer, Wiggins wrote, was "Justice for all." In another column Wiggins wrote that "politicians and leaders in this country [are] turning their backs to the resurgence of Nazism, hatred and bigotry," and that "Gov. Clinton and Rev. Jackson" and other politicians should "speak about this kind of injustice" by taking issue publically with "the David Dukes of the world" and "the hate groups who are training young White children to shoot guns and kill 'niggers' and 'Jews.'"[99] With such discourse Wiggins constructed the mainstream controversy over Sister Souljah's supposedly racist words as insignificant and even insulting compared to the realities of racism.

In framing the mainstream controversy around Souljah's dissent as a distraction from more crucial issues, this frame also made calls for community self-sufficiency and black self-determination. *Los Angeles Sentinel* columnist Jim Cleaver suggested that rather than concerning themselves with the controversy, the black community would be better off "setting up our priorities and taking functional control of our neighborhoods" since "white America" only responds temporarily "when black folk take to the streets" but always "slip back to business as usual."[100]

Similarly, *Essence* magazine, which specifically targets African American women readers, dedicated a five-page report to questions of what the black community could do in the wake of the Rodney King verdict and the continued "hegemony of the white world." This report contained an interview with Sister Souljah that did not touch on her controversial words or the criticism by Clinton but rather how "African people" as "victims of white supremacy" could "move to more collective action."[101] By completely ignoring the controversy that had been at the forefront of coverage on Souljah for months leading up to its publication, the editorial staff of *Essence*'s July issue made a point about what was important to their readers by simply ignoring what was not.

Ultimately, through frames that presented the controversy over Souljah's words as an unfair distraction created by both Clinton and the mainstream media and resulting in the neglect of important issues and real instances of racism, the black press argued that, as the *New York Amsterdam News* put it, "the community should make their own decisions regarding the Sister Souljah/Bill Clinton controversy."[102]

CONCLUSIONS

Unlike Eartha Kitt before her, Sister Souljah was largely not limited by explicitly gendered discourse in coverage of her dissent. More implicitly, however, both the mainstream and black press subsumed coverage of Souljah in a discussion of the political relationship between Bill Clinton and Jesse Jackson and freely compared her dissent to the lyrics and actions of male rappers. This focus on male figures significantly limited the agency available to Souljah to shape the conversation by pushing her and her dissent to the margins of a space dominated by better-known (and more powerful) men.

Interesting in this case is the large amount of coverage Souljah received in the mainstream press despite her marginal celebrity. Souljah acknowledged herself that "many White people had not heard of her prior to Clinton's condemnation of her post-riot comments."[103] Thus, like Tommie Smith and John Carlos, Souljah's celebrity persona was primarily constructed for mainstream audiences *after* her dissent was denounced by white elites. This, in addition to dominant cultural denunciations of rap music, likely contributed to mainstream constructions of Souljah as a one-dimensional and dangerous public figure who embodied the supposed deviance of inner-city African American culture.

On the other hand, the more friendly treatment of Souljah by black press members reflects their recognition of her as a community member. These journalists allowed Souljah both complexity and agency by covering her good works in the African American community and her firsthand responses to criticisms of her dissent. This, in addition to a more complex understanding of hip hop that recognized its activists roots and increasing role as a major player in the black public sphere, allowed black newsmakers to see around both the militant persona Souljah's words reflected and the Clinton/Jackson political power struggle.

Notably, this case represents the first examined in this volume to take place in a so-called post-civil-rights America. The more (though certainly nowhere near fully) integrated newsrooms of the mainstream press in 1992 compared to their 1949 and 1968 counterparts speak to this.[104] Notably however, coverage of Souljah reflects not only a continued reliance on elite white sources well into the close of the twentieth century, but also an ongoing mischaracterization of African American dissent and expressive forms. The failure of mainstream newsmakers to locate Souljah's dissent in the context of a viable musical storytelling tradition that hinges on the use of rhetorical exaggeration, irony, and nuance to express anger and point out social inequalities is striking. Similarly mainstream journalists' reliance on fear-based narratives of mass black violence demonstrate that dominant racialized discourse continued to assume—some forty-plus years after Robeson was accused of "instigating" a "travelling riot"—that black Americans were ready and willing to follow dissenting black celebrities into all sorts of mayhem. These findings certainly present a pessimistic view of how well the post-civil-rights mainstream news force informed its audience about fundamental issues of race and nation.

Likewise, my findings here support work that details the implicit way post-civil-rights politicians, and the media that cover them, use colorblind rhetoric to prime ideologies that insist on the deviance of black culture while simultaneously claiming investment in anti-racist philosophy. While earlier cases in this study demonstrate that the discursive equation of black political dissent with forms of white institutionalized oppression was well in place long before Sister Souljah arrived on the scene, the strength of the "reverse racism" frame in mainstream coverage of Souljah reveals a lack of complex understandings of racial power and hierarchy in the 1990s and an especially well-entrenched ideological strategy for silencing radical black critique.

While, like the black press of the time, some scholars and social commentators have come to regard Clinton's reinterpretation of Sister Souljah's dissent, as enabled and enflamed by mainstream journalists, as a tool of racialized political manipulation in the same vein as Reagan's "welfare queens" and "crack babies," and Bush's Willie Horton ad, others continue to celebrate it a stroke of political (albeit manipulative) genius.[105] As evidenced by the 2008 public labeling of comments by the Reverend Jeremiah Wright as Barack Obama's "Sister Souljah moment," mainstream interpretations of Souljah's dissent continue to be used in the service of colorblind ideologies that demonize black pain and expressive forms. That Souljah's name has become synonymous with political controversies that pit the supposedly divisive racial critiques of African Americans against the wooing of white voters is a clear signal of the lasting impact of mainstream framing.

On the other hand, the national conversation about the experiences of young people in America's urban centers and the role of race and class in the valuing of their lives is yet to be had.

NOTES

1. Sister Souljah, "Killing Me Softly: Deadly Code of Silence," *360 Degrees of Power*, Epic Records, 1992.
2. Mark Anthony Neal, *Soul Babies: Black Popular Culture and the Post-Soul Aesthetic* (New York: Routledge, 2002); Nelson George, *Post-Soul Nation: The Explosive, Contradictory, Triumphant and Tragic 1980s as Experienced by African Americans* (New York: Penguin Books, 2004).
3. Manning Marable, "Affirmative Action and the Politics of Race," in *Race Critical Theories*, ed. Philomena Essed and David Theo Goldberg (Malden, MA: Wiley-Blackwell, 2001): 344–354.
4. Sut Jhally and Justin Lewis, *Enlightened Racism: The Cosby Show, Audiences and the Myth of the American Dream* (Boulder, CO: Westview Press, Inc., 1992).
5. Tali Mendelberg, *The Race Card: Campaign Strategy, Implicit Messages and the Norm of Equality* (Princeton, NJ: Princeton University Press, 2001); Douglas Hartmann, *Race, Culture, and the Revolt of the Black Athlete: The 1968 Olympic Protests and Their Aftermath* (Chicago: The University of Chicago Press, 2003).
6. Robert Entman, "Modern Racism and the Images of Blacks in Local Television News," *Critical Studies in Media Communication* 7, no. 4 (1990): 332–345, doi: 10.1080/15295039009360183; Jhally and Lewis, *Enlightened Racism*; Eduardo Bonilla-Silva, *White Supremacy and Racism in the Post-Civil Rights Era* (Boulder: Lynne Reinner Publishers, Inc., 2001); Eduardo Bonilla-Silva, *Racism Without Racists: Colorblind Racism and the Persistence of Racial Inequality in America* (Lanham, MD: Rowman and Littlefield, 2006).
7. Cornel West, "A Genealogy of Modern Racism," in *Race Critical Theories*, ed. Philomena Essed and David Theo Goldberg (Malden, MA: Wiley-Blackwell, 2001): 90–112.
8. Howard Winant, *The New Politics of Race: Globalism, Difference, Justice* (Minneapolis: University of Minnesota Press, 2004).
9. Robert Gooding-Williams, *Reading Rodney King/Reading Urban Uprising* (New York: Routledge, 1993): 2.
10. Ronald Jacobs, *Race, Media and the Crisis of Civil Society: From Watts to Rodney King* (Cambridge, England; New York: University Press Cambridge, 2000): 127.
11. Judith Butler, "Endangered/Endangering: Schematic Racism and White Paranoia," in *Reading Rodney King/Reading Urban Uprising*, ed. Robert Gooding-Williams (New York: Routledge, 1993): 15–22; Kimberlé Crenshaw and Gary Peller, "Real Time/Real Justice," in *Reading Rodney King/Reading Urban Uprising*, ed. Robert Gooding-Williams (New York: Routledge, 1993): 56–70.
12. Jacobs, *Race, Media and the Crisis of Civil Society:* 114.
13. David Mills, "Sister Souljah's Call to Arms: The Rapper Says Riots Were Payback. Are You Paying Attention?" *The Washington Post*, May 13, 1992, Style sec.: B1, www.washingtonpost.com/wp-dyn/content/article/2010/03/31/AR2010033101709.html (accessed Mar. 1, 2014).

14. "In Her Own Disputed Words: Transcript of Interview That Spawned Souljah's Story," *The Washington Post*, Jun. 16, 1992, sec. 1: A7.
15. Richard Cohen, "Sister Souljah: Clinton's Gumption . . ." *The Washington Post*, Jun. 16, 1992: A21.
16. In fact, only two stories on Souljah in the mainstream press presented portions of the interview from which the quote was drawn at any length, and one of these was the original article reporting on the interview.
17. In particular, George Lipsitz has labeled California, the state where the Rodney King events and riots took place, "the Mississippi of the 1990s" because of the way in which institutionalized racism was not only largely accepted but furthered by the political reforms of 1990s (George Lipsitz, *The Possesive Investment in Whiteness: How White People Profit from Identity Politics* [Philadelphia: Temple University Press, 2006]).
18. Vinette K. Pryce, "Sister Souljah Raps Dems and Clinton," *New York Amsterdam News (1962–1993)*, Jun. 20, 1992: 1.
19. For example, Dan Quayle had publicly attacked Ice-T's "Cop Killer"; Ice Cube's "Black Korea" had been labeled racist and 2 Live Crew had recently been tried for obscenity.
20. Mills, "Sister Souljah's Call to Arms."
21. Eve Zibart, "Defending Rap Rights," *The Washington Post*, Jul. 3, 1992, www.lexisnexis.com/hottopics/lnacademic (accessed Dec. 1, 2013); Courtland Milloy, "A Music Rapped in Insincerity," *The Washington Post*, June 28, 1992, www.lexisnexis.com/hottopics/lnacademic (accessed Dec. 1, 2013).
22. Tricia Rose, *The Hip Hop Wars: What We Talk about When We Talk about Hip Hop—and Why It Matters* (New York: Basic Books, 2008).
23. Greg Braxton, "Cover Story: The Voices of Rap—Politics or Just Music?" *Los Angeles Times*, Jun. 19, 1992.
24. Stewart E. Tolnay and E.M. Beck, *A Festival of Violence: An Analysis of Southern Lynchings, 1882–1930* (Champaign University of Illinois Press, 1995).
25. Neal, *Soul Babies*; Todd Boyd, *The New H.N.I.C. (Head Nigga in Charge): The Death of Civil Rights and the Reign of Hip Hop* (New York: New York University Press, 2003).
26. Melissa Harris-Lacewell, *Barbershops, Bibles, and BET: Everyday Thought and Black Political Thought* (Princeton, NJ: Princeton University Press, 2004).
27. For this chapter, stories published between May 13, 1992, the date the interview with Souljah was published by *The Post*, and July 13, 1992 were examined. Data was collected from *The New York Times, The Washington Post, Los Angeles Times, Time,* and *Newsweek* in the mainstream press and the *New York Amsterdam News, Washington Informer, Los Angeles Sentinel, Jet, Essence,* and *Ebony* in the African American press.
28. In particular, Patrick Scott Washburn, Catherine R. Squires, and Todd Vogel have noted the way national and community-level economic downturns in combination with post–civil rights era attempts at integrating mainstream newsrooms and communities led to significant decreases in black newspaper publication and circulation. Notably, however, the magazines *Ebony*, which revised its content and appearance to meet the demands of different eras, and *Essence*, which was founded in 1970 after the heyday of the black press and like *Ebony* sustains itself economically primarily through advertising, have seen significant increases in circulation in the same period. Patrick Scott Washburn, *The African American Newspaper: Voice of Freedom* (Evanston, IL: Northwestern University Press, 2006); Catherine Squires, *African Americans in the Media* (Malden, MA: Polity Press, 2009); Todd Vogel, ed., *The Black*

Press: New Literary and Historical Essays (New Brunswick, NJ: Rutgers University Press, 2001).
29. Richard Cohen, "Racist Rappings of Sister Souljah," *The Washington Post*, May 15, 1992, www.lexisnexis.com/hottopics/lnacademic (accessed Nov. 26, 2013); Jon Pareles, "Dissing the Rappers Is Fodder for the Sound Bite," *The New York Times*, Jun. 28, 1992, www.lexisnexis.com/hottopics/lnacademic (accessed Nov. 26, 2013); Anna Quindlen, "Public & Private; All of These You Are," *The New York Times*, June 28, 1992, www.lexisnexis.com/hottopics/lnacademic (accessed Nov. 26, 2013).
30. William A. Baker, "Hard-Core Haters," *The New York Times (1923–Current File)*, Jul. 1, 1992: 1; Mills, "Sister Souljah's Call to Arms."
31. Colman McCarthy, "For Grim Rapper, Hatred Is a Cash Crop," *The Washington Post*, June 23, 1992, www.lexisnexis.com/hottopics/lnacademic (accessed Nov. 26, 2013).
32. Cohen, "Racist Rappings."
33. Jackie Smith, John McCarthy, Clark McPhail, and Boguslaw Augustyn, "From Protest to Agenda Building: Description Bias in Media Coverage of Protest Events in Washington, DC," *Social Forces* 79, no. 4 (2001): 1397–1423; Feagin, Joe, Vera, Hernán, and Batur, Pinar. *White Racism* (New York: Routledge, 2001).
34. Jack Nelson, "Democrats Call for National Renewal, Rip Bush, Perot, *Los Angeles Times*, Jul. 14, 1992.
35. "Sister Souljah Is No Willie Horton," *The New York Times (1923–Current File)*, Jun. 17, 1992: A24; Anthony Lewis, "Black and White: Perceptions and the Politics of Race," *The New York Times (1923–Current File)*, Jun.18, 1992: A27; Pareles, "Dissing the Rapper"; Russell Baker, "Back from the Dead," *The New York Times (1923–Current File)*, Jun. 23, 1992: A21.
36. Jack E. White, "Sister Souljah: Capitalist Tool," *Time*, Jun. 29, 1992, http://content.time.com/time/magazine/article/0,9171,159990,00.html (accessed Nov. 17, 2013); Sam Fulwood III, "Clinton Chides Rap Singer, Stuns Jackson," *Los Angeles Times*, Jun. 14, 1992; Dorothy Gilliam, "Clinton's Low Blow to Black Aspirations," *The Washington Post*, Jun. 17, 1992.
37. Sheila Rule, "Rapper, Chided by Clinton, Calls Him a Hypocrite," *The New York Times (1923–Current File)*, Jun. 17, 1992: A1; Gwen Ifill, "Clinton Stands by Remark on Rapper," *The New York Times (1923–Current File)*, Jun. 15, 1992: A16; Ifill, "Clinton at Jackson Meeting: Warmth, and Some Friction," *The New York Times (1923–Current File)*, Jun. 14, 1992: 31.
38. Sam Fulwood III, "New Barbs Fly in Clinton-Jackson Feud: Democrats: Risk Arises That Squabble, Which Began with Remarks about Rap Singer, Will Intrude on Party Convention," *Los Angeles Times*, Jun. 20, 1992; Eve Zibart, "Defending Rap Rights."
39. *Los Angeles Times*; David S. Broder and Thomas B. Edsall, "Clinton Finds Biracial Support for Criticism of Rap Singer," *The Washington Post*, Jun. 16, 1992.
40. Cohen, "Racist Rappings."
41. Lipsitz, *The Possessive Investment in Whiteness*.
42. Lynne Duke, "Souljah's Meaning, Refracted Through Racial Prism: Rapper's Post-Riot Words on Killing Whites Are Subject of Wildly Different Interpretations," *The Washington Post*, Jun. 22, 1992; A.M. Rosenthal, "Jesse Jackson's Enemy," *The New York Times (1923–Current File)*, Jun. 23, 1992: A21.
43. See, for example, R.W. Apple Jr., "The 1992 Campaign: Democrats; Jackson Sees a 'Character Flaw' in Clinton's Remarks on Racism," *The New York Times (1923–Current File)*, Jun. 19, 1992: A1.

44. Marable, "Affirmative Action and the Politics of Race."
45. "Gov. Clinton's Remarks." *The Washington Post,* Jun. 16, 1992.
46. William T. Parker, "Rap Artists and Racism," *Los Angeles Times,* Jul. 13, 1992.
47. Jeffrey Schmalz, "Midwest: Fertile Region for Politics of Disgust," *The New York Times (1923–Current File),* Jul. 1, 1992: A1.
48. Tim Rutten, "Politicians Sow Double Standards on Race," *Los Angeles Times,* Jul. 9, 1992.
49. Sam Fulwood III, "92 Democratic Convention: Jordan's Words Seen as a Shock to Blacks," *Los Angeles Times,* Jul. 16, 1992.
50. See, for example, Sam Fulwood III, "Clinton Carves New Strategy with Double-Edged Sword," *Los Angeles Times,* Jun. 16, 1992.
51. See Catherine Squires and Sarah J. Jackson, "Reducing Race: News Frames in the 2008 Primaries," *The Harvard International Journal of Press Politics* 15, no. 4 (2010): 375–400; Robert M. Entman and Andrew Rojecki, *The Black Image in the White Mind: Media and Race in America* (Chicago: University of Chicago Press, 2000); Limor Peer and James S. Ettema, "The Mayor's Race: Campaign Coverage and the Discourse of Race in America's Three Largest Cities," *Critical Studies in Media Communication* 15, no. 3 (1998): 255–278.
52. Baker, "Back from the Dead."
53. Apple Jr., "The 1992 Campaign"; Ifill, "Clinton at Jackson Meeting."
54. Mary McGrory, "Backing Jackson into a Corner," *The Washington Post,* Jun. 16, 1992.
55. Thomas B. Edsall, "Clinton Stuns Rainbow Coalition; Candidate Criticizes Rap Singer's Message," *The Washington Post,* Jun. 14, 1992.
56. Maralee Schwartz and E.J. Dionne Jr., "Clinton Tells Municipal Workers He'd Cut Federal Jobs, Not Theirs," *The Washington Post,* Jun. 18, 1992.
57. Gwen Ifill, "For Clinton, Attention Grows, Problems Remain," *The New York Times (1923–Current File),* Jun. 21, 1992: 21.
58. David Lauter, "Clinton Endorsement Avoided by Jackson," *Los Angeles Times,* Jun. 22, 1992.
59. David S. Broder, "Clinton's Gamble with Jesse Jackson," *The Washington Post,* Jun. 17, 1992.
60. Dan Balz, "Clinton Says Jackson Is Rewriting History; Candidate Reacts to Remarks in Controversy Concerning Rap Singer Sister Souljah," *The Washington Post,* Jun. 20, 1992.
61. Original emphasis. Joe Klein, "The Jesse Primary," *Newsweek,* Jun. 22, 1992.
62. Michael Kramer, "The Political Interest: The Green-Eyed Monster," *Time,* Jun. 29, 1992, www.time.com/time/printout/0,8816,975892,00.html (accessed Apr. 20, 2010).
63. Richard Cohen, "The Rap on Jesse Jackson," *The Washington Post,* Jun. 23, 1992.
64. Mendelberg, *The Race Card*; Nicolas Valentino, Vincent Hutchings, and Ismail White, "Cues That Matter: How Political Ads Prime Racial Attitudes During Campaigns," *American Political Science Review* 96, no. 1 (2002): 75–90.
65. Jon Pareles, "Dissing the Rappers": H20.
66. Dorothy Gilliam, "Clinton's Low Blow to Black Aspirations," *The Washington Post,* Jun. 17, 1992; Alexander Cockburn, "The Stupidity of Believing in Nothing: Clinton's Utterly Calculated Slap at Jesse Jackson Cost Him Many Votes and Gained None," *Los Angeles Times,* Jun. 22, 1992, http://articles.latimes.com/1992-06-22/local/me-512_1_jesse-jackson (accessed May 1, 2013).
67. Abiola Sinclair, "Media Watch: Clinton, Jackson, Souljah and You," *New York Amsterdam News (1962–1993),* Jul. 4, 1992: 24.

114   Black Celebrity, Racial Politics, and the Press

68. More forcefully, black press veteran Jim Cleaver denounced Souljah's statements but simultaneously legitimized the "anger and dispair" of the black community (Jim Cleaver, "Kleaver's Klippings: Far Too Much Ado about Nothing," *Los Angeles Sentinel*, Jul. 2, 1992: A7).
69. For example, see Pryce, "Sister Souljah Raps Dems and Clinton"; and Esther G. Walker, "Sister Souljah Electrifies Audience at Abyssinian," *New York Amsterdam News*, Jul. 11, 1992: 4.
70. "Sister Souljah to Keynote Malcolm X Celebration," *Washington Informer*, May 20, 1992: 1; "Vantage Point," *Los Angeles Sentinel*.
71. Esther G. Walker, "Sister Souljah Electrifies."
72. Sinclair, "Media Watch"; Lillian Wiggins, "Wake Up My Brothers and Sisters," *Washington Informer*, Jun. 24, 1992: 12.
73. See, for example, Carl Bloice, "Clinton Drops a Bomb beneath the Rainbow Sign: Attacks Popular Rap Singer as Racist," *New York Amsterdam News*, Jun. 20, 1992: 3.
74. "Vantage Point," *Los Angeles Sentinel*.
75. J.R. Black, "Clinton's Attacks on Sister Souljah Are Misleading," *New York Amsterdam News (1962–1993)*, Jul. 4, 1992: 12; Pryce, "Sister Souljah Raps Dems and Clinton."
76. See, for example, "Vantage Point," *Los Angeles Sentinel*; and "Bill Clinton's Dilemma," *Los Angeles Sentinel*, Jul. 9, 1992.
77. The NNPA, also known as the Black Press of America, was founded in 1940 as a federation of more than 200 black community newspapers from across the United States, see the National Newspaper Publishers Association, www.nnpa.org.
78. Alvin Peabody, "Clinton, Blacks Squaring off as Campaign Heats Up," *Washington Informer*, Jun. 24, 1992: 1.
79. Pryce, "Sister Souljah Raps Dems and Clinton."
80. J. Zamgba Browne, "Rangel, Rivera Say Clinton Insulted Jesse and the Rainbow," *New York Amsterdam News (1962–1993)*, Jun. 20, 1992: 3.
81. Browne, "Rangel, Rivera Say Clinton"; Bloice, "Clinton Drops a Bomb."
82. "Vantage Point," *Los Angeles Sentinel*; "Bill Clinton's Dilemma," *Los Angeles Sentinel*.
83. "Vantage Point," *Los Angeles Sentinel*.
84. Ibid.
85. The mainstream press tended to treat this "misguided belief" as fact. Calvin Rolark, "Clinton's Sister Souljah Rap," *Washington Informer*, Jun. 24, 1992: 12.
86. "Bill Clinton's Dilemma," *Los Angeles Sentinel*.
87. "Rev. Jackson Holds Summit Meeting; Clinton Blasts Rap Star Sister Souljah," *Jet*, Jun. 29, 1992: 6; Black, "Clinton's Attacks on Sister Souljah."
88. Eleanor Brown, "Clinton and Sister Souljah," *Los Angeles Sentinel*, Jul. 2, 1992: A6.
89. "Bill Clinton's Dilemma," *Los Angeles Sentinel*.
90. Sinclair, "Media Watch."
91. Browne, "Rangel, Rivera Say Clinton"; Sinclair, "Media Watch."
92. Bloice, "Clinton Drops a Bomb"; "Rev. Jackson Holds Summit Meeting," *Jet*.
93. David R. Jones, "The Urban Agenda," *New York Amsterdam News (1962–1993)*, Jun. 27, 1992: 5.
94. Carl Bloice, "Big Demonstration Planned for Democratic Convention," *New York Amsterdam News (1962–1993)*, Jun. 27, 1992: 1.
95. Dennis Schatzman, "Motorcycle Cop Removed from Streets after Fatal Shooting," *Los Angeles Sentinel*, Jul. 9, 1992: A1.
96. Ibid.
97. Black, "Clinton's Attacks on Sister Souljah."

98. Lillian Wiggins, "A Case of Blatant Discrimination by the Navy," *Washington Informer*, Jul. 1, 1992: 16.
 99. Wiggins, "Wake Up My Brothers and Sisters."
100. Jim Cleaver, "Kleaver's Klippings: Far Too Much Ado About Nothing."
101. William Strickland, "After the Verdict," *Essence*, Jul. 1992: 46.
102. Walker, "Sister Souljah Electrifies."
103. Vinnette K. Pryce, "Sister Souljah Visits the AmNews," *New York Amsterdam News (1962–1993)*, Jul. 11, 1992: 4.
104. Pamela Newkirk has detailed the ways in which the goal of a fully integrated press, inspired by the civil rights movement, was largely abandoned by the 1990s because of the dismal progress that had been made (Pamela Newkirk, *Within the Veil: Black Journalists, White Media* [New York: New York University Press, 2000]).
105. Monte Piliawsky, "Racism or Realpolitik? The Clinton Administration and African-Americans," *The Black Scholar* 24, no. 2 (1994): 2–10; Clarence Lusane, "Rhapsodic Aspirations: Rap, Race and Power Politics," *The Black Scholar* 23, no. 2 (1993): 37–51; Claire Jean Kim, "Managing the Racial Breach: Clinton, Black-White Polarization, and the Race Initiative," *Political Science Quarterly*, 117, no. 1 (2002): 55–79; Robert. C. Smith, *We Have No Leaders: African Americans in the Post-Civil Rights Era* (Albany: SUNY Press, 1996); Ta-nehisi Coates, "Fear of a Black President," *Atlantic Monthly (10727825)* 310, no. 2 (Sep. 2012): 76–90.

5 Mahmoud Abdul-Rauf and "The Star-Spangled Banner," 1996

Just because I can do it doesn't make it a dream. The American Dream is when it's fair.[1]

For the majority of the 1995–1996 NBA season, Mahmoud Abdul-Rauf (née Chris Wayne Jackson), a well-regarded player for the Denver Nuggets, had remained seated or in the locker room during the playing of the national anthem. By his own account, Abdul-Rauf quietly sat out "The Star-Spangled Banner" for over sixty games without much public attention. However, in early March, a Nuggets fan raised the question of Abdul-Rauf's whereabouts during the anthem during an on-air call with Denver talk radio personalities. The disc jockeys ran with the story.

When directly questioned by the media, Abdul-Rauf made public his reasons for avoiding the anthem. The point guard had converted to Islam in 1991 and told reporters that standing for the anthem conflicted with his conscience and religious beliefs. Abdul-Rauf stated that Islam forbid him to worship idols, as reverence was reserved for Allah, and that he considered the singing of "The Star-Spangled Banner" and accompanying reverence shown to the American flag a form of worship. The devout basketball star went on to state:

> The flag is a symbol of oppression, of tyranny. This country has a long history of that. I don't think you can argue the facts. You can't be for God and for oppression. It's clear in the Koran, Islam is the only way. I don't criticize those who stand, so don't criticize me for sitting. I won't waiver from my decision.[2]

Facing immediate criticism of this statement from local media, Abdul-Rauf offered more specifics on his critique of patriotic traditions in the United States in a subsequent television interview:

> In my religion, in my way of life, Islam, when another brother hurts, when another brother is oppressed, I feel the same. I'm able to make a lot of money in the United States. I'm from here and I'm not saying,

Mahmoud Abdul-Rauf and "The Star-Spangled Banner," 1996

again, that it represents everything bad. I never said that. I'm just saying that it also represents the bad. I just don't look at the Muslim issue; I look at the Caucasian American and I look at the African American being oppressed in this country and I don't stand for that.[3]

These statements generated intense discussion among journalists and sports fans and professional scrutiny of the usually private player from the National Basketball Association. Citing a rule that all players must stand "in a dignified posture" for the national anthem, the NBA suspended Abdul-Rauf without pay.[4] League officials contended, "All our rules apply equally to all our players."[5] The suspension was brief; two days later Abdul-Rauf and the NBA reached a compromise in which the point guard would stand with other players for the national anthem while closing his eyes, lowering his head, and offering "prayer for those who are suffering"[6] (Figure 5.1). The NBA agreed to repay Abdul-Rauf all of the salary he was docked under the suspension.

Abdul-Rauf finished the season with the Nuggets, the target of occasional death threats and fan booing, and was promptly traded (despite being dubbed earlier in the year as "having the best season of his career") to the Sacramento Kings.[7] He played with the Kings for two seasons and then

Figure 5.1 Mahmoud Abdul-Rauf prays during the national anthem at his first game post-suspension, March 15, 1996. (AP Photo / Michael S. Green)

left the NBA to play basketball in Europe, returning for one season to play with the Vancouver Grizzlies and then moving on to an overseas basketball career that took him to Russia and Saudi Arabia.

According to journalist Robert Sanchez, Abdul-Rauf's "not standing for the anthem virtually killed his career."[8] The point guard would eventually return to the United States and open a now abandoned (thanks to damage caused by Hurricane Katrina) mosque in Mississippi. His return to Mississippi, the state where he was born, was also plagued by a series of unsolved crimes including his home being vandalized, marked with white supremacist symbols, and eventually burned down. He currently lives in Atlanta with his family.

Abdul-Rauf is unique among the figures examined here because his dissent, by his own admission, was intended only as a private and personal embodiment of his conscience. The publicization of this dissent was led by zealous talk radio disc jockeys, and Abdul-Rauf had little opportunity to arrange or plan public comment. Once under public scrutiny however, Abdul-Rauf did not shy away from clearly communicating his beliefs. Thus, much of the public, including newsmakers, reacted to his dissent as an orchestrated public protest.

As in the case of Sister Souljah, mainstream journalists took a significant interest in Abdul-Rauf's dissent, publishing 126 stories. On the other hand their counterparts in the black press presented marginal coverage of Abdul-Rauf, with only 7 stories.[9] Given the frequency of coverage of Souljah in the black press just four years prior, this minimal coverage may reflect both the continued publication decline of black newspapers and a deeming of Abdul-Rauf's dissent as not particularly newsworthy in comparison to other issues affecting African Americans. Trends in mainstream and black press coverage of Mahmoud Abdul-Rauf reveal how, at the end of the twentieth century, critiques of black disenfranchisement and American patriotism were framed for the public. While clearly such critiques by black athletes, combining issues of religion, race, imperialism, and sport, were not new to American newsmakers, Abdul-Rauf's dissent has gone largely uninterrogated in scholarly work.

RELIGION, RACE, AND THE RISE OF ISLAMOPHOBIA

A week after the anthem controversy erupted, a producer and sound engineer from Denver radio station KBPI, along with a listener, barged into the mosque Abdul-Rauf was known to frequent. The group played "The Star-Spangled Banner" on a trumpet and boom box while disc jockeys egged them on live from the studio. One of the men reportedly wore a mock turban.[10] According to the *Denver Post*, "the radio station employees tried to put headsets on two Muslims who asked them to vacate the mosque to force them into a live interview, then laughed at them because of the way they spoke English."¹¹ After arguing that the incident was simply a "prank" reflecting "extremely poor judgment," and agreeing to apologize on air, the disc jockeys were allowed to keep their jobs. *The New York Times* reported that "the station also agreed to develop an internship program for Muslims who aspire to be broadcasters," but did not expand on how the station expected to woo Muslims to work alongside those who mocked them.¹²

As this incident reveals, the historical moment of Abdul-Rauf's dissent was marked by an increased public awareness and demonization of Islam. The historical othering and denigration of Islam in Western discourse is well documented; moreover, proximate events like the 1993 World Trade Center bombing and the Gulf War had created a cultural atmosphere in which Islam was regularly linked to violence and anti-American sentiment.¹³ Further, just a few months prior to Abdul-Rauf's dissent becoming public, mainstream newsmakers throughout the nation had constructed the Million Man March as a reflection of deviant black political ideology through their focus on controversial Black Muslim leader Louis Farrakhan.¹⁴

The outing of Abdul-Rauf on local talk radio also coincided with the announcement that Timothy McVeigh would be tried for the Oklahoma City bombing in Denver, and a few journalists made this connection. Jim Hodges and Larry B. Stammer of the *Los Angeles Times* reported, "The issue became public through local talk radio shows that were discussing patriotism and the Oklahoma City bombing trial, which has been moved to Denver. Callers said they had noticed Abdul-Rauf's lack of attendance at pregame ceremonies."¹⁵ While Abdul-Rauf's location during the anthem and the Oklahoma City bombing were entirely unrelated, Amy Bass suggests that public scrutiny of Abdul-Rauf's interpretations of Islamic law "likely filled a symbolic void left by Timothy McVeigh," whose white, Christian background did not align with dominant discourses that linked terrorism and anti-democratic ideals to the foreign Other.¹⁶

Such contexts are particularly important to this case because of the well-documented ways Islam has been racialized in the public sphere. In this process, the supposedly deviant threat of Islam has been articulated with larger dominant discourses that frame Arabs, those with Arab-sounding names, and black and brown Muslims regardless of ethnicity and nationality as an "always foreign" group.¹⁷

Such othering is apparent in the thirteen percent of mainstream coverage that constructed Abdul-Rauf's dissent as a particularly deviant form of Islam. Much like previous mainstream narratives that delineated the behavior of "bad" and "good" expressions of blackness, this discourse depended on highlighting critiques of Abdul-Rauf levied by Muslims labeled "mainstream." The *Los Angeles Times* printed the opinion of one Muslim leader that Abdul-Rauf's dissent "will damage the Muslim position in this country," and the editors of the *Denver Post* contended that "mainstream Muslims deplored Abdul-Rauf's protest," without giving any evidence to this effect.¹⁸ Further, at least one story in every mainstream source quoted

NBA "superstar" and "fellow Muslim" Hakeem Olajuwon's sentiment that Abdul-Rauf's perspective was "hard to understand" and "misunderstood the tenants of Islam."[19]

Through such discourse Muslims with beliefs like, or sympathies for, Abdul-Rauf are constructed as outside definitions of national belonging regardless of their citizenship. Further "good Muslims" are defined within a binary that offers little to no space for the public expression of their experiences, identity, or connections to a diverse Islamic community since these, in and of themselves, are deemed threatening.[20] Thus, mainstream coverage of Abdul-Rauf's dissent constructing him as "bad" and foreign because of an unwillingness to embrace displays of patriotisms also reinforced to "good" Muslims like Olajuwon that such displays were non-negotiable to their still-marginal acceptance in society.[21]

Notably, while this comparison of Abdul-Rauf to other Muslims is a reflection of the entrenchment of contemporary colorblind racial narratives that embrace token members of marginalized groups to legitimize the neglect and denigration of others, the scope of this research shows that such narratives were well in place as early as 1949 when mainstream newsmakers, serving an unabashedly segregated public, wrote that Robeson's "Communist propaganda had been vigorously repudiated by members of his own race."[22]

Finally, the contemporary hold of discourses of colorblind racism, and their intersection with Islamophobia, evidenced itself four months later as Muhammad Ali was celebrated as an American hero during the opening ceremonies of the summer Olympic Games in Atlanta. As discussed in the introduction to this volume, by 1996, Ali's 1960s-era political dissent—largely based on his own Islamic conversion and conscience—had been buried within amnesiac dominant discourses that depoliticized the boxer while celebrating his contemporary acceptance as evidence of an inclusive American culture.[23] Despite this amnesiac celebration of a Parkinson's-riddled Ali some thirty years after his religiously based dissent was framed as violently un-American, simultaneous scrutiny of Abdul-Rauf reflects American society's continued refusal to accept either Islam or black dissent (and especially the two in combination) as legitimate.

CONTEMPORARY CONTAINMENT OF HISTORICAL DISSENT

Despite comparisons of Abdul-Rauf to other Muslims and African Americans, a surprisingly few, only eight percent, of mainstream stories drew any kind of comparison between the point guard and histories of dissent among African American athletes in their coverage. When such recollections did appear they tended to lack historical context and several were factually inaccurate. Jason Diamos of *The New York Times* incorrectly asserted that Tommie Smith and John Carlos were "stripped of their Olympic medals," and Jim Hodges and Larry B. Stammers of the *Los Angeles Times* incorrectly listed Smith and Carlos with Muhammad Ali "among Muslim athletes" who had ignited controversies in sport.[24]

While small, the passing inclusion of Ali, Smith, and Carlos suggests some awareness by mainstream newsmakers of a tradition of dissent among African American athletes. For example, John Young of the *Denver Post* wrote, "in a controversy with the same tones and undertones of Muhammad Ali's refusal to fight in Vietnam, the National Basketball Association suspended Abdul-Rauf without pay for refusing to stand for the American flag."[25]

Most apparent in these comparisons, however, is the discursive work journalists did to contain the possibility that Abdul-Rauf's dissent would be perceived too similarly to that of now-celebrated historical figures. Several discussions suggested that because Abdul-Rauf compromised with the NBA on his original position, he was not comparable to Ali or Smith and Carlos. *Denver Post* columnist Mark Kiszla stated that Abdul-Rauf was "badly miscast as a rebel, when he was far too confused and fragile to be the next John Carlos."[26] Kiszla's colleague Terry Frei concluded that Abdul-Rauf's position was "more egocentric and less deeply rooted" than protests by athletes in the 1960s.[27]

As evidence of the amnesia (or perhaps willful ignorance) with which contemporary mainstream journalists remember past black dissent, Frei also contended that the Smith and Carlos' "incident" at the Olympics "didn't set off the international media firestorm that Abdul-Rauf's non-standing stance did."[28] Such contentions contradict the historical fact of the immense public response to the 1968 Olympic stand demonstration (as well as the detailed findings of this and other scholarly studies). Further, this contention sensationalizes contemporary dissent in a manner that constructs it as more disruptive to the status quo than that which occurred during the 1960s. Like contemporary nostalgia around Martin Luther King Jr. that conveniently forgets the role of mainstream media in framing him as an agitator and Communist, Smith and Carlos are framed within a sanitized, inaccurate vision that masks how severely their actions were feared and sanctioned.[29] These constructions can be understood as a "strategic rhetoric of whiteness," enabling modern racism through the selective retelling of the past.[30]

Only Robert Lipsyte of *The New York Times* (who had sympathetically covered Ali, Smith, and Carlos thirty years before) contextualized Abdul-Rauf's dissent and later compromise with the NBA as understandable when compared to dissenting sports legends. Lipsyte wrote that contemporary athletes like Abdul-Rauf:

> Had seen what happened to great athletes who thought they were free to express their individualism. The refusal of Muhammad Ali on religious grounds to be drafted and the relatively mild Olympic black power demonstrations of Tommie Smith and John Carlos were met with brute power; Ali lost nearly four years of work, and Smith and Carlos never

received the endorsement contracts that their medals and personalities deserved. Athletes got the message; you can paint your hair blue and draw pictures on your backside, talk trash or sniff it, even wear clown pants so long as you don't get too big for them.[31]

FRAMING MAHMOUD IN THE MAINSTREAM

Of the 126 stories about Abdul-Rauf's dissent published in the mainstream press, a tiny five-and-a-half percent of mainstream coverage critiqued the inclusion of the anthem at NBA games and/or critiqued those who demonized the player. While a small minority of the coverage of the controversy, these critiques, presented mostly in columns and letters to the editor, presented a clear alternative discourse by characterizing the inclusion of the anthem at basketball games as "anachronistic" and critics of Abdul-Rauf as "bigots." This coverage also tended to focus on Abdul-Rauf's biography by discussing his "rise from poverty in Mississippi" and his struggle to overcome the effects of Tourette's syndrome.[32]

Conversely, forty-five percent of mainstream characterizations of Abdul-Rauf and his dissent regarding the national anthem were explicitly negative. These characterizations included a range of descriptions of Abdul-Rauf that framed him as either a "militant" "deserter" or a "misguided" "kid" (despite being twenty-seven at the time). Similarly, while most negative coverage of Abdul-Rauf agreed that his position on the anthem was "disrespectful" and "insulting," this supposed lack of respect was sometimes likened to "treason," while other times simply constructed as "bad judgment."[33] Thus, mainstream news coverage of Abdul-Rauf contained tones of both outrage and paternalism.

The *Denver Post*, which might be expected to offer the greatest context to the story given their familiarity with Abdul-Rauf, published the most explicitly and strongly negative coverage. For example, while other sources rarely had anything bad to say about Abdul-Rauf as a player even when critiquing his dissent, the *Denver Post* contained multiple denigrating descriptions of his athleticism. *Denver Post* writers frequently implied the injuries that kept Abdul-Rauf from playing for several games after the controversy were faked. Woody Paige snarkily wrote, "Abdul-Rauf's sore foot is as sincere as Babe Ruth's belly ache," going on to call him a "quitter" twelve times in a single column.[34]

Perhaps most interestingly, there was an almost complete disregard of any discussion of race, racism, or racial inequality in mainstream coverage of Abdul-Rauf's dissent despite his explicit mention of the "oppression" experienced by African Americans. Mainstream newsmakers showed no interest in addressing "tyranny" either. The sidelining of inequality as a valid topic altogether in this case, as compared to that of Sister Souljah, suggests the reluctance of contemporary mainstream newsmakers to interrogate race without a clear script of racial fear and controversy and the legitimization (and limiting) of an elite white figure. Coverage of Abdul-Rauf also suggests that neoliberal economic philosophy and religious and national identities operate as surrogates for race in the mainstream public sphere by functioning as acceptable vectors through which to demean the voices of people of color.

Accordingly, two primary frames for understanding Mahmoud Abdul-Rauf's dissent about the national anthem were presented by mainstream newsmakers; these included (1) a focus on Abdul-Rauf's income and economic value as evidence of the irrationality of his dissent, and (2) a valuation of religious freedom and constitutional rights that contradictorily sought to undermine their application to Abdul-Rauf.

It's All about the Benjamins, Baby

This frame—that at its core the issue of whether Abdul-Rauf should stand for the national anthem was one of economics—was presented in thirty percent of stories in the mainstream press. Iterations of this frame implied that because of the millions of dollars Abdul-Rauf made as an NBA player he was unreasonable and ungrateful to criticize the U.S., that his eventual compromise with the NBA evidenced greed and a lack of conviction, and that Abdul-Rauf's public role as a sports commodity disallowed political dissent.

Every mainstream source examined here reported repeatedly on the $11.2 million contract under which Abdul-Rauf played, often breaking it down in detail to "$2.6 million dollars a year, $665,653 for the remainder of the 1996 season, and $31,707 a game."[35] *The New York Times* reported that "Denver fans" were "complaining that a player making $2.6 million this year should be more appreciative of the United States."[36] The *Denver Post* interviewed a local high school sociology teacher who felt that "if the United States was so oppressive, Abdul-Rauf would not have become a multimillion-dollar professional athlete."[37] Similarly, Woody Paige wrote that "by not standing for the national anthem, [Abdul-Rauf] is showing disrespect to others, the flag and the country in which he was born—the same country where he has no problem taking $2.6 million this year to play a game."[38] Fellow *Denver Post* columnist Mark Kiszla sardonically wrote, "when a U.S. citizen who drives a Ferrari and lives in a big house hears the lyrics to the 'Star Spangled Banner,' tyranny and oppression somehow come rushing to Abdul-Rauf's tortured mind."[39]

Similarly, *Newsweek's* Frank Deford described Abdul-Rauf as "bereft of any obligation to the public that pays him $2.6 million a season," and *Los Angeles Times* columnist Allan Malamud found it "extremely difficult to sympathize with Mahmoud Abdul-Rauf when he is making $2.6 million a year and being treated like a hero in a country whose flag he says is a 'symbol of oppression, of tyranny.'"[40] *Denver Post* columnist Mike Rosen, after contending that Abdul-Rauf's "religious argument was unfounded," argued that "Mahmoud's fallback argument—oppression—didn't hold up very well, either, coming from a millionaire who dropped out of college."[41]

What every one of these stories implies is that oppression and tyranny do not exist because of Abdul-Rauf's individual economic success *and* that he should be exceptionally grateful and patriotic as a result of this success. Such narratives clearly reflect neoliberal colorblind ideologies that highlight the wealth and fame of individual celebrities to mask the ongoing, large-scale inequalities the terms "oppression" and "tyranny" imply. Further narratives of Abdul-Rauf's economic success discursively justified severe sanctions against him, ignored sport as a form of labor, and called on stereotypes that define African Americans as naturally athletic.

For example, the *Los Angeles Times* reported on the position of a Methodist pastor who, while more sympathetic toward Abdul-Rauf than most commentators on the subject, undermined this sympathy almost immediately—"Abdul-Rauf, likely the victim of some oppression, has also been able to earn millions of dollars in America essentially engaging in a recreational activity."[42] A letter to the editor published by the *LA Times* stated that "the United States of America" had "afforded him the opportunity to capitalize on his natural athletic ability to achieve a level of economic success the average citizen can only dream of," suggesting that Abdul-Rauf be "barred from professional sports in this country" for his dissent.[43]

Letters published by the *Denver Post* contended "everything Abdul-Rauf has achieved, his education, the millions of dollars he makes every year playing basketball . . . he owes to this country . . . he should have his citizenship revoked and bank accounts frozen"; that "the man formally known as Chris Jackson is a hypocrite who professes Muslim beliefs while enjoying a well-paid celebrity lifestyle"; that he should consider moving to "Iran, Iraq or Saudi Arabia" but "it's doubtful he would be making millions of dollars in any of those countries"; and called Abdul-Rauf a "driveling, dribbling millionaire who has no idea how privileged he is to live in the United States."[44]

Here, Abdul-Rauf is framed as the beneficiary of an idealized American system in which he became a millionaire with little to no effort and therefore should model uncritical patriotism. The framing of Abdul-Rauf's dissent as illegitimate because of his large salary also reflects what Bass has described as the way the treatment of athletes as commodity works in conjunction with larger dominant discourses of racial citizenship.[45] This narrative was starkly apparent in mainstream coverage that advocated for the disciplining of Abdul-Rauf through his physical removal from the Denver community.

For example, Mark Kiszla argued, "His protest against the national anthem sent one, clear message to the Nuggets, Denver fans and the NBA: Abdul-Rauf is more trouble than he's worth," and flippantly rhymed, "The Stars and Stripes are forever. Mahmoud Abdul-Rauf is done in Denver."[46] *Denver Post* columnists also stated, "Surely the Nuggets can get something for Abdul-Rauf" in trade, and argued that his "weak character" and "fragile psyche" "need proper handling" "somewhere—anywhere—outside of Denver."[47] Sports column Pike's Peek wrote that the Nuggets "will be able to get something of value for the little fella when they shop him around the NBA at year's end," and Woody Paige wrote that Abdul-Rauf "must never be permitted to play in Denver again."[48]

Such narratives reproduced dominant discourses that place the value of black life purely in its benefit to the status quo—in this case white Christian economic interests—and justify the institutional reprimanding of black bodies.[49] Further, these narratives disturbingly mirror slave-era rhetoric that normalized the reprimanding of "unruly" slaves by selling them away from their homes and families, supporting the work of scholars like John Hoberman, who argue that contemporary sport has subsumed the role of slavery in the objectification and controlling of black masculinity.[50]

Once Abdul-Rauf agreed to stand for the anthem, his decision was framed as the result of a desire not to lose pay, simultaneously disciplining the point guard for what might have otherwise been regarded as a perfectly reasonable compromise and delegitimizing the beliefs behind his dissent. Michael Booth of the *Denver Post*, for example, wrote that "Nuggets star Mahmoud Abdul-Rauf says he won't stand for the national anthem because of loyalty to his Islamic beliefs, but he reverses that decision . . . . Why press the point when your self-described loyalty could cost you your paycheck?"[51] The *Post*'s sports column Pike's Peek contended that "Abdul-Rauf rethought his religious philosophies and decided that a silent prayer is probably worth $30,000-plus a night after all."[52]

Columnist Gil Spencer wrote, "If Mahmoud remained riveted to his principles, he wouldn't be playing basketball at $31,000 a game for a long time. So he's back to playing basketball."[53] A letter to the editor published by the *Los Angeles Times* stated that it was "abundantly clear that money supersedes his declared faith."[54] Similarly, *Denver Post* sportswriter Terry Frei argued that despite Abdul-Rauf's assertion that "my beliefs are more important than anything," when "called on it and told that it would cost him nearly $32,000 for each worknight he missed . . . he rationalized an accommodation."[55]

Woody Paige wrote that "Abdul-Rauf, who converted to the Islamic faith in 1991, didn't stand on his religious principles, but he can stand on his wallet now." His colleague Kevin Simpson wrote "Abdul-Rauf's respect for dead presidents curiously fits into his personal, religious and political ideology where the national anthem does not." Such framing puts Abdul-Rauf in a lose/lose situation wherein both his "religious principles" and "accommodation" are constructed as signifiers of negative personality characteristics.[56] Further, this frame totally disregarded the fact that Abdul-Rauf had not given up his perspective on the flag or anthem and that his "compromise" of performing an Islamic prayer during the anthem—something he had not been doing before—might alternatively be viewed as an ideological victory on his end.

Together, this frame reflects a modern iteration of that which appeared in coverage of Smith and Carlos in 1968, linking token opportunity in sport for African Americans to a required patriotism. In Smith and Carlos' case, the expectation was to be grateful and patriotic for the mere opportunity to participate and to embrace primary identities based on national citizenship. In Abdul-Rauf's case, because of the modern commercialization of sport and neoliberal economic narratives, he is framed as ungrateful and unpatriotic because of his economic success and refusal to identify as a sports commodity. Entirely ignored in this frame is any legitimation of Mahmoud Abdul-Rauf's experiences or his larger critique of American oppression and tyranny.

On Being Deserving of the Constitution

This second most common frame in the mainstream press appeared in twenty-seven percent of stories and reflected the deep contradictions mainstream journalists faced in denouncing Mahmoud Abdul-Rauf's dissent while maintaining a commitment to the American value of individual freedom. Every occurrence of this frame reaffirmed freedoms of religion and speech. Thus, Abdul-Rauf was commonly said to be "within his constitutional rights" as an American citizen not to stand for the anthem, to express his political views, and to observe his religious consciousness as he saw fit. While it might be expected that this frame and its required acknowledgement of Abdul-Rauf's rights would result in sympathetic framing of his actions, this was not necessarily the case.

In fact, many of the journalists who contributed to this frame constructed Abdul-Rauf as being wrong for using his rights. In a critique of the NBA's suspension of Abdul-Rauf, Woody Paige wrote, "The United States was born on the principles of freedom of speech and religion" and, thus, "the league acted improperly and, probably, unconstitutionally." Despite this, Paige, who as discussed previously was especially demeaning in his characterizations of Abdul-Rauf, also contended that the point guard "could have prevented the action weeks ago by choosing to avoid a confrontation."[57]

Paige's fellow columnists at the *Denver Post* also attempted to walk this line. John Young wrote, "The American flag is worthy of respect, and of saluting. Abdul-Rauf wins no allies calling it 'a symbol of oppression,'" but that, "at its root," America is all about "the freedom to differ,"; Kevin Simpson observed that Abdul-Rauf's dissent "could well end up being about high-minded concepts in contract and constitutional law," but was also "the latest in a long line of exhibits pointing to the death of common courtesy."[58] Simpson went on to call Abdul-Rauf a "delusional," "pathetic," "artless boor" but concluded, rather reluctantly, that "acting like a lout during the anthem isn't criminal."[59]

Through such discourse, columnists constructed constitutional rights and concepts related to performing patriotism like "manners" and "respect" as equally valuable to society. In order to justify such logic, these constructions inaccurately suggested that Abdul-Rauf engaged in explicitly confrontational acts during the playing of the anthem despite the reality of his quiet bench sitting and invisible locker room waiting.

Further, much of this framing implied a hatred of dominant American values by Abdul-Rauf that the player had never expressed. A *Los Angeles Times* interviewee offered that while "like religious belief, patriotism is a matter of personal choice" that "cannot be legislated," Abdul-Rauf was "hiding his anger against a group of people under a religious façade."[60] The interview did not elucidate what group of people Abdul-Rauf was apparently angry with, but the clear implication is Christians and/or whites. The *LA Times* also published a letter to the editor informing Abdul-Rauf, "The constitution of the land you so despise gives you the right not to stand up when the national anthem is sung or when the flag is saluted."[61] Similarly, Mark Kiszla wrote, "Every American should be entitled to freedom of expression. But it is Abdul-Rauf's privilege to be cast as ungrateful and hateful in newspapers from sea to shining sea."[62] These narratives undermined Abdul-Rauf's legitimate access to constitutional freedoms by appropriating pro-First-Amendment and patriotic discourse to "cast" him as undeserving.

The message of such framing, as detailed by Kenji Yoshino, is that while mainstream society has come to consensus that people should not be legally penalized for their cultural differences, they should concede to "covering" or muting these differences if they present challenges to mainstream culture.[63] This discourse, while condemning violations of First Amendment rights, required Abdul-Rauf, as a Muslim and a black man, to appease social expectations defined in white, Christian citizenship by keeping his beliefs invisible and far from spaces deemed sacred in American customs.

The majority of letters to the editor published by *The New York Times* also made religious freedoms and individual rights their main point and reflected the contradictions of critiquing Abdul-Rauf for using them. According to one reader, "The reason why I stand up during the playing of the national anthem is that we have the right to sit down." And while one writer found the NBA's actions a "blatant example of discrimination on the basis of religious belief," another felt, "regardless of individual freedom of expression if some standards of respect are not adhered to, all rules of conduct will fall by the wayside."[64]

More negative letters published in the mainstream press contended, "Abdul-Rauf has the Constitutional right . . . but he would do well to ponder what would happen to him if he attempted a protest against the Government in some Islamic countries."[65] Another argued, "Abdul-Rauf has forgotten the very reason for the founding of this country: religious freedom. He should be praising God that he lives in a country where he can worship openly. If he dislikes this country that much, he should live in those countries that are truly oppressive."[66] Such discourse repeats a theme common in public narratives around alternative political and religious perspectives, and especially around Islam, that suggests political dissenters should leave America if they find anything about it objectionable *and* that Islamic countries are barbaric, backward, and despotic. Thus, despite a rhetorical attachment to the sacredness of First Amendment rights for American citizens, mainstream journalists and commentators framed Abdul-Rauf as outside of this citizenship via the othering of his religious beliefs.

A "Manhattan attorney" was quoted in *The New York Times* that while freedom of religion is "an absolute right," "to the extent that the religious and political become intertwined, you may find yourself in a situation where there is a clear and present danger," suggesting that such a "situation" may lead to a "riot" and thus might meet an "exception" of First Amendment protection.[67] The suggestion that Abdul-Rauf's perspective on the anthem might cause violence is particularly sensationalistic but notable given that dissent by African Americans, and the mere presence of Islam, are linked to imagined violence.

Alternatively, mainstream stories in this frame sometimes quoted the ACLU or player's union, both organizations siding with Abdul-Rauf's unequivocal freedoms of religion and expression. The editors of *The New York Times* wrote that "a lawsuit would have put the NBA on shaky legal ground," and the *Los Angeles Times* reported that "the law may be on Abdul-Rauf's side if he decides to press the issue in court."[68] Mark Heisler of the *Los Angeles Times* commented, "A court would have to decide if his [Abdul-Rauf's] contractual pledge to obey unspecified rules [in the NBA operations manual] abrogates First Amendment rights."[69] The *Los Angeles Times* also published a rather long and very thorough letter to the editor that directly quoted the Supreme Court's finding regarding the illegality of requiring Jehovah's Witness school children to recite the Pledge of Allegiance.[70] Through such inclusions, this frame allowed for the presentation of some alternative discourses for understanding patriotism, with several opinion-based pieces comparing Abdul-Rauf being forced to stand for the anthem to anti-Democratic ideals.[71]

Calling the inclusion of the national anthem at sporting events an "absolutely idiotic tradition," columnist Harvey Araton of *The New York Times* wrote, "You want to renounce what Abdul-Rauf is saying, go right ahead. Boycott his games. You don't have to go any more than he has to stand up."[72] Robert Lipsyte wrote that Abdul-Rauf's "religious freedom can't be in question."[73] Lipsyte's colleague, Peter Steinfels, reported that "the NBA's action might violate the Civil Rights Act, which requires employers to accommodate the religious beliefs of employees if it can be done without hardship" and praised "the devout athlete" for giving "the nation a moment of reflection on religion, politics, patriotic rituals and the demands of conscience."[74] A letter to the editor published by *The New York Times* commented that the reaction to Abdul-Rauf's not standing was "troubling" and "makes you contemplate the thin line between patriotism and the conditions for totalitarianism."[75]

A scathing critique of the NBA's actions, published by the editors of *The New York Times,* stated:

> The [national anthem] ceremony is meant to honor a nation that respects freedom of expression, and the right of individuals to hold personal and religious beliefs that may depart from the mainstream. . . . The real issue in the dispute all along was not the wisdom or accuracy of Mr. Abdul-Rauf's view of the flag. . . . It was the NBA's blindness to the fact that trying to force participation in a patriotic exercise undermines democratic values.[76]

While these alternative discourses of patriotism are notable and clearly offered readers in the mainstream public sphere some access to ideological diversity, only one story of the 126 included in mainstream coverage of Abdul-Rauf's dissent actually acknowledged the "history of oppression and tyranny" of which Abdul-Rauf spoke. Andrew Tonkovich of the *Los Angeles Times* listed "My Lai, Manzanar, slavery" and the experiences of Native Americans as examples of just that, noting that the "attack on Abdul-Rauf inspires the unlikeliest flag waver (me) to wrap himself in one. If only to point out that it's how you use it."[77]

THE BLACK PRESS FRAMES ABDUL-RAUF

While minimal, none of the coverage of Abdul-Rauf's anthem dissent in the black press condemned it. Rather, journalists in the black press offered alternative readings of Islam to those found in the mainstream press and, like the mainstream press, engaged in a debate about the application of freedom of expression. Unlike mainstream coverage however, this later frame was contextualized amid conversations of race-based double standards.

Abdul-Rauf's Islam

The most popular frame in the black press, found in nearly sixty percent of coverage, focused on legitimizing Mahmoud Abdul-Rauf's relationship with Islam. This frame constructed Muslims as rightful citizens and contended that diverse interpretations of Islamic faith were legitimate.

The *Denver Urban Spectrum,* which unlike many of its counterparts was founded in the late-1980s, long after the heyday of the black press, ran two articles about Abdul-Rauf in their March issue. The issue, which focused on the topic "Religion and Spirituality: Is It the Question or the Answer?" would have been on newsstands when the national anthem controversy erupted in mid-March. Montoya Clemmons, author of both articles, constructed Abdul-Rauf as accomplished both athletically and personally by detailing the evolution of Abdul-Rauf's relationship with Islam and extensively quoting the player about his "soul searching," "discipline," and "striving for knowledge."[78] In an article titled, "Religious Diversity Unifies Team," Clemmons reported that Abdul-Rauf's Muslim identity "only makes for dynamic conversation and greater unity over the course of the season," quoting one of Abdul-Rauf's Christian teammates, LaPhonso Ellis, saying, "anything that teaches sound, moral values is fine with me . . . hopefully someone will see our light so that someone may say 'I want to be like Mahmoud.'"[79]

Particularly striking in this coverage of Abdul-Rauf compared to that in the mainstream press is both the construction of Islam as aspirational and the voices that are given agency to speak. In particular, both Abdul-Rauf and Ellis—a black teammate who worked closely with Abdul-Rauf and supported his religious beliefs—are treated as valid interpreters of religious and moral principle. Notably however, newsmakers at the *Denver Urban Spectrum* choose not to address Abdul-Rauf's dissent in their April or May issues, perhaps reflecting the local tensions that arose once mainstream media picked up the story.

Other black press sources also focused stories on legitimizing Abdul-Rauf's interpretation of Islam. The *Los Angeles Sentinel,* for example, highlighted opinions of "Islamic leaders" in regard to the national anthem controversy, leading with the statement that "Mahmoud Abdul-Rauf's decision not to stand for the national anthem should be respected as an act of religious conscience." In this article, the belief of "some" Islamic leaders that "standing for the national anthem is a secular act that does not contradict Islamic principles," is characterized as an "opinion" rather than fact.[80] This framing provided an alternative to the limited representation of "mainstream" Islam in the mainstream press and allowed for the individuality and agency of its worshippers.

Further, the *Sentinel* included beliefs from religious scholars and Muslim leaders that were notably excluded from mainstream representations of Islam. These included that Abdul-Rauf "should not be pushed to go beyond what his beliefs dictate," that "the decision of whether to stand for the anthem and flag is a subjective one, believers are responsible to their own consciences," and that "we should support him in his conviction, whether we agree with his specific interpretation or not." Ultimately, the *Sentinel* explained, "The decision [to observe or not observe the national anthem] is one Muslims must make for themselves since Islam is a monotheistic religion that teaches all acts of worship are special only to God."[81]

Sentinel staff also dedicated an article to discussing the positive influence Islam had on Abdul-Rauf's life. It began, "He recites five obligatory prayers every day, faithfully observes his religion's holy days and helps tutor younger Muslims in the tenants of Islam."[82] Immediately, such discourse constructs Abdul-Rauf's relationship with Islam as legitimate and not only reflective of his own positive "faithful" characteristics but also as a positive force in other people's lives.

The article goes on to describe Abdul-Rauf's "embrace" of Islam and reports that Abdul-Rauf "has managed to thrive in the glitzy world of pro basketball while drifting closer to the spiritual Islamic world in which he feels increasingly more comfortable." Given Abdul-Rauf's faith, the article reports, "It came as no surprise to his Denver Nuggets teammates and friends that when it came down to either basketball or his religion, Mahmoud Abdul-Rauf chose Islam."[83] This discourse is particularly important considering the way Abdul-Rauf's interpretation of Islam was constructed as a rejection of his American citizenship in the mainstream press. Instead, the black press simply suggests not that Abdul-Rauf was choosing Islam over his country but over his career, a choice that allows for much more understanding (and admiration).

The *Sentinel* article also reported that before the controversy, Abdul-Rauf had lost both money and personal relationships as a result of his faith. "His religion apparently made him less marketable" given the shoe contract Nike chose not to renew after his conversion, and, "his faith also cost him his first marriage."[84] Here Abdul-Rauf is constructed as a figure with staunch personal convictions and a history of choosing his "commitment" to Islam over privileges he might otherwise be afforded as a result of his fame. The article also reported that "the name Mahmoud Abdul-Rauf means 'Elegant and praise worthy, most merciful, most kind,'" noting that soon the name "Mujahid," meaning "striver for truth," would be added to Abdul-Rauf's first name.[85]

This concluding nod to "truth" echoes discourses found in black press coverage of Eartha Kitt, Tommie Smith, John Carlos, and Sister Souljah, all of whose dissent was framed within the black press as representative of some basic truth within black experience.

Together, these articles construct Abdul-Rauf's relationship with Islam as sincere, and his interpretation of its tenets legitimate. Notably, Islam is presented as a generally positive force that leads Abdul-Rauf to be more faithful, humble, and self-sacrificing than the average person or average player in "the glitzy world of pro-basketball." Thus, while mainstream constructions of Islam tended to separate supposedly dissention-free "mainstream Islam" from Abdul-Rauf's version, which was constructed as illegitimate, insincere, and incompatible with American democracy, black newsmakers constructed Abdul-Rauf as a model (Islamic) citizen.

The Racial Contradictions of Patriotism and Rights

This frame, making up just over thirty percent of black press coverage, was found in the opinion columns of both the *New York Amsterdam News* and *Los Angeles Sentinel,* and focused on how race and other socially constructed identities influenced both historic and contemporary understandings and applications of the freedoms guaranteed by the First Amendment.

In a scathing column titled "When Black Men Try to Leave the Plantation," David Andrew Love deemed the mainstream characterization of Abdul-Rauf as "unpatriotic when his religious convictions precluded him from standing during the playing of the national anthem," as one example of a larger trend in the way "this country always has sought to control the thoughts and movements of Black folks." Love explicitly linked this treatment of Abdul-Rauf to "the tenets of white supremacy."[86]

Several things are immediately evident in this characterization of Abdul-Rauf's dissent. First, Abdul-Rauf's "religious convictions" are treated as legitimate and his not standing for the anthem as a logical consequence of them. Further, unlike mainstream journalists who avoided addressing issues of race in their coverage and who provided no structural critique of any type of inequality, Love makes these things his explicit goal.

Focusing on what he calls the "contradictions in a land that preaches freedom of speech yet changes the rules when Black folks try to exercise that right," Love cites examples of blacks being denied the rights of "self-ownership" from slavery through the present. These examples included a discussion of the efforts made to silence figures like Marcus Garvey, Paul Robeson, Malcolm X, and Martin Luther King, along with Louis Farrakhan and Robert Johnson ("the first Black D.A. in New York State history").[87] Ultimately, Love suggests that the "attacks" on all these figures represent a race-based "hypocrisy" in the application of American laws and rights.

In specific regard to the "negative attention in the mainstream media" about Abdul-Rauf, Love wrote:

> The situation of Mahmoud Abdul-Rauf exemplifies the racist image of the ungrateful, unpatriotic Negro. In this country, people of color are good enough to strut their stuff on the basketball court, but are not allowed to use their mind and formulate an opinion. . . . While whites cite the countless people that died for this country, others take note of those who died in this country. Besides, how can any young African-American man in 1996 (especially one aware of the current assault on his people) engage in some empty, false sense of patriotism? We built this country, and others should not dictate how we interpret our own reality.[88]

In a similarly framed column in the *Los Angeles Sentinel* titled "Autopsy Not Pretty," Al Brown suggests that Abdul-Rauf's stance regarding the anthem has "placed America on an autopsy table" and "brought the term 'patriotism' before the nation for evaluation."[89] Brown goes on to point out that Abdul-Rauf's position "is well within his constitutional right—the one that talks about the freedom of religion" and "is similar to another common kind of freedom of expression called 'flag-burning,' which has stood up to many legal challenges."[90] Like Love, Brown points out that the player "has withstood some vile media abuse," including "one writer suggesting he take his ball and move to a more perfect country. I wonder if that same writer will tell the Klansman in South Carolina, who recently opened a KKK novelty shop, to pack up his crosses and robes and take them to a more perfect country?"[91] By comparing the treatment of Abdul-Rauf to that of flag burners and Klansmen—whose freedoms of expression are upheld and whose actions he constructs as much more un-American than those of Abdul-Rauf—Brown succinctly critiques the hypocrisy of mainstream discourses around the anthem controversy.

In an interpretation of Abdul-Rauf's dissent far more complex than those offered by mainstream journalists, Brown explained:

> [Abdul-Rauf] points out that to stand during the playing of the national anthem in a country that treats its majority population of poor people with disfavor in its economic, judicial, and educational arenas, is against his religious beliefs. . . . Abdul-Rauf choose to expose an ugly side of America—a side patriotic extremists don't want to discuss. The truth is that America is a nation far from getting over 400 years of discrimination and racial degradation. The truth is we are a nation intoxicated by arrogance and power. Not the power of freedom, which so many of us profess; but the power of control.[92]

By labeling Abdul-Rauf's position as reflective of "the truth," Brown again presents the contradictory nature of a nation that values "freedom" but seeks to "control" any who point out it failures. For Brown and Love the main takeaway from Mahmoud Abdul-Rauf's dissent and reactions to it is the unequal way basic American rights are applied to raced figures. Further, by locating the persecution of Abdul-Rauf amid historical and contemporary trends in silencing marginalized voices, these authors reflect what Houston Baker calls the "critical memory" of the black public sphere and name mainstream media makers among those most guilty of oppressive behavior.[93]

CONCLUSIONS

The majority of mainstream news coverage in this case presented an image of America in which the existence of millionaire black athletes and oppression were mutually exclusive, and Islam (or at least the visible kind that influences how its worshippers understand and interact with the world) could only exist at the fringe. Thus, the moment when Mahmoud Abdul-Rauf's dissent was outed can be understood as one in which the contradictions of race and religion in a society that is dominated by white, Christian, capitalistic values erupted. Notably, some mainstream responses to Abdul-Rauf evidenced an early (and now seemingly mild) version of the Islamophobic rhetoric that has become rampant in America since September 11, 2001.

For the first time in this volume, two of the primary frames used by the mainstream and black press had a similar focus—guaranteed freedoms. However, the discourses used across the two presses resulted in different understandings of their application. In the mainstream press, the guarantee of individual freedoms for all was treated as existent even as some newsmakers struggled to reconcile this with their silencing of Abdul-Rauf. In the black press, individual freedoms were also idealized, but there was an explicit discussion of how American culture continued to fail to fulfill these ideals—particularly for racial and religious minorities—despite rhetorical guarantees.

A visible handful of mainstream press columnists challenged the dominant versions of patriotism and nation that their colleagues embraced and pointed out the hypocrisy of valuing the freedoms on which the nation was founded while persecuting Abdul-Rauf. While the presence of these voices is meaningful, only one—less than one percent—attempted to address the "oppression" and "tyranny" Abdul-Rauf spoke of in any depth. Further a small number of sympathetic voices in the mainstream press is not unique, a handful of mainstream journalists offered Eartha Kitt and Tommie Smith and John Carlos some sympathy, yet were also overwhelmed by their colleagues' denigrations of dissent.

Thus, like Paul Robeson some fifty years earlier, Abdul-Rauf's critiques of dominant understandings of nation were met with severe sanctioning in the majority of mainstream discourse. Certainly, the sanctioning of Robeson that led to the literal revocation of his citizenship rights was more severe and based in more explicitly anti-black narratives. Yet it is clear from mainstream responses to both Abdul-Rauf and Sister Souljah that the late-twentieth-century discursive sanctioning of black dissidents, embedded in new discourses that claim to embrace equality while denigrating alternative ways of knowing, have real impact on livelihoods and access to symbolically constructed rights and spaces.

If the question is how much things changed in twentieth-century press coverage of African American celebrity dissent, my work here suggests that the more significant changes can be seen in the black press. In 1992, the black press felt free to openly and vigorously defend Sister Souljah against a high-profile white politician despite the clearly intense and unapologetic nature of her words. Likewise, in 1996 members of the black press felt free to offer a scathing critique of white supremacy while coming to the defense of an African American whose religious views did not match those of most members of their community. Such coverage is clearly less limited than the careful and often implicit ways in which black newsmakers discussed the hypocrisies that existed in dominant responses to the politics of Paul Robeson, and the way black newsmakers were compelled, in 1949, to offer denunciations of Communism as unrepresentative of the ideologies of the African American community. Greater journalistic freedom from censorship and sanctioning is clear within the black press of the late twentieth century.

However, questions regarding the role of various journalistic sources in constructing meaning for citizens of the nation remain tangled. As the traditional black press has progressively experienced more editorial freedom, it has also seen a sharp decline in readership and resources. While mainstream newsmakers continue to fail to offer their readers sustained interrogation of sociocultural dissent based on black perspectives, more Americans of every background depended on them for information. If the presence of some alternative perspectives in the mainstream press is evidence of social progress, we must ask ourselves how much. Why do these perspectives remain so few that their frequency nearly mirrors that which occurred during 1968? We must also consider how strategic rhetorics of racial hegemony have or have not been embraced by mainstream newsmakers, and if and how black celebrities can successfully levy challenges to them.

In the next chapter I turn to the twenty-first century with a keen eye to these questions.

NOTES

1. Mahmoud Abdul-Rauf, quoted in Robert Sanchez, "The Conversion of Chris Jackson," *5280 Magazine,* www.5280.com/magazine/2007/10/conversion-chris-jackson (accessed March 7, 2014): Oct. 2007.
2. Jason Diamos, "Abdul-Rauf Vows Not to Back Down from the N.B.A.," *The New York Times,* Mar. 14, 1996.
3. CBS Morning News, "Sports Report," Mar. 13, 1996; and Jim Hodges, "N.B.A. Sits Abdul-Rauf for Stance on Anthem," *Los Angeles Times,* Mar. 13, 1996.
4. Associated Press, "Pro Basketball; NBA Suspends Rauf," *The New York Times,* Mar. 13, 1996: B15.
5. Ibid.
6. "Abdul-Rauf Tells Why He'll Stand," *USA Today,* www.lexisnexis.com/hot topics/lnacademic (accessed Nov. 26, 2013).
7. Jackie MacMullan, "The NBA," *Sports Illustrated,* Jan. 22, 1996, http://vault.sportsillustrated.cnn.com/vault/article/magazine/MAG1007681/2/index.htm (accessed Dec. 2, 2008).
8. Sanchez, "Conversion of Chris Jackson."
9. The data in this analysis was published between March 12, 1996—the day Abdul-Rauf's suspension was announced—and May 12, 1996. Sources searched include *The New York Times, Los Angeles Times, Denver Post, Time,* and *Newsweek* in the mainstream press and the *New York Amsterdam News, Los Angeles Sentinel,* Denver-based magazine *Urban Spectrum, Jet,* and *Ebony* in the African American press. Special thanks to Terry Nelson at the Blair-Caldwell African American Research Library in Denver, Colorado, for helping me locate back issues of the *Urban Spectrum.*
10. Larry Stewart, "Angels Add Some Spark to Prime Team," *Los Angeles Times,* Mar. 22, 1996: 1.
11. Virginia Culver, "Faiths Unite in Outrage over Mosque Defilement," *Denver Post,* Mar. 22, 1996: A1.
12. "Disc Jockeys will apologize for mosque incident," *The New York Times,* Mar. 30, 1996: A1, 21.

13. Jack Shaheen, *Reel Bad Arabs: How Hollywood Vilifies a People* (New York: Olive Branch Press, 2001); Melani McCallister, *Epic Encounters: Culture, Media, & U.S. Interests in the Middle East* (Berkeley: University of California Press, 2002).
14. S. Craig Watkins, "Framing Protest: News Media Frames of the Million Man March," *Critical Studies in Media Communication* 18, no. 1 (2001): 83–101.
15. Jim Hodges and Larry B. Stammer, "NBA and Abdul-Rauf Are Standing Firm; Pro Basketball: Area Islamic Leaders Disagree with Nuggets' Guard for Decision on Anthem," *Los Angeles Times*, Mar. 14, 1996: 1.
16. Amy Bass, *Not the Triumph but the Struggle: The 1968 Olympics and the Making of the Black Athlete* (Minneapolis: University of Minnesota Press, 2002).
17. Nadine Naber, "Ambiguous Insiders: An Investigation of Arab American Invisibility," *Ethnic & Racial Studies* 23, no. 1 (2000): 37–61; Mehdi Semati, "Islamophobia, Culture and Race in the Age of Empire," *Cultural Studies* 24, no. 2 (2010): 256–275.
18. Hodges and Stammer, "NBA and Abdul-Rauf Are Standing Firm"; "Desecration of Mosque Defiles All Faiths," *Denver Post*, Mar. 22, 1996: B6.
19. See, for example, "A Puzzled Olajuwon Speaks Out on Citizenship," *The New York Times (1923–Current File)*, Mar. 14, 1996: B19.
20. Mahmood Mamdani, *Good Muslim, Bad Muslim, the Cold War, and the Roots of Terror* (New York: Pantheon Books, 2004).
21. Evelyn Alsultany, "Selling American Diversity and Muslim American Identity through Nonprofit Advertising Post-9/11," *American Quarterly* 59, no. 3 (2007): 593–622. While Mamdani and Alsultany locate the popularity of such discourse as having primarily taken root post–September 11th, these findings reveal that discourse requiring the explicit stating of allegiance to the nation by American Muslims in order to be (relatively) free from social sanction was well in place before that tragic event.
22. Eduardo Bonilla-Silva, *Racism without Racists: Colorblind Racism and the Persistence of Racial Inequality in the United States* (USA: Roman & Littlefield Publishers, Inc., 2003); "The Riot That Interests Governor Dewey," *Chicago Daily Tribune (1923–1963)*, Sep. 3, 1949.
23. Donald Spivey, *Sport in America: New Historical Perspectives* (Westport, CT: Greenwood Press, 1985); Alina Bernstein and Neil Blain, eds., *Sport, Media, Culture: Global and Local Dimensions* (New York: Routledge, 2003).
24. Jason Diamos, "Basketball; Abdul-Rauf's Plan: Stand, Pray and Play," *The New York Times*, www.lexisnexis.com/hottopics/lnacademic (accessed Nov. 26, 2013); Hodges and Stammers, "NBA and Abdul-Rauf Are Standing Firm."
25. John Young, "Who Stands for the Right to Sit?" *Denver Post*, Mar. 17, 1996.
26. Mark Kiszla, "Final Verse Near on Nugget," *Denver Post*, Mar. 26, 1996.
27. Terry Frei, "Mahmoud Abdul-Rauf's Short-Lived Stand against Standing for the Anthem Cause for a . . . Flashback," *Denver Post*, Mar. 24, 1996.
28. Terry Frei, "Mahmoud Abdul-Rauf's Short-Lived Stand."
29. Houston A. Baker Jr., "Critical Memory and the Black Public Sphere," *Public Culture* 7, no. 3 (1994): 3–33.
30. Thomas K. Nakayama and Robert L. Krizek, "Whiteness: A Strategic Rhetoric," *Quarterly Journal of Speech* 81, no. 3 (1995): 291–309.
31. Robert Lipsyte, "Athletes Standing Up as They Did Before," *The New York Times*, Mar. 17, 1996.
32. For example, see Harvey Araton, "Sports of the Times; An Issue of Religion and Respect," *The New York Times*, accessed Nov. 26, 2013, www.lexisnexis.com/hottopics/lnacademic (accessed Nov. 26, 2013); and Chris Foster, "Pros Can't Escape the Glare" *Los Angeles Times*, Mar. 19, 1996.

33. For example, see Hodges, "N.B.A Sits Abdul-Rauf"; and "A Puzzled Olajuwon Speaks Out on Citizenship," *The New York Times*.
34. Woody Paige, "Rauf Takes a Lame Exit," *Denver Post*, Mar. 29, 1996.
35. For example, see "Editorials: Abdul-Rauf's Selective Objection Doesn't Meet Religious Tests," *Denver Post*, Mar. 14, 1996; Hodges, "N.B.A. sits Abdul-Rauf."
36. "A Puzzled Olajuwan Speaks Out on Citizenship," *The New York Times*; Peter Steinfels, "March 10–16: Anthems, Islam and Basketball," *The New York Times*, Mar. 17, 1996.
37. Alan Snel, "Students Speak Out on Issue," *Denver Post*, Mar. 14, 1996: A10.
38. Woody Paige, "Abdul-Rauf Has a Right Not to Stand," *Denver Post*, Mar. 13, 1996.
39. Mark Kiszla, "Abdul-Rauf: Nuggets' Rebel without a Clue," *Denver Post*, Mar. 14, 1996.
40. Frank Deford, "Of Stars and Stripes," *Newsweek*, Mar. 25, 1996: 64; Allan Malamud, "Notes on a Scorecard," *Los Angeles Times*, Mar. 14, 1996.
41. Mike Rosen, "Dissing the Flag," *Denver Post*, Mar. 22, 1996.
42. K. Connie Kang, "A Rotating Panel of Experts from the Worlds of Philosophy, Psychology and Religion Offer Their Perspective on the Dilemmas That Come with Living in Southern California," *Los Angeles Times*, Mar. 20, 1996.
43. Paul Kneipp, "Oh, Say Can You See the Argument Here?" *Los Angeles Times*, Mar. 16, 1996.
44. "Letters to the Post," *Denver Post*, Mar. 31, 1996.
45. Bass, *Not the Triumph*.
46. Kiszla, "Abdul-Rauf: Nuggets Rebel without a Clue"; Kiszla, "Final Verse Near on Nugget."
47. Woody Paige, "Seven-Point Plan for Resurrection," *Denver Post*, Apr. 22, 1996; Mark Kiszla, "They Don't Listen to Bickerstaff," *Denver Post*, Apr. 6, 1996: C1; Post Office, "Nuggets Need New Coach Not a Purge of Their Roster," *Denver Post*, May 6, 1996: C3; Paige, "Rauf Takes a Lame Exit"; Kiszla, "Final Verse Near on Nugget."
48. "Nuggets Not in the Mahmoud: Abdul-Rauf Can Lead Team in a Silent Prayer," Pike's Peek, *Denver Post*, Mar. 17, 1996; Paige, "Rauf Takes a Lame Exit."
49. Ronald Jackson II, *Scripting the Black Masculine Body: Identity, Discourse, and Racial Politics in Popular Media* (Albany: The State University of New York Press, 2006).
50. John Hoberman, *Darwin's Athletes: How Sport Has Damaged Black America and Preserved the Myth of Race* (New York: Houghton Mifflin Company, 1997).
51. Michael Booth, "Is Loyalty Dead?" *Denver Post*, Mar. 17, 1996.
52. "Nuggets Not in the Mahmoud," *Denver Post*.
53. Gil Spencer, "United We Stand, Sometimes," *Denver Post*, Mar. 24, 1996.
54. Bill George, "Oh, Say Can You See the Argument Here?" *Los Angeles Times*, Mar. 16, 1996.
55. Frei, "Mahmoud Abdul-Rauf's Short-Lived Stand."
56. Woody Paige, "Cash Gets Nugget on His Feet." *Denver Post*, March 16, 1996: A1; Kevin Simpson, "Oh, Say, Can You See . . . The Decline of Manners?" *Denver Post*, Mar. 14, 1996: B1. Jason Diamos of *The New York Times* was the only mainstream journalist to report that "the decision to go back to work had nothing to do with money" but "was based on a better understanding of the situation" (Jason Diamos, "Abdul-Rauf Is Calm in Face of Controversy," *The New York Times*, Mar. 21, 1996: B9).
57. Paige, "Abdul-Rauf Has a Right."

58. Young, "Who Stands for the Right to Sit?"; Simpson, "Oh, Say, Can You See . . . The Decline of Manners?" *Denver Post,* Mar. 14, 1996.
59. Ibid.
60. Kang, "A Rotating Panel of Experts."
61. Paul Wasserman, "Oh, Say Can You See the Argument Here?" *Los Angeles Times.*
62. Kiszla, "Abdul-Rauf: Nuggets' Rebel without a Clue."
63. Kenji Yoshino, *Covering: The Hidden Assault on Our Civil Rights* (New York: Random House, 2006).
64. "The Issue Is Respect; Lest We Forget," *The New York Times,* Mar. 24, 1996, www.lexisnexis.com/hottopics/lnacademic (accessed Nov. 26, 2013); "The Issue Is Respect; Respect, Part 2," *The New York Times,* Mar. 24, 1996, www.lexisnexis.com/hottopics/lnacademic (accessed Nov. 26, 2013); "The Issue Is Respect; Respect, Part 3," *The New York Times,* Mar. 24, 1996, www.lexisnexis.com/hottopics/lnacademic (accessed Nov. 26, 2013).
65. "The Issue Is Respect; And Elsewhere?" *The New York Times,* Mar. 24, 1996, www.lexisnexis.com/hottopics/lnacademic (accessed Nov. 26, 2013).
66. Ibid.
67. Jason Diamos, "Abdul-Rauf Vows Not to Back Down from the NBA." *New York Times,* March 14, 1996: B14. However, separating religion from politics is an impossible enterprise, see Robert J. Higgs and Michael C. Braswell, *An Unholy Alliance: The Sacred and Modern Sports* (Macon, GA: Mercer University Press, 2004); John Hargreaves, "Globalisation Theory, Global Sport, and Nations and Nationalism," in *Power Games: A Critical Sociology of Sport,* ed. John Sugden and Alan Tomlinson (New York, NY: Routledge, 2002): 25–43; and Robert Higgs, *God in the Stadium: Sports and Religion in America* (Lexington, KY: The University Press of Kentucky, 1995).
68. "Star-Spangled Coercion," *The New York Times,* Mar. 15, 1996, www.lexisnexis.com/hottopics/lnacademic (accessed Nov. 26, 2013); Hodges, "N.B.A. Sits Abdul-Rauf."
69. Mark Heisler, "Top Pro Prospects Run Hot, Cool," *Los Angeles Times,* Mar. 17, 1996.
70. Fred Okrand, "NBA Rules and the National Anthem," *Los Angeles Times,* Mar. 24, 1996.
71. See, for example, Ronald O. Richards, "Oh, Say Can You See the Argument Here?" *Los Angeles Times,* Mar. 16, 1996; " 'The Land of the Free?' " *Newsweek,* www.lexisnexis.com/hottopics/lnacademic (accessed Nov. 25, 2013).
72. Harvey Araton, "An Issue of Religion and Respect," *The New York Times,* Mar. 14, 1996: B13.
73. Robert Lipsyte, "Athletes Standing Up as They Did Before."
74. Peter Steinfels, "Anthems, Islam and Basketball."
75. "The Issue Is Respect; Why Not Sit?" *The New York Times,* Mar. 24, 1996, www.lexisnexis.com/hottopics/lnacademic (accessed Nov. 26, 2013).
76. "Star-Spangled Coercion," *The New York Times.*
77. Andrew Tonkovich. "Oh, Say Can You See the Ironies Here?" *Los Angeles Times,* Mar. 24, 1996: 7.
78. Montoya Clemmons, "Denver Nugget Finds Solace in Islam," *Denver Urban Spectrum,* Mar. 1996.
79. Montoya Clemmons, "Religious Diversity Unifies Team," *Denver Urban Spectrum,* Mar. 1996.
80. "Islamic Leaders: Standing for Anthem a Matter of Conscience," *Los Angeles Sentinel,* Mar. 21, 1996: B2.
81. Ibid.

82. "Mahmoud Abdul-Rauf: A Very Private Person in the Spotlight," *Los Angeles Sentinel,* Mar. 21, 1996: B2.
83. Ibid.
84. Ibid.
85. Ibid.
86. David Andrew Love, "When Black Men Try to Leave the Plantation," *New York Amsterdam News,* May 11, 1996: 13.
87. Ibid.
88. Ibid.
89. Al Brown, "Autopsy Not Pretty," *Los Angeles Sentinel,* Apr. 4, 1996: A6.
90. Ibid.
91. Ibid.
92. Ibid.
93. Baker, "Critical Memory and the Black Public Sphere."

6 Kanye West and Hurricane Katrina, 2005

Middle America packed in
Came to see me in my black skin[1]

Five years after Hurricane Katrina devastated the Gulf Coast of the United States, the media, and the President tasked with responding to the disaster, were still talking about the brief off-script moment of a rising hip hop star. On November 8, 2010, former President George W. Bush told NBC's Matt Lauer that being "called a racist" by Kanye West in the aftermath of Hurricane Katrina was the worst moment of his presidency. Lauer corrected the president—noting that West never used the term "racist"—and accurately predicted that Bush would receive criticism for describing the moment as the "all time low" of his presidency in his book *Decision Points*. "You're not saying that the worst moment in your presidency was watching the misery in Louisiana. You're saying it was when someone insulted you because of that," Lauer noted. Bush stood by the account in his book, saying that West's words had made him feel "disgust."[2]

That a President had such a strong reaction to an African American celebrity's critique of structural inequality reveals much about the rules that dictate how race can be talked about, and by whom, in twenty-first-century America. After all, Kanye West was certainly not the first, or the last, high-profile American to criticize the U.S. government's response to Katrina or to suggest its sluggishness and lack of preparedness was related to the race and class of the residents of New Orleans. Yet West's indignation—located at a specific moment in the rise of his cultural capital, balking normative telethon behavior and neoliberal colorblind scripts of black celebrity—is what the former President, and much of the nation, most remembers.

In the fall of 2005, Kanye West was experiencing an unprecedented rise in popularity that would foreshadow his establishment as one of the most famous (and sometimes infamous) rappers of the twenty-first century. His sophomore album, *Late Registration*, debuted at number one on the Billboard charts, selling a stunning 860,000 copies in just one week.

West's first single from the album, "Gold Digger," was the number one Billboard single for over two months. Both Pepsi and the NFL had hired West for ongoing public campaigns. Among a wave of media coverage of West, *Time* magazine featured a cover story on the rapper/producer on August 29, 2005—the same day Hurricane Katrina made landfall in New Orleans—with the headline "Hip-Hop's Class Act: Defying the Rules of Rap, Kanye West Goes His Own Way. Why He's the Smartest Man in Pop Music."

Given this meteoric rise, it was no surprise NBC chose West as one of a handful of celebrities to play a lead role in their "Concert for Hurricane Relief" to benefit Red Cross efforts to aid victims of Katrina. During the telethon, which aired live on the East Coast and Midwest, Kanye West went off-script to provide personal commentary on what he saw as racial disparity in media coverage of hurricane victims (Figure 6.1). West began, "I hate the way they portray us in the media. If you see a black family it says they're looting. If you see a white family, it says they're looking for food." Actor Mike Meyers, West's co-presenter, was clearly surprised and attempted to return to the script, but West ignored him. He continued by criticizing himself for not donating to the relief efforts sooner, and then offered an

Figure 6.1 Kanye West and Mike Meyers appear on NBC's "A Concert for Hurricane Relief," September 2, 2005. (Screenshot)

institutional-level critique of American racial and economic inequality, the ongoing Iraq war, and racialized state violence:

> You know it's been five days because most of the people are black . . . America is set up to help the poor, the black people, the less well-off as slow as possible. . . . We already realize a lot of the people that could help are at war right now. . . . And now they've given them permission to go down there and shoot us.[3]

Despite the complexity and length of these comments, the portion most replayed by the mainstream media—and thus remembered by the public—was West's closing sentence: "George Bush doesn't care about black people." While an overwhelming majority of mainstream coverage of West's dissent—seventy-five percent—directly quoted or paraphrased the line, few reporters included any other portion of his remarks.[4] Not a single mainstream press source I examine here quoted or discussed the portion of West's comments in which he pointed out that members of the National Guard who might have otherwise been helping the citizens of New Orleans were instead in Iraq, or the portion of his statement in which he drew attention to the very real violence that was occurring at the hands of authorities against Katrina survivors.[5]

In this chapter I examine what newsmakers did talk about when they covered West's dissent to gauge how understandings of one of the most striking examples of twenty-first-century black celebrity dissent are both unique from and similar to that of the twentieth century.[6] Given the contemporary celebration of "diversity" in the mainstream press and all-time-low readership of the black press, reporting of West's dissent reflects a complex, and at times conflicting, moment of framing in which the realities of contemporary inequality came head to head with pre-established neoliberal scripts of black celebrity and national crisis. Here I consider the larger context of coverage and conversations about Hurricane Katrina in the public sphere with an eye to how race and inequality have or have not been addressed. Then, I discuss the ways Kanye West's rise in hip hop reflects particular trends in discourses of multiculturalism, colorblindness, and interracial consumption of rap music that attempted to set him apart from other black MCs. Finally, I delineate the frames reporters deployed to explain West's Katrina dissent to mainstream audiences and those who continue to engage the black public sphere.

COVERING KATRINA

Cedric Johnson and his contributors have extensively detailed the ways the social and economic conditions at the crux of twenty-first-century neoliberalism contributed to the benign neglect visited upon the most vulnerable residents of New Orleans before, during, and after Katrina.[7] At the writing of this volume, countless other academics, public intellectuals, journalists, and cultural critics have addressed the failures that existed in both the response to Hurricane Katrina and media coverage of the disaster.[8] The overwhelming consensus among these critics is that, without doubt, American citizens, mostly black and poor, many elderly, were dehumanized, displaced, and in many cases died as a result of both local and federal failures in preparedness and response.

Examinations of media coverage of the man-made disaster that followed the natural disaster of Katrina recognize that some mainstream journalists, particularly those on the ground in New Orleans experiencing the devastation and human suffering firsthand, broke with traditional dehumanizing frames of the black poor and made visible the victimhood of Katrina's survivors.[9] Unfortunately, this type of sympathetic coverage was less frequent and less lasting than media narratives that reproduced and perpetuated racialized narratives of black incivility and criminality.[10] In particular, the media's focus on "looting" and acts of violence in New Orleans in the wake of Katrina has been roundly criticized both because reports of these activities were later discovered to be wildly exaggerated and because this focus framed the post-Katrina story as one of law and order rather than one of human need, suffering, and resolve.[11] Kanye West, then, justifiably hated "how they portray us in the media."

The perpetuation of racist stereotypes was not the only consequence of the media's willingness to spread rumors of black incivility in Katrina's wake; these narratives also influenced how lawmakers responded (or failed to respond) to hurricane victims.[12] When West stated, "And now they've given them permission to go down there and shoot us," he was referring to Governor Kathleen Blanco's September 1, 2005, "shoot to kill" order, which Linda Robertson has described as "the State of Louisiana declar[ing] war on the survivors in New Orleans."[13] Notably, after focusing heavily on sensationalized reports of violence in New Orleans, some members of the media reported on these "shoot to kill" orders directed at desperate American citizens as "good news."[14]

Today the continuing conversation about the failures surrounding Katrina in the public sphere tend to singularly highlight the Bush administration's slow response in a way that limits critique to a specific administration at a specific moment, thereby displacing the ongoing legacy of racial and economic neglect in New Orleans. While it is certainly fair to critique the individual failures of figures like FEMA's Michael Brown, these mainstream critiques have yet to interrogate the entrenched structural inequalities that such failures laid bare.[15] Further, media reports on solutions to the post-Katrina disaster tend to celebrate recovery efforts that align with neoliberal narratives of individualism and entrepreneurship, like the charity of private organizations and the bootstrapping of individual figures, rather than acknowledging or even considering the necessity of legislative and/or mass social change for Katrina "recovery."[16] And of course, in certain segments of the media, particularly those dominated by unabashedly conservative voices, the racialized mythologies that blame the victims of Hurricane Katrina for their own misfortune continue to be spread as if they are indisputable.[17]

Together, sociological examinations of Katrina's aftermath have demonstrated that, as shirts printed by Color of Change, a grassroots online political organization that sprung up in response to the political disempowerment of African Americans post-Katrina, read, "Kanye was right."[18] The media perpetuated stereotypes, local government officials okayed violence against survivors, the Iraq War depleted possible resources, and the federal government, headed by George W. Bush, failed to respond in a timely manner.

HIP HOP CELEBRITY IN THE TWENTY-FIRST CENTURY

To understand the hows and whys of news framing of West's dissent it is valuable to consider the ways the subaltern and radical potentials of hip hop as a cultural phenomenon intersect with the commodification of black cultural expression and the entrenchment of neoliberal narratives of colorblindness in the twenty-first century. As well documented by scholars and critics, in the thirteen years between the 1992 Los Angeles uprising and the human disaster that would follow Hurricane Katrina—both moments that made visible the economic and racial Others that contemporary American politics had otherwise rendered invisible—the culture wars that once attempted to exorcise rap music from the public sphere had been replaced by the consumption of urban black "cool."[19]

As mainstream culture repackaged the art forms of disenfranchised people of color for consumption through entertainment and style choices, twenty-first-century hip hop became embedded, as Imani Perry notes, "with both the possibilities of the history of black American resistance and struggle and the vacuousness, conspicuous consumption, and negative '-isms' of American culture."[20] Accordingly, the visible successes of black rappers and the proliferation of white hip hop fandom have helped to both break down boundaries in popular culture and perpetuate neoliberal mythologies of a colorblind America in which society is no longer limited by institutional inequalities or individual prejudices.[21]

The rise of Kanye West's celebrity was in many ways a microcosm of these conflicting potentials. West easily fulfilled neoliberal narratives because he appeared to embrace middle-class white values through his pink-polo-shirt-wearing aesthetic and suburban, educated, middle-class background. Further, West's lyrics reflected a multiculturalism that included both references to easily identifiable scripts of black urban life and signifiers of "high" culture like European travel and philosophy. As *Time* magazine reminded us, by "defying the rules of rap" (rules that were classed and raced through presumptions that rappers only reflect an inner-city aesthetic) Kanye was a "class act."[22] His perceived location outside of a poor black aesthetic considered "class"-less allowed West to be tokenized as a success story; it made him "the smartest man in pop music."[23] West's occasional rebellious public behavior was treated much like that of the young rising star Cassius Clay many generations before—the symptom of youthful indiscretion and ego but a reflection of legitimate talent and not a threat. (This would change in September of 2009 when West interrupted Taylor Swift, whose celebrity had been carefully constructed to embody virginal white womanhood, during an acceptance speech at the MTV Video Music Awards.)

Notably, West's *Late Registration,* like his first album *The College Dropout,* contained plenty of sociopolitical critique, however this anti-establishment expression was treated as a style choice, or when too inconvenient, altogether ignored by the mainstream media. In fact, when NBC edited Kanye West's Hurricane Katrina dissent from their West Coast re-air of the "Concert for Hurricane Relief," it was not the first time the very corporate institutions that sought to profit from West's particular brand of cool had silenced a critique from the star. Throughout 2005, as mainstream pop music stations played West's "We All Fall Down," they edited "white man" from the (clearly critical of racialized economic exploitation) lyric, "Drug dealers buy Jordans, crackheads buy crack/And the white man get paid off of all of that."[24]

As this example demonstrates, West and his fellow hip hop artists were introducing counternarratives into mainstream spaces even as the neoliberal nature of consuming raced experience attempted to render these narratives moot. In spite of—and in many ways because of—the ways contemporary culture commodifies hip hop artists, they have become the most visible voices for alternative readings of America's most sacred institutions. Even as corporate control and cultural appropriation limit the diversity of hip hop artists and narratives on pop radio, it continues to introduce generations of young people to the idea that challenging the establishment can not only be cool but can allow them access to experiences and spaces in which to explore issues of identity and power.[25]

As Jeff Chang details, despite frequent complaints that the "hip hop generation" has become obsessed with consumption and themselves, this generation is more politically engaged by the numbers than any before, including the civil rights generation. Chang reminds us that activism rooted in hip hop communities and protest using hip hop–inspired expressive forms were widespread in the years leading up to Kanye West's dissent.[26] Challenges to the status quo are made available both through such activism and through hip hop communities that many of the artists who find success in the mainstream maintain allegiance to.[27] Thus, despite West's mainstreaming, it should be no surprise that a hip hop artist—who is also the son of a former Black Panther/black press photojournalist and an English professor educated in and around historically black colleges and universities—would introduce the alternative discourse of these communities into the mainstream public sphere.

GOING OFF-SCRIPT: KANYE WEST AND THE MAINSTREAM PRESS

The mainstream press included forty-two stories on Kanye West's dissenting comments regarding Hurricane Katrina. Despite the frequency with which the mainstream press reported on the infamous quote about George Bush's "care" for black people, coverage of West's dissent was framed as an interpersonal conflict with the president in less than ten percent of stories—a distinction that perhaps only Eartha Kitt could fully appreciate. Rather, coverage fell into two primary frames: (1) a focus on constructing West's dissent only in relation to his growing value as an entertainment commodity, and (2) the idea that conversations about inequality should not coexist with fundraising, especially celebrity fundraising. Both of these frames minimized the content of West's critique, turning his dissent into a question of celebrity behavior that mattered only to prop up or diminish his status or as a distraction from supposedly more valid, apolitical charity efforts. While these frames limited conversations about inequality in the mainstream press, it is notable that the first is the least negative—though no less evasive—of those discovered in this project. Further, West's dissent received less coverage from mainstream newsmakers than that of any other figure examined in this volume. Both these findings reveal a shift in how the discursive agency of black celebrities is limited in twenty-first-century mainstream media discourse.

A long-form essay in *Newsweek* by Jonathan Alter, titled "The Other America," was the only source in the mainstream press to mention West's dissent as part of an in-depth discussion on class and race inequality in the aftermath of Hurricane Katrina. This single mainstream article acknowledged histories of race and class disenfranchisement and the continuing existence of what Alter described as "the old evasions, hypocrisies, and not-so-benign neglect" in American society.[28]

In comparison, a quarter of mainstream stories about West's dissent explicitly described it as volatile, aggressive, and inappropriate, with many of the very same terms used to describe the dissent of West's antecedents. Mainstream journalists also frequently avoided making explicit value judgments of West's dissent by simply ignoring its content all together in favor of reporting on his music and fame. The occasional mainstream journalist even explicitly sympathized with West's "frustration" and framed his intentions as sincere while simultaneously insisting on his dissent as inappropriate. Mainstream newsmakers then appeared to be navigating raced historical narratives that demonize black celebrity challenges to the status quo, contemporary neoliberal expectations for the (superficial) inclusion of black perspectives, and, at times the very real emotions that many Americans, black and white, felt in response to Katrina.

Are You Not Entertained?

Rather than interrogating the content of his words, mainstream coverage of West's dissent presented a unique frame not seen in the other cases examined in this project: a discussion of the entertainment value offered by West in spite of (and sometimes exactly because of) his dissent. This frame, appearing in forty-five percent of stories, located West's dissent in relation to his larger career trajectory, his involvement with other telethons for Katrina relief, the opinions of other celebrities about his comments, and the West-inspired protest song titled "George Bush Doesn't Care about Black People" by Houston rap group Legendary K.O.

The reliance on this "West as entertainment commodity" frame resulted in the majority of mainstream coverage of Kanye West's post-Katrina dissent appearing in infotainment stories in arts, entertainment, and culture sections of newspapers rather than sections on national news or politics.[29] For example, columnist Geoff Boucher of the *Los Angeles Times* focused on the impact, or lack thereof, of West's dissent on his career, asking, "How can Kanye West go on national television and passionately accuse Bush of not caring about blacks one week and still be riding high the next as a best-selling rapper and corporate pitchman?" Boucher spent the remainder of the lengthy column answering this question with explanations about how West's fans view him as an "independent-minded artist" and suggesting that West's "popularity" and cultural "credibility" made him irresistible to corporate interests and fans alike.[30] Not surprisingly in this context, Boucher spent no time interrogating questions of institutional racial or economic inequality in the wake of Katrina. Such coverage reflects the way celebrity culture in the twenty-first century—with a focus on the trajectory of fame in and of itself as news—and neoliberal narratives that render anti-establishment discourse in hip hop as existing largely for trendy consumption, influenced the meaning-making process of mainstream journalists covering the story.

When addressed by the mainstream press, West's work as a musician and producer was nearly always characterized positively. West was described as a "popular" "bestselling artist" with an "explosive career" and a "mix of bluster, earnest and creative reach," an "innovator" with "remarkable passion and charisma" and "immense range."[31] The *Los Angeles Times* ran two "Pop Music Reviews" of West's concert performances, one occurring a week after his dissenting statements and another a month later. In both, the authors, Steve Hochman and Robert Hilburn, offer complimentary descriptions of West's musical style and focus on reviewing the content of his concerts. The authors do mention "the controversy that followed" West's "criticism of President Bush." In both cases, West's dissent is framed as relevant only in relation to the content of his musical performances. Hilburn, after a long and highly complimentary review of West's concert, noted that West "paused after one number and expressed sympathy for the Katrina victims, but he didn't mention Bush again," and Hochman wrote that at an "MTV-sponsored concert" West "provided context for his earlier swipe at Bush."[32]

Similarly, *The New York Times* mentioned West's dissent in passing in their review of the 2005 Emmy Awards, noting that "there were few unscripted moments, and nothing came close to Kanye West's impromptu 'George Bush doesn't care about black people' outburst on NBC's recent hurricane relief telethon," then shifting to a discussion of the winners of the evening.[33] In announcing the Madison Square Garden Katrina fundraiser concert, "From the Big Apple to the Big Easy," the paper briefly noted: "The disaster and its aftermath gives musicians plenty to talk about, as Kanye West memorably demonstrated."[34]

The New York Times also ran entertainment articles about television appearances and concerts by rappers David Banner, Nelly, and Reverend Run that contained brief and largely agreeable comments from their subjects on West's dissent. In fact, the small number of explicitly approving characterizations of West's dissent in the mainstream press were generally the result of reports on other hip hop celebrities' opinions. *The New York Times* reported that Joseph Simmons (aka Reverend Run of Run-DMC) felt that "Kanye is a prophet. . . . There was lots of wisdom to what he said."[35] The *Los Angeles Times* reported that hip hop mogul Russell Simmons felt "that's what rappers are supposed to do—say what the masses are thinking."[36] The *Chicago Tribune* reported that R&B singer Usher felt that "if it wasn't for his comments, there would not be an open dialogue about the underserved people in the Gulf region."[37]

The reporting of mostly positive opinions from African American celebrities in response to West's dissent stands in sharp contrast to the way black public figures were pitted against one another in mainstream discourse in the other cases examined here. However, the mainstream press largely ignored reactions to West's dissent from African American politicians, community activists, academics, and citizens, revealing a tendency to only view celebrities as newsworthy representatives of the black community. This finding demonstrates the unique power and access to mainstream conversations that come with black celebrity while revealing how black political voices are limited in the mainstream more generally.

Every mainstream newspaper dedicated at least one entertainment article to the West-inspired rap song "George Bush Doesn't Care about Black People" by Houston rap group Legendary K.O. and the various YouTube video mash-ups it subsequently inspired. These stories focused on the technological and copyright angles of the story along with histories of sampling "in the rap world" rather than issues of political expression, protest music, race, or class.[38] What is interesting about these "tech" stories is that so much of the user-generated content inspired by West offered explicit critiques of American inequality, yet such critiques were sidelined in order to discuss copyright law, a topic not particularly relevant to Americans trying to make sense of the aftermath of Hurricane Katrina. Further, while coverage of the Legendary K.O. song allowed for the acknowledgement of the production of alternative narratives around West's dissent, no discussion of the unique ideological work done by African Americans through technology was offered.

Together, mainstream journalists' focus on entertainment news resulted in a frame that, while not explicitly negative in its representation of West's actions, ignored the complicated issues at their root. West's dissent was treated as tangential to the central going-ons of the entertainment world and rarely reported on in any detail—a new construction of black celebrity dissent that, while different from the strong condemnations of the past, continues to undermine its relevance. Rather than treating West's comments as dangerous, subversive, or even especially newsworthy, framing them as simply entertainment-worthy reflects a larger neoliberal context that celebrates black public figures while ignoring that the artistic contributions of such figures often arise from experiences based in continued racial, economic, and political disparity. By refusing to treat West's dissent as a political story, mainstream newsmakers displaced claims that might have otherwise required a sustained critique of the racial and economic status quo.

The Incompatibility of Charity and Politics

In addition to largely framing West's dissent as an entertainment story, the mainstream press constructed a frame that was strikingly similar to the "incompatibility of sport and politics" frame applied to the 1968 Olympic dissent of Tommie Smith and John Carlos. Within nearly thirty percent of mainstream stories, successful charity, in the benefit of the nation, was framed as being mutually exclusive to conversations about inequality. Here, the mainstream press framed West's comments as untimely, inappropriate, and a distraction to efforts to help the people of the Gulf Coast following Hurricane Katrina.

In the *Chicago Tribune* for example, the editors, while sympathizing with West's "frustration," argued, "that can wait for later ... the present, however, is the time for banding together, not for divisiveness."[39] Similarly, a letter to the editor published by the *Chicago Tribune* named West as one of "many people" who were "wasting too much time attacking the government" and who should "focus on the priority: rescuing people and helping the Gulf states return to some semblance of normalcy."[40] In addition to undermining West's concerns, such language individualizes responsibility for Hurricane Katrina victims rather than acknowledging the possibility of institutional solutions to their disenfranchisement.

Likewise, *Time* magazine published a letter to the editor that argued, "West is certainly entitled to his opinion, but there's a time and place for that . . . our first priority should be rescue and recovery," while another more forcefully argued, "Now is not the time to play the race card. Kanye, please sit down, shut up and get out your wallet."[41] Here the suggestion is clear, West cannot criticize the government *and* fulfill his obligation to help Katrina victims. Further, pointing out inequality is derailed as the "playing" of a "card" and something that should be "shut up" and replaced with spending. Such discourse reflects well-entrenched dominant expectations that black celebrities behave publically in a way comfortable to the majority regardless of what their own "first priority" is. West is expected to cater to dominant decorum by reading words written for him and avoiding challenges to the status quo just as Eartha Kitt was expected to "act" like a "lady" at the White House, and Smith, Carlos, and Abdul-Rauf were expected to perform patriotism and gratefulness at the Olympics and in the NBA.

Additionally, such framing presumes no legitimate space for institutional-level critique or blame in the effort to immediately aid Americans. This discourse is dependent on neoliberal rhetoric that labels attempts to acknowledge inequality "divisive" while suggesting that the market can solve complex social issues. Presenting charity as an apolitical and positive social force perpetuates what critics have labeled "disaster capitalism" and derails discussion of oppression and structural intervention into dominant social institutions.[42] As many have pointedly argued, such intervention is likely the only thing that could have solved the issues at play in New Orleans both before and after the landfall of Hurricane Katrina.

Along these lines, every mainstream news source except *Newsweek* printed suggestions that West's dissent could pose a "distraction" to fundraising efforts and/or deter potential donors. Columnist Ned Martel of *The New York Times* suggested that after his initial dissent, other broadcast network producers worried that West might "need to be muted lest he drop some polemic" noting that his "role was to perform, not pontificate."[43] The use of the loaded terms "polemic" and "pontificate" by the author suggest that the inclusion of political and social criticism by West into his public appearances was combative, condescending, and dogmatic—and thus censorship-worthy. Such discourse in 2005 reflects a mainstream impulse to silence and reprimand the political dissent of black celebrities that parallels that from over half a century before.

In a similar narrative, the *Chicago Tribune* and *The New York Times* ran articles about West's appearance at the National Football League's opening weekend events, noting that West "would stick to entertainment" by making his appearance "more about music than politics."[44] Here West's musical appearances, like his fundraising potential, are constructed as needing to be void of political critique to reach their full value. One *Tribune* column even snarked that West's appearance on the NFL's kickoff show proved that ABC "does indeed care about hip-hop artists in preppy clothing."[45]

In several articles on the censoring of West's comments from the West Coast broadcast of the NBC telethon, the *Los Angeles Times* reported that "producers feared his comments would distract from the aim of the program," and that "to politicize the concert" might "dissuade viewers from donating."[46] These articles quoted the executive producer of another telethon on which West appeared who contended that "people know that politicizing will certainly not be a smart thing to do as far as inspiring people to want to call in and rally around this cause."[47] The *Los Angeles Times* also reported that other telethons had "an emphasis on music rather than commentary" and kept "the focus on victims' needs rather than politics."[48] The obvious misnomer here being that "victims' needs" and "politics," particularly race and class politics, had nothing to do with each other when the experiences of Hurricane Katrina victims were the direct result of legacies of political neglect.

Besides the neoliberal assumption that charity was the best way to help Katrina survivors, that so many mainstream outlets assumed West's dissent would cost the people of the Gulf Coast aid certainly does not give the generally charitable American public much credit. At their core, such concerns about the audience for Katrina fundraisers assumed the public was largely made up of white supporters of President Bush who did not see inequality in the wake of Katrina as a relevant issue. Given that between September and November of 2005 between fifty and sixty percent of Americans disapproved of the job Bush was doing, more Americans identified themselves as Democrats or Independents than Republicans, and around thirty-five percent of Americans identified racially as non-white or as Latino, such assumptions certainly did not reflect the political or demographic realities of the nation's potential Red Cross donors.[49] At no point did any member of the mainstream press entertain the possibility that West's comments might actually inspire some members of the population to take action.

While it was frequently suggested that West's statements were a distraction from the goal of raising money for hurricane relief and "may have offended you," it was also reported that West was "obviously impassioned," and a handful of stories included follow-up quotes from West who insisted he had said "what I really feel" and "let my heart speak."[50] The *Los Angeles Times*, which contained the most positive characterizations of West, also sympathetically reported that he felt "heartache over the struggle of the flood victims" and credited his dissent to an "underdog impulse."[51] This coverage of West by mainstream journalists alongside negative constructions of his dissent likely reflects some sympathy with his response to Katrina despite an overarching dominant narrative that his dissent was inappropriately timed and placed.

Together the framing of West's dissent as a violation of charitable values and as purely based in entertainment reinforced systems of domination through silence and diversion.[52] In this case, rather than producing explicitly racialized denunciations like those that often regulated past celebrity dissent, mainstream narratives avoided discussion of race while making claims of larger progressive goals, facilitating implicit ideological disavowal of structural inequality.

WHEN POETS BECOME EMPOWERED: THE BLACK PRESS AND KANYE WEST

Black press coverage, which totaled ten stories, most commonly presented West's dissent within frames of (1) community debates about African American uplift and self-sufficiency, and (2) legacies of institutional inequality. Notably, both frames included an in-depth discussion of the *content* of West's dissent regarding raced and classed oppression in the wake of Katrina unavailable to readers of the mainstream press.

Defining Community Uplift and Self-Sufficiency

A frame that highlighted a debate about the best means to aid Katrina's victims and the larger African American community was constructed in sixty percent of black press stories. While this frame was articulated in different ways among the various papers and journalists—sometimes with a more conservative call for community bootstrapping and sometimes via a legitimation of hip hop's activist roots—the idea that readers of the black press were members of the same community as the victims of the disaster that followed Katrina, and thus had a special responsibility to their them, was uniformly articulated.

African American Self-Sufficiency

As demonstrated at various points in other cases examined in this volume, the black press is certainly not free from the influence of dominant ideological narratives. At times the inclusion of these narratives has been a matter of survival, however they also reflect community debates about the usefulness of racial agitation and appeals to the state versus accommodation and bootstrapping.[53] In the twenty-first century these debates continue to surface in ways that sometimes reflect class elitism and concerns about respectability politics among African American elites. In this case, such debates appeared via a frame that embraced a call to action in response to Katrina that rejected the idea of placing any expectations or demands on mainstream institutions in favor of improving the self-reliance and standing of the black community.

Every story that mentioned West's dissent in the *Chicago Defender*, for example, focused on a larger concept of community self-sufficiency. James Muhammad reported that Illinois Department of Human Services secretary Dr. Carol Adams' felt that "Kanye told the truth, but we don't have time to be insulted. It's time to get busy and prepare for ourselves."[54] While West's comments are regarded as "truth," the overall frame of the article suggests that rather than focus on agitating against the negligence of the federal government, the black community must "get busy" taking care of themselves. Muhammad presented a detailed discussion of "Operation Save Us," a program run by the Reverend Al Sampson that focused on "mobilizing a Black response" to Hurricane Katrina. This program is explained as including black mayors, ministers, contractors, architects, and lawyers in an effort "for Blacks to take control of their own destiny."[55]

More forcefully, two columns in the *Chicago Defender* by Joseph C. Phillips argued that even if "West is correct. Who cares? . . . Government is not supposed to be our friend," but is simply supposed to fulfill "a duty to protect our lives and property," something that it failed to do "at every level." Phillips contends that "it is better for intellectuals and entertainers to ask: do Black people care about Black people . . . ?" and that "the difference between" that question and "those of Mr. West is that one places responsibility and the power to change our communities in the hands of Black people—Black men—and does not rely on the benevolence on the government." Phillips also characterizes West's dissent as "the petulant complaint of a child to a parent."[56]

Such discourse in the black press is striking because of the ways it dovetails with conservative critiques of the "welfare state" as a debilitating force that infantilizes citizens and robs them of their initiative. In particular this approach suggests that black civil society alone can and should solve problems rooted in legacies of institutional neglect, and implies that rather than pressuring the government to correct these legacies and ongoing neglect, African Americans should simply accept the shortcomings of the status quo and take sole "responsibility" for the current state of their communities.

Further, the patriarchy explicit in Phillips' discourse is troubling because of the way it positions black men as the singular leaders of the black community and their individual actions as the solution to legacies of neglect. This embrace of patriarchal bootstrapping discourse reflects the realities of conservative discourses of black uplift in the twenty-first-century black public sphere. While not ignoring the neglect of the government in fulfilling their responsibilities to the citizens of New Orleans and acknowledging a history of "pernicious racism" in the United States, Phillips' framing suggests that ultimately anti-establishment discourse like West's is childish, and that black men in particular, with or without social support, must rally their resources to provide for an entire community rather than waiting on "the lords of the administrative state."[57]

Conversely, a column by A. Asadullah Samad in the *Los Angeles Sentinel* addressed West's comments as "truth," but suggested that "we know the deal, and now all of America knows the deal. We, as Black Americans, have to step up like never before, in contributions, donations, giving up rooms in our homes, to help our people while they are in the process of being 'helped.'"[58] This call to "Black Americans" to help "our people" alongside the contention that West's dissent is something that has always been known in the black community presents a frame centered in a philosophy of community self-sufficiency and cynicism of mainstream institutions that is far less dismissive of demands for mainstream change.

Samad constructs the "help" provided from outside the black community as suspect (as demonstrated by his insertion of quotation marks around the word), and after discussing the ways in which "the government and the media got us lookin' real crazy right now," notes that "it's time for all Black America to step up to demonstrate that we're not as crazy as they're trying to make us look."[59] The repeated use of "us," "we," and "our people" constructs the plight of the victims of Hurricane Katrina as being one experienced by all of "Black America" while also expressing concern that the inaccurately perceived actions of hurricane victims will impact every African American. Thus Samad's "got us lookin' real crazy" narrative walks a line between explicit critique of mainstream media representations, acknowledgement of the inequalities in existence in New Orleans, and a respectability politics that seeks to control what types of black images are made available in the mainstream public sphere in an effort to protect the reputation of the black community.

Hip Hop as Black Uplift
Within the frame of black self-sufficiency and community uplift, newsmakers in the black press took as a given that a rapper with a platform like West's not only would, but should, challenge the political and economic status quo that enabled the human suffering following Katrina. This framing stands in clear contrast to the mainstream marginalization of discourses that treated black celebrity and hip hop as inherently political. An article by Margena Christian of *Jet*, for example, quoted Congresswoman Maxine Waters as hoping that "he [West] will serve as an inspiration to other hip-hoppers who are making money and have forgotten how to open their mouths and talk about what they said was on their minds when then got into hip hop."[60] Similarly, Dr. Michael Eric Dyson was quoted as feeling that West's dissent "was hip hop at its best. Thank God hip hop took a break from the booze, the broads and the bling to once again find its conscience and to raise up a voice that is clear, blunt and articulate in the best of its hip-hop tradition."[61]

This framing of West acknowledges the conflict that exists between the commodification of hip hop culture in the mainstream and its political potential and history as an art rooted in black desires for uplift and social change. Such coverage in the black press took as a given the role hip hop plays as "the black CNN," and in doing so legitimated not only its political value but the validity of anti-establishment critiques from artists like West.[62]

Framing hip hop as a tool of black uplift thus lead to frequent descriptions of West's dissent as a form of truth-telling and West as a spokesperson for those who were otherwise voiceless. Damaso Reyes of the *New York Amsterdam News* described West as "one of the more politically aware artists," and an article in the *Chicago Defender* labeled West's comments "truth."[63] *Jet*'s coverage, which also included the opinions of Al Sharpton,

Russell Simmons, and Cornel West, referred to West's dissent as "absolutely right," and reflecting "bravery," "courage," and a "passion and care for his people."[64] Multiple interviewees in the black press expressed in some form the idea that, as reported in *Jet*, "Kanye said what a lot of us have been saying and should be supported and protected for having the nerve to say it."[65] Thus, West was constructed as having contributed a valuable and traditionally ignored perspective to mainstream post-Katrina discussions while his motivations were treated as rooted in a genuine concern for the status of the black community.

While, like the mainstream press, the black press reported on the support of black celebrities like Russell Simmons in their coverage of West's dissent, there are notable differences in how this support was framed. First, despite the occasional quote from a black celebrity, the black press mostly presented responses from black government officials, intellectuals, and community leaders, revealing a different understanding of who black America's spokespeople are and who should be included in the national conversation about Katrina. Second, because of the larger context, the stories that included celebrity quotes in the black press were located in news sections and stories about politics, race, and national disasters, thus the opinions of celebrities were not relegated to stories that commodified back artistic expression.

Reyes, of the *New York Amsterdam News,* presented a similar version of this frame through a focus on what West and New Orleans rapper Juvenile were personally doing to help those affected by Hurricane Katrina. The article briefly mentions West's line about George Bush but the majority of space is dedicated to discussing West's charity work with Live 8. Unlike mainstream newsmakers who did not report on West's self-criticisms about hesitating to give to the relief efforts and his subsequent commitments to help, *Amsterdam News* coverage reported on West "calling my business manager to see what is the biggest amount I can give."[66]

Reyes also explained that although rapper Juvenile lost his house in the hurricane, he considered himself "one of the fortunate ones" compared to those who "have nobody to reach out to for support." Juvenile is quoted with the request to "please keep our city, its people and our families in your prayers." While this coverage of West's and Juvenile's personal crusades for the victims of Hurricane Katrina embraces an individualistic charity tone, it also constructs these two figures as part of a larger communal initiative to recognize the people of New Orleans as deserving Americans, encouraging readers to lend "support to their fellow citizens."[67]

This version of the community uplift frame presumes the responsibility of black hip hop artists to those who have less institutional access because of a shared set of experiences in the African American community. Notably, as Zenia Kish has detailed, "a veritable subgenre of Katrina hip-hop was born on [the] waves of backlash against unnecessary suffering and institutional failure" that followed Katrina.[68] Like West, rappers nationwide who were not as high profile saw themselves as responsible for contributing discursive dissent that drew attention to the ways inequality, oppression, and neglect influenced the experiences of Katrina survivors.[69]

Legacies of Institutional Inequality

Forty percent of black press coverage of Kanye West's post-Katrina dissent framed his remarks within discussions of the institutional neglect and discrimination experienced by African Americans and the poor throughout American history. The frequency of this frame reveals that while the black press included some conservative voices calling for individual- and community-level solutions, it also provided a large-scale context and critique that held American institutions very much responsible for black suffering. This frame constructed West's comment that "America is set up to help the poor, the black ... as slowly as possible," as old news to the African American community and something still experienced in everyday life.

For example, Christian's *Jet* article quoted NAACP President Bruce Gordon that "Kanye's description of the way the media treats us is absolutely right. The double standard in the mainstream media when it comes to Black folk and others is long standing. This is just the Katrina version of bias."[70] By characterizing a mainstream media "double standard" as being "long standing," Gordon and *Jet* provide a context for West's dissent that was largely overlooked by mainstream journalists who, unsurprisingly, were not keen on critiquing themselves. According to this frame, racist media depictions are only one example of an ongoing institutional "bias" against African Americans.

Gordon is further quoted that "the likelihood of those on the bottom" of the "income scale" being black "is pretty high," and that therefore the aftermath of Hurricane Katrina in New Orleans reflects "that poor people are not at the table ... and their needs are not taken seriously." Again, *Jet*, via the words of the leader of the nation's oldest civil rights organization, contextualizes the aftermath of Hurricane as being the result of institutional factors whereby those who are "at the table" ignore of the "needs" of the poor and black.[71]

More specifically, articles in the *Chicago Defender* and *Los Angeles Sentinel* compared Katrina's aftermath with other documented cases of racial neglect and abuse. In these cases, West's dissent was framed as part of a larger critique of institutional racism. James Muhammad quoted Representative Bobby Rush saying, "We have never seen Black bodies lying in the streets, even during the heyday of the Ku Klux Klan and lynchings," and Joseph Phillips cited "the 1940s and 50s" as a period of specific neglect of "Black people."[72] Reflecting on the lack of government response to the victims of Hurricane Katrina, A. Asadullah Samad wrote that "Blacks, historically, have never gotten their fair share out of government assisted relief efforts," going on to describe the failures of the Freedman's Bureau after the Civil War, National Recovery Assistance during the Great Depression, riot relief in the 1960s and 1990s, and recovery efforts around other natural disasters that affected the lives of African Americans.[73]

Thus the black press validated West's dissent through critical historical documentation and memories of lived experience within the African American community. This type of large-scale, pattern-establishing, institutional critique of racial inequality was absent in mainstream coverage of West's comments.

Members of the black press also linked historic and contemporary neglect of the African American community to individual misunderstanding of race and poverty among those with social and political power. The *Sentinel*'s main editorial on West's dissent discussed the impact and implications of comments by two high-profile white figures as compared to West's. The *Sentinel* editors reported on Barbara Bush's feelings that because Katrina survivors being housed in the Houston Astrodome were "underprivileged anyway" things were "working very well for them," and those of "a Republican Louisiana politician" who had reportedly stated that "Katrina cleaned up all these black people in the projects like we have been trying to do for years."[74]

Sentinel editors did not particularly laud West, noting that he was not necessarily "an effective on-the spot [sic] spokesperson for the African American community," but instead argued that both Barbara Bush and the unnamed Louisiana politician clearly "lived in the public/political arenas" and thus reflected the racist and classist views of American institutions. This focus on the continued misunderstanding of and outright revulsion to the black poor within elite government circles allowed *Sentinel* editors to implicitly support West's observations about the "setup" of America. Ultimately, the editors argued, the comments of Bush and the Louisiana politician should be treated with much more ire than those of West because of their potential to do real harm to the African American community.[75]

Together, frames of West's dissent in the black press offered readers much greater nuance and diversity of perspective by revealing multiple readings of hip hop as a powerful, albeit commodified, political tool, conservative ideologies of black self-sufficiency that did not deny the government failures in the wake of Katrina, explicit criticism of mainstream representations of black suffering and dissent, and evidence of the ongoing legacy of racial and economic inequality. The black press' refusal to disconnect the story of Kanye West's dissent from the experiences of those in the Gulf and histories of oppression provided a clear alternative to what Eric Ishiwata calls the "antiracial, ahistorical lens of neoliberalism" in mainstream narratives.[76]

CONCLUSIONS

Findings in this case suggest both the continuing influence of historic narratives that limit black celebrity dissent and the presence of unique narratives tied to twenty-first-century political contexts. First, while the black press continues to contribute to counternarratives that directly interrogate issues affecting racially marginalized members of American society, contemporary neoliberal political discourse has clearly imbedded itself in mainstream *and* black public spheres.[77]

Of the cases I examined for this volume, this marks the first and only in which conservative post-Reagan-era rhetoric that contends government has no unique responsibility to the African American community appeared in black press responses to black celebrity dissent. While black press journalists at times critiqued Paul Robeson, Eartha Kitt, and Tommie Smith and John Carlos, they never implied as part of these critiques that the government should take a hands-off approach to inequality. Rather, in these cases, black press narratives reflecting more conservative or accommodationist takes on racial politics used frameworks that explicitly maintained the need for institutional-level interventions.

Further, in the 1990s, journalists in the black press offered open expressions of exhaustion and contempt toward mainstream narratives that suggested America had rid itself of inequality and presented virtually no negative framing of even highly dramatic black dissent. Thus, the significant presence of narratives of black self-sufficiency in the black press in this case evidences a phenomenon in which mainstream conservative narratives that demonize the "welfare state" exist alongside those that explicitly interrogate state-sponsored inequality and legitimate black expressive forms.

On the other hand, contemporary ideologies in mainstream press framing of West compounded the entrenched ways black dissent has been demonized in the public sphere, offering an extremely homogeneous set of understandings. Framing of West's dissent as incompatible to charity efforts reflect both historic narratives, like those that sanctified sport in coverage of Smith and Carlos, and the ongoing entrenchment of the neoliberal economic narratives that evidenced themselves in dismissals of Mahmoud Abdul-Rauf because of his salary. In this case, rather than sport or token economic success, solutions to social problems based in neoliberal capitalism are sanctified.

Second, this case suggests mainstream framing of black celebrity dissent has evolved in new ways that reflect the work colorblind narratives do to limit challenges to the status quo. Here, less explicitly negative framing of Kanye West evidences the way hip hop's antagonistic relationship with the status quo had come to be accepted, and sometimes celebrated, in public discourse in the twenty-first century.[78] Specifically, the twenty-first-century treatment of celebrity as news and the commodification of hip hop's anti-establishment leanings contributed to a media environment in which West's Katrina dissent was framed as entertainment rather than a radical threat like that of Sister Souljah. Thus, it appears that as black expressive forms have been increasingly consumed in the twenty-first century, dominant discourses have developed both less explicitly raced strategies for the marginalization of black perspectives and the construction of "safe" spaces in which black dissent is made non-threatening.

Despite these limitations, it is significant that prior to West's dissent, African American leaders were not successful in introducing a sustained discussion of inequality into mainstream coverage of the hurricane's aftermath. Rather, West's celebrity created a visibility that led mainstream newsmakers, and the President for years to come, to feel it necessary to respond to the larger claims of inequality being levied from the margins at the time. Because mainstream audiences were familiar with West and witnessed his dissent live, mainstream newsmakers, while ignoring West's agency as a producer of political thought, nevertheless eventually had to tackle his claims and those like them in some way. In the weeks after Katrina's human disaster, mediamakers made attempts at directly addressing issues of racial and economic inequality in New Orleans, though without acknowledging the role West played in making these topics newsworthy.[79]

Thus, coverage of West, both its problematics and potentials, reflect Neal's assertion that hip hop as a third stream of black thought has been more successful at penetrating mainstream discourses than more traditional institutions of the black public sphere.[80] Further, my findings suggest that while mainstream discourses remain problematic in constructing the acceptable public role of African American celebrities, hip hop's mainstreaming in the twenty-first century, and the simultaneous mainstream commodification of black cultural expression, may be creating a space in which black rappers in particular are less penalized for dissent than their counterparts in other realms of the entertainment industry. At the same time, mainstream newsmakers' explicit refusal to take West's comments seriously in their coverage demonstrates that this mainstreaming does not necessarily result in progressive understandings of African Americans as social agents.

As a testament to this, Kanye West's celebrity has skyrocketed since 2005 alongside growing mainstream critiques of his self-expression. When he agreed to a rare in-depth interview with Joe Caramanica of *The New York Times* in June of 2013—a point at which he had become not only one of the most successful rappers in America but a significant tastemaker of popular culture and fashion trends—West had already been widely labeled as "arrogant," "immature," and "obnoxious" in various mainstream media outlets. Reactions to the *Times* interview were no different, with quite a few commentators labeling West mentally unstable.[81] Yet, as Heben Nigatu points out, West's so-called arrogance and intentional push of dominantly sanctioned boundaries of black celebrity behavior can be understood as a political act that uses self-love and satire as a method of self-preservation in the face of a culture always seeking to control and limit expressions of blackness.[82]

In the frequently maligned *Times* interview, West clearly stated his commitment to challenging mainstream structures and expectations: "I'm going to use my platform to tell people that they're not being fair. Anytime I've had a big thing . . . it was a fight for justice. Justice. And when you say justice, it doesn't have to be war. Justice could just be clearing a path for people to dream properly."[83] Soon thereafter West gave another interview to radio DJ Zane Lowe in which he connected his successes to legacies of civil rights activism and black celebrities who broke down cultural barriers, and expressed frustration at being shut out of elite spaces within the fashion industry and the expectation that people "who look like me" be "quiet as fuck."[84] Comedian Jimmy Kimmel, playing off the mainstream narrative that given his success West was irrational, egotistical, and immature to believe that he continued to experience any type of marginalization, parodied the Lowe interview by having children reenact it on his late-night television show.[85] When West later appeared on Kimmel's show insisting, "Whenever I went up and spoke my mind whether it put my career in jeopardy or whatever it was always what I thought was the truth" and contending that mediamakers "treat celebrities like zoo animals," these comments were similarly denigrated as "lampoon-able and ridiculous."[86]

What is notable in the interviews with Caramanica, Lowe, and Kimmel is that West expresses a very clear awareness of mainstream limitations placed on his creative and political agency alongside an explicit desire to be understood outside these limitations. Yet in each case his attempts at self-definition were met with pushback via neoliberal colorblind ideologies that suggest West's success disproves any claim of marginalization, and that his boundary-pushing actions are to be treated only as spectacle. Thus, West's ongoing celebrity illustrates quite plainly the intersection of a twenty-first-century entertainment culture that relies on and consumes black celebrity and a racial order that continually seeks to restrain permissible forms of black expression. It is worth asking how different these phenomena are from those faced by Paul Robeson, Muhammad Ali, and the other subjects examined in this volume.

NOTES

1. Kanye West, "Black Skinhead," *Yeezus*, Roc-a-Fella/Def Jam, 2013.
2. "Matt Lauer Reports," NBC, Nov. 8, 2010.
3. "*A Concert for Hurricane Relief*," NBC Studios, Sep. 2, 2005.
4. Seventy-five percent of the coverage of West's dissent I examined mentioned his Bush-related comment, versus just twelve percent that included a quote or paraphrase of his criticisms regarding media inequality in covering black "looters" versus white "finders" and the under five percent that made reference to the portion of West's statements claiming structural inequality in the way "America is set up."
5. Perhaps the most high profile of these incidents became known as the Danziger Bridge shootings, in which police open-fired on and killed civilians, including a mentally disabled man, attempting to flee from Katrina's aftermath. (John Burnett, "What Happened on New Orleans' Danziger Bridge?" *All Things Considered*, NPR, Sep. 12, 2006, http://www.npr.org/templates/story/story.php?storyId=6063982 (accessed Feb. 25, 2014).
6. The data analyzed in this chapter was published between September 2, 2005, the day West made his comments, and November 2, 2005. My sources

include *The New York Times, Chicago Tribune, Los Angeles Times, Time,* and *Newsweek* in the mainstream press and the *New York Amsterdam News, Chicago Defender, Los Angeles Sentinel, Jet,* and *Ebony* in the African American press.
7. Cedric Johnson, ed., *The Neoliberal Deluge: Hurricane Katrina, Late Capitalism, and the Remaking of New Orleans* (Minneapolis: University of Minnesota Press, 2011).
8. See, for example, Kirk Johnson, Mark Dolan, and John Sonnett, "Speaking of Looting: An Analysis of Racial Propaganda in National Television Coverage of Hurricane Katrina," *The Howard Journal of Communications* 22 (2011): 302–318; Hemant Shah, "Legitimizing Neglect: Race and Rationality in Conservative News Commentary about Hurricane Katrina," *The Howard Journal of Communications* 20 (2009): 1–17; Alice Gavin, "Reading Katrina: Race, Space and an Unnatural Disaster," *New Political Science* 30, no. 3 (2008): 325–346; Michael Eric Dyson, *Come Hell or High Water: Hurricane Katrina and the Color of Disaster* (New York: Basic Books, 2007); Carole Stabile, "No Shelter from the Storm," *South Atlantic Quarterly* 106, no. 4 (2007): 683–708; Douglas Brinkley, *The Great Deluge: Hurricane Katrina, New Orleans, and the Mississippi Gulf Coast* (New York: Morrow, 2006); Samuel R. Sommers, Evan P. Apfelbaum, Kristin N. Dukes, Negin Toosi, and Elsie J. Wang, "Race and Media Coverage of Hurricane Katrina: Analysis, Implications, and Future Research Questions," *Analysis of Social Issues and Public Policy* 6, no.1 (2006): 39–55.
9. Stabile, "No Shelter."
10. Linda Robertson, "News Coverage of Post-Katrina New Orleans and the 2008 Midwest Floods," in *The Neoliberal Deluge: Hurricane Katrina, Late Capitalism, and the Remaking of New Orleans,* ed. Cedric Johnson (Minneapolis: University of Minnesota Press, 2011): 269–299.
11. Dyson, *Come Hell or High Water*; Sommers et. al., "Race and Media Coverage."
12. Robertson, "News Coverage of Post-Katrina."
13. Ibid.
14. Johnson, Dolan, and Sonnett, "Speaking of Looting."
15. Robertson, "News Coverage of Post-Katrina."
16. Ibid.
17. Ibid.
18. Color of Change, http://colorofchange.org/.
19. Eric Ishiwata, "'We Are Seeing People We Didn't Know Exist': Katrina and the Neoliberal Erasure of Race," in *The Neoliberal Deluge: Hurricane Katrina, Late Capitalism, and the Remaking of New Orleans,* ed. Cedric Johnson (Minneapolis: University of Minnesota Press, 2011): 32–59; Imani Perry, *Prophets of the Hood: Politics and Poetics in Hip Hop* (Durham: Duke University Press, 2004); Jeff Chang, *Can't Stop Won't Stop: A History of the Hip-Hop Generation* (New York: Picador, St. Martin's Press, 2005); Tricia Rose, *The Hip Hop Wars: What We Talk about When We Talk about Hip Hop—and Why It Matters* (New York: Basic Books, 2008); S. Craig Watkins, *Hip Hop Natters: Politics, Pop Culture, and the Struggle for the Soul of a Movement* (Boston: Beacon Press, 2005).
20. Perry, *Prophets*: 15.
21. Rose, *Hip Hop Wars*.
22. Josh Tyrangiel, "Why You Can't Ignore Kanye," *Time,* Aug. 21 2005, http://content.time.com/time/magazine/article/0,9171,1096499,00.html (accessed Mar. 2, 2014).
23. Ibid.

24. Rose, *The Hip Hop Wars*; Bakari Kitwana, *Why White Kids Love Hip Hop: Wankstas, Wiggers, Wannabes, and the New Reality of Race in America* (New York: Basic Books, 2005).
25. Kitwana, *Why White Kids*.
26. Chang, *Can't Stop Won't Stop*.
27. Perry, *Prophets*.
28. Jonathan Alter, "The Other America," *Newsweek*, Sep. 19, 2005.
29. In *The New York Times*, nine of the fifteen total mentions of West's dissent were published from the Arts/Culture desk and only two from the National Desk. In the *Los Angeles Times*, seven of the nine total articles on West's dissent were in the "Entertainment" section of the paper with only two published in Section A. Fifty percent of the *Chicago Tribune*'s coverage also included West's dissent in entertainment-based stories.
30. Geoff Boucher, "Celebs or Saviors: Kanye West a Critic with Cred," *Los Angeles Times*, Sep. 9, 2005.
31. For example, see Geoff Boucher, "Celebs or Saviors"; Steve Hochman, "Kanye West Continues His Rap on Bush," *Los Angeles Times*, Sep. 12, 2005; Robert Hilburn, "He's Energizing and Enthralling: Kanye West Puts the 'New' Back in Concerts as He Opens His U.S. Tour in Florida," *Los Angeles Times*, Oct. 13, 2005.
32. Hochman, "Kanye West Continues His Rap on Bush"; Hilburn, "He's Energizing and Enthralling."
33. Alessandra Stanley, "A Good-Natured show in the Shadow of Turbulent Times," *The New York Times (1923–Current File)*, Sep. 19, 2005: E9.
34. Kelefa Sanneh, "Pop/Jazz," *The New York Times (1923–Current File)*, Sep. 18, 2005: A33.
35. "The Second Coming of Reverend Run," *The New York Times (1923–Current File)*, Oct. 9, 2005: A4.
36. Matea Gold and Chris Lee, "Kibosh on Telethon Artist Comments?" *Los Angeles Times*, Sep. 9, 2005.
37. "Hold the Beef," *Chicago Tribune*, Sep. 14, 2005.
38. For example, John Leland, "Art Born of Outrage in the Internet Age," *The New York Times*, Sep. 25, 2005.
39. S.C. Lewis, "Finger-Point Later," *Chicago Tribune*, Sep. 9, 2005, http://articles.chicagotribune.com/2005–09–09/news/0509090325_1_finger-gulf-coast-cities-wait (accessed Nov. 13, 2013).
40. Tony Yaniz, "Wrong Priorities," *Chicago Tribune*, Sep. 9, 2005, http://articles.chicagotribune.com/2005-09-09/news/0509100019_1_wrong-priorities-hillary-clinton-wicker-park (accessed Nov. 23, 2013).
41. "Letters: Sep. 19, 2005." *Time*, Sep. 19, 2005, http://content.time.com/time/magazine/article/0,9171,1103596,00.html (accessed Nov. 25, 2013).
42. Nandini Gunewardena and Mark Schuller, eds., *Capitalizing on Catastrophe: Neoliberal Strategies in Disaster Reconstruction* (Walnut Creek, CA: AltaMira Press, 2008).
43. Ned Martel, "On a Telethon Weekend, Restraint from an Unlikely Source," *The New York Times (1923–Current File)*, Sep. 12, 2005: E7.
44. "Kanye Sticks to the Script," *Chicago Tribune*, Sep. 8, 2005, http://articles.chicagotribune.com/2005-09-08/news/0509080387_1_george-bush-doesn-t-care-concert-sticks (accessed Nov. 23, 2013); Kate Aurthur, " . . . But No More Politics," *The New York Times (1923–Current File)*, Sep. 8, 2005: E2.
45. Whizzer, "Canine Lines," *Chicago Tribune*, Sep. 7, 2005.
46. Matea Gold and Chris Lee, "Kibosh on Telethon Artist Comments?" *Los Angeles Times*, Sep. 9, 2005, http://articles.latimes.com/2005/sep/09/entertainment/

et-telethon9 (accessed Nov. 23, 2013); Matea Gold and Scott Collins, "NBC Deletes Rap Star's Remarks on Telethon," *Los Angeles Times,* Sep. 4, 2005, http://articles.latimes.com/2005/sep/04/nation/na-telethon4 (accessed Nov. 23, 2013).
47. So much for being "the smartest man in pop music."
48. Richard Cromelin, "TV Fundraisers Focus on Storm Victims Instead of Politics," *Los Angeles Times,* Sep. 10, 2005, http://articles.latimes.com/2005/sep/10/entertainment/et-pop10 (accessed Nov. 23, 2013).
49. "Presidential Approval Ratings—George W. Bush," Gallup, www.gallup.com/poll/116500/presidential-approval-ratings-george-bush.aspx (accessed Oct. 18, 2010); "Party Affiliation," Gallup, www.gallup.com/poll/15370/party-affiliation.aspx (accessed Oct. 18, 2010); and U.S. Census Bureau, accessed Oct. 18, 2010.
50. See Boucher, "Celebs or Saviors"; Cromelin, "Katrina's Aftermath."
51. Robert Hilburn, "Too Much of a Good Thing?" *Los Angeles Times,* Sep. 12, 2005, http://articles.latimes.com/2005/sep/12/entertainment/et-critics12 (accessed Nov. 24, 2013); Hilburn, "He's Energizing and Enthralling."
52. Paul Gilroy, "The End of Antiracism," in *Race Critical Theories,* ed. Philomena Essed and David Theo Goldberg (Malden, MA: Wiley-Blackwell, 2001): 249–264; Howard Winant, *The New Politics of Race: Globalism, Difference, Justice* (Minneapolis: University of Minnesota Press, 2004).
53. For an early example, see the ways in which the black press was both structured by and facilitated the political perspectives of W.E.B. Du Bois and Booker T. Washington at the turn of the twentieth century: Jacqueline M. Moore, *Booker T. Washington, W.E.B. Du Bois, and the Struggle for Racial Uplift* (Lanham, MD: Rowman & Littlefield Publishers, 2003); Patrick Scott Washburn, *The African American Newspaper: Voice of Freedom* (Evanston, IL: Northwestern University Press, 2006); Todd Vogel, ed., *The Black Press: New Literary and Historical Essays* (New Brunswick, NJ: Rutgers University Press, 2001).
54. James G. Muhammad, "Hurricane Katrina on Everybody's Mind at Football Classic," *Chicago Defender,* Sep. 5–6, 2005.
55. Ibid.
56. Joseph C. Phillips, "A Government That Cares," *Chicago Defender,* Sep. 16–18, 2005; Joseph C. Phillips, "Government That Cares—Part Two," *Chicago Defender,* Sep. 22, 2005.
57. Phillips, "Government That Cares—Part Two."
58. A. Asadullah Samad, "Between the Lines; America Got Us Lookin Real Crazy Right Now," *Los Angeles Sentinel,* Sep. 15, 2005: A7.
59. Ibid.
60. Margena A. Christian, "Black Leaders Sound Off: Did Race Delay Relief to Disaster Areas?" *Jet,* Sep. 26, 2005, www.lexisnexis.com/hottopics/lnacademic (accessed Nov. 28, 2013).
61. Ibid.
62. This description of hip hop is widely credited to Public Enemy founder Chuck D as early as his "Yo! MTV Unwrapped," *Spin* magazine, September 1991 interview.
63. Damaso Reyes, "Hip-Hop Stars Speak Out on Katrina," *New York Amsterdam News,* Sep. 8–14, 2005; Muhammad, "Hurricane Katrina on Everybody's Mind."
64. Christian, "Black Leaders Sound Off."
65. Ibid.
66. Reyes, "Hip-Hop Stars Speak Out on Katrina."

67. Ibid.
68. Zenia Kish, "'My FEMA People': Hip-Hop as Disaster Recovery in the Katrina Diaspora," *American Quarterly* 61, no. 3 (Sep. 2009): 671–692.
69. Ibid.
70. Christian, "Black Leaders Sound Off."
71. Ibid.
72. Muhammad, "Hurricane Katrina on Everybody's Mind."
73. Samad, "Between the Lines."
74. "We All Live in Glass Houses," *Los Angeles Sentinel,* Sep. 15, 2005: A6.
75. Ibid.
76. Ishiwata, "We Are Seeing People We Didn't Know Exist": 48.
77. Catherine R. Squires has also identified the foothold of neoliberal discourses in the black public sphere as related to questions of the 2007–2008 subprime lending crisis. See her article "Coloring in the Bubble: Perspectives from Black-Oriented Media on the (Latest) Economic Disaster," *American Quarterly* 64, no. 3 (2012): 543–570.
78. Melissa Harris-Lacewell, *Barbershops, Bibles, and BET: Everyday Thought and Black Political Thought* (Princeton, NJ: Princeton University Press, 2004).
79. Sarah J. Jackson, "Hurricanes Don't Care about Black People: Hurricane Katrina, Racial Inequality and News Media Response," (MA thesis, University of Michigan, 2007).
80. Mark Anthony Neal, *Soul Babies: Black Popular Culture and the Post-Soul Aesthetic* (New York: Routledge, 2002).
81. For example, see "Kanye West Gives the Most Humble and Self-Effacing Interview of His Career: JK! 'Ye is still gloriously arrogant in 'New York Times' Q&A," *Spin,* Jun. 12, 2013, www.spin.com/articles/kanye-west-new-york-times-interview-caramanica-yeezus/ (accessed Dec. 12, 2013); Aly Weisman, "The Most Gag-Worthy Quotes from Kanye West's *New York Times* Interview," *Business Insider,* Jun. 12, 2013, www.businessinsider.com/quotes-from-kanye-wests-nyt-interview-2013-6 (accessed Dec. 12, 2013).
82. Heben Nigatu, "In Defense of Kanye's Vanity: The Politics of Black Self-Love," *Buzzfeed,* Jun. 20, 2013, www.buzzfeed.com/hnigatu/in-defense-of-kanyes-vanity-the-politics-of-black-self-love (accessed Dec 12, 2013).
83. Joe Caramanica, "The Visionaries: Behind Kanye's Mask," *The New York Times,* Jun. 11, 2013.
84. Edwin Ortiz, "Here's Pt. 1 of Kanye West's Interview with Zane Lowe," *Complex Music,* Sep. 23, 2013, www.complex.com/music/2013/09/kanye-west-zane-lowe-interview-part-1 (accessed Dec. 12, 2013).
85. Lauren Nostro, "Two Kids Spoof Kanye West's Interview with Zane Lowe on 'Jimmy Kimmel Live,'" *Complex Music,* Sep. 25, 2013, www.complex.com/music/2013/09/kimmel-spoofs-kanye-interview (accessed Dec. 12, 2013).
86. Brian Lowry, "Jimmy Kimmel, Kanye West Parley Twitter 'Feud' into PR," *Variety,* Oct. 10, 2013, http://variety.com/2013/voices/columns/jimmy-kimmel-kanye-west-parlay-twitter-feud-into-pr-1200709142/ (accessed Dec. 12, 2013); Katie Van Syckle, "Kanye West's 12 Best Tangents on 'Kimmel,'" *Rolling Stone,* Oct. 10, 2013, www.rollingstone.com/music/videos/kanye-west-and-jimmy-kimmel-make-up-after-spat-20131010 (accessed Dec. 12, 2013).

Conclusion
Black Celebrity, Racial Politics, and the Press: Going Forward

I don't like people who like me because I'm a Negro; neither do I like people who find in the same accident grounds for contempt. I love America more than any other country in the world, and, exactly for this reason, I insist on the right to criticize her perpetually.[1]

The press is a political instrument. . . . It orders, shapes and directs the collective consciousness of its readers. . . . The newspaper or periodical is not only a collection of facts and attitudes, it is a social experience, and its continual publication is itself a political process. . . . One could accurately regard a newspaper as a printed rally.[2]

Without a doubt, the social location and power of black celebrities has shifted since Paul Robeson faced down violent crowds in Peekskill, New York. These shifts, linked to social and political upheaval, resistance, and adaptation, highlight how both celebrity and blackness are defined and consumed in our society at particular historical moments. The actions of the subjects at the core of my research are a reminder that members of oppressed collectives regularly resist dominant understandings of race and nation through communicative acts. Those who gain access to dominant spaces and opportunities to publicize such acts challenge journalists and the publics they serve to define and redefine the boundaries of national discourse. The cases in this volume clearly demonstrate that African American celebrities, while limited in institutional power and bound by particular political moments, are active agents using their bodies, access, and personas to interject counterdiscourses rooted in blackness into spaces and conversations that are otherwise constructed as having no place for non-national identities.

At the same time, my work here re-illustrates that the creation and dispersal of news is inherently political. Journalists, despite professional ideals of objectivity, bring very specific and clearly raced worldviews to decisions of what to report, how to report it, and who to report it for when it comes to covering the dissent of African American celebrities. Given this value-laden process, and what we know about the potential for news framing of raced topics to have profound effects on political and social behavior, my research offers specific insight into understanding the role various segments of the press have played in supporting the evolution of worldviews at the intersection of black celebrity and racial politics for over half a century.[3]

OVERALL FRAMING TRENDS

Table 7.1 lists the frequencies of primary frames each press constructed for understanding the cases I examine in this study.[4] Several trends are apparent. First, mainstream journalists present frames that (1) construct African American celebrities who present challenges to the status quo as physical and/or ideological threats to an idealized nation and its representatives, and (2) fixate on how the introduction of discourses based in black experience violate dominantly defined expectations of behavior. These frames uniquely disadvantage black celebrity dissent by situating it within raced narratives and assumptions.

Further, mainstream framing tends to severely overestimate the power black celebrities have over other African Americans and the fate of the nation as a whole: Paul Robeson is constructed as having the power to cause riots and spread communism, Sister Souljah is constructed as having the power to initiate a murderous uprising, Kanye West is constructed as having the power to stop donations to those in need. Additionally, mainstream press frames suggest that the mere existence of African American celebrities, especially in sport, undermines the validity of claims of inequality—in Smith and Carlos' case, sport is treated as a sort of Eden of fairness and understanding in which race should not be acknowledged, while Mahmoud Abdul-Rauf's ability to make millions of dollars through athletic competition is assumed to be a contradiction to the existence of oppression.

Primary frames in each case in the black press also reflect some consistency across time. Newsmakers serving the black public sphere tend to contextualize black celebrity dissent within (1) critical memory about, and the ongoing reality of, institutional inequality; and (2) community-level debates about the appropriate means to, and possibilities for, racial progress in American society. Both of these constructions are largely absent from the mainstream press across time and, at their root, focus on treating black experiences as valid and important. The primary frames in the black press also regularly seek to specifically respond to dominant discourses by pointing out hypocrisies, double-standards, and distractions in the mainstream public sphere. Conversely, at no historical moment herein did mainstream newsmakers take up the task of responding to discourses within the black public sphere, a reflection of the privilege at work in the relationship between the two.

Table 7.1 Framing Trends and Frequency of Occurrence by Press and Subject

	1949	1968	1968	1992	1996	2005
Mainstream Press Frames	Robeson	Kitt	Smith & Carlos	Souljah	Abdul-Rauf	West
	Ideological Battle Ground 40%	Antagonistic Attacker 33%	Incompatibility of Sport & Politics 45%	Reverse Racist/ Violence Instigator 43%	Black Economic Success = No Oppression 30%	Entertainment Value Only 45%
	Communist Instigator 30%	Breach of Etiquette 28%	Unpatriotic 40%	(Racial) Politics as Usual 30%	Tenuousness of Guaranteed Rights 27%	Incompatibility of Charity & Politics 30%
Black Press Frames	Robeson	Kitt	Smith & Carlos	Souljah	Abdul-Rauf	West
	Racist Climate 45%	Truth-telling re Inequality 40%	Black Unity/Uplift 65%	Bill Clinton Betrayer 62%	Islam = Complex/ Valid 60%	Black Self-Sufficiency / Hip Hop as Uplift 60%
	Complicity of Officials 30%	Freedom of expression 20%	Truth-telling re Inequality 65%	Mainstream Distraction 45%	Unequal Application of Guaranteed Rights 30%	Legacies of Racial Neglect/Inequality 40%

SHIFTS AND STALEMATES IN FRAMING BLACK CELEBRITY

In every case I examined here, African American celebrities were reprimanded in mainstream news for introducing counterdiscourses into traditionally dominant spaces. The non-normative forms and spaces of the dissent examined in this project became central to how the messages being communicated by the celebrities in question were understood. Dissent expressed by black celebrities that fell outside of the expected and limited norms of protest traditionally assigned to African Americans was consistently constructed as a threat to normative concepts of nation. Mainstream media makers framed concert stages, White House dinners, Olympic podiums, newspaper interviews, basketball courts, and disaster fundraisers as spaces that should be entirely void of dissenting political opinion. Such frames ignore both the innately political nature of these spaces and leave essentially no public location in which it is acceptable for a black public figure to express dissent. Thus, while there has, at times, been a shift in the physical and material consequences faced by dissenting black celebrities, there has been little mainstream discursive change in the sharply negative reaction to those who leverage their access to explicitly address racism and other inequalities outside of dominantly sanctioned locations.

At the same time, cases like those of Kitt and West illustrate that dominant constructions of decorum, tradition, and ritual play a significant role in mainstream understandings of black celebrity dissent and a violation of any of these reason enough for severe denunciation, even if that dissent is deemed in any way sympathetic. Further, the forms of these denunciations clearly depend upon the social identities of the celebrity in question, with intersectional factors like gender and religion playing a significant role in how presumed violations are constructed. In Kitt's case, framing of her dissent reflects discursive sanctioning based in patriarchal Eurocentric definitions of womanhood and civility. Likewise, Abdul-Rauf's position on the anthem was framed as illegitimate via definitions of citizenship based in hegemonic white Christianity that construct Islam as foreign.

In every case the inclusion of African American celebrities was only celebrated in mainstream discourse so long as their visibility did not result in a violation of the dominant gaze. While mainstream discourses suggested that the opportunities and successes of the likes of Smith and Carlos and Abdul-Rauf demonstrated the nation's commitment to egalitarian values, any dissent that used this opportunity and success to suggest such values were mythical and unfulfilled was constructed as unreasonable, unrealistic, and dangerous. At the same time, such constructions clearly transformed over time in ways that aligned with specific political events and hegemonic shifts in racial representation and discourse.

Thus, black celebrities have been and continue to be subject to a unique set of political criteria for mainstream acceptance that expects them to always perform according to sanctioned scripts while sidelining their identities as members of a still-oppressed group. The severe sanctions that befell once-celebrated figures like Robeson and Abdul-Rauf demonstrate, as Amy Bass has contended, "how quickly the rules of national belonging change if an individual does not subscribe to the tenets of citizenship in the sanctioned way."[5] Together, mainstream news coverage continues to suggest that in order to be free of social sanction by dominant white society, black celebrities must remain silent on the issues that affect their communities most.

Sixty-five years after Paul Robeson was demonized and reprimanded for refusing to shut up and sing, black celebrities are still reprimanded for being true to themselves while alternative discourses rooted in black experience are still treated as unreasonable. Crossover fame allowed every one of my subjects the opportunity to insert alternative ways of knowing into dominant discourse, yet these cases reflect that once a moment of alternative expression by a black celebrity is over they have limited power to influence how it is reinterpreted, rarely being called upon by mainstream journalists to offer further comment or explanation.

Certainly, the limitations placed on the dissent of black celebrities have opened up in positive ways in the mainstream public sphere—Kanye West was never in danger of being lynched as Paul Robeson was and was even regarded with some friendly, albeit derailing, sympathy. However, severe economic sanctions, as well as real physical threats, continue to befall some black celebrities who speak out against dominant ways of understanding—Mahmoud Abdul-Rauf could most certainly speak to this. At the same time, it appears that in the case of a celebrity like West, whose moment of dissent occurred within a very specific context that made space for (limited) expressions of blackness, it is possible for a black public figure to insert counterdiscourses into the mainstream public sphere while retaining his or her livelihood. In the contemporary era, however, these counterdiscourses may be simply ignored or belittled rather than demonized.

Notably, in 1949 and 1968, no portion of the entertainment industry was dependent economically on the production of black superstars, as music and sports industries are today, and Paul Robeson in particular had no cohort of institutionally empowered celebrity or political power players to come to his aid. By the late twentieth and early twenty-first centuries, black celebrities undoubtedly had more cultural capital and the increasing integration of political and entertainment realms allowed for their backing by powerful allies like Jesse Jackson (in Souljah's case) and Russell Simmons (in West's). Further the hip hop generation's consumption of black cool alongside anti-establishment narratives has demonstrated quite clearly to mediamakers, marketers, and political elites alike that black celebrity is where the money is.

As for the black press, my findings in this volume support the work of those who have identified its contribution to a counterpublic sphere that offers members counternarratives unavailable in dominant media.[6] In particular, coverage of dissent by black celebrities is given a level of credibility and validity in African American news sources that remains absent from dominant spaces. By providing the black experience and black cultural expression primacy, the black press accepts racism and institutional histories of neglect as a given. This larger contextualization of inequality in America makes the black press a space where actions like Kitt's, Smith and Carlos', West's, and Souljah's are not seen as out of place, dangerous, purely entertainment, or inappropriate.

Rather, the black press consistently treats the non-traditional dissent of African American celebrities as part of a larger effort to advance the needs of the black community and the nation. In this context, black celebrity dissent is not always celebrated, in fact some members of the black press, as in the cases of Robeson and Smith and Carlos, have found such dissent counterproductive to the larger battle for racial equality. Other times, journalists in the black press have not found the dissent of black celebrities particularly relevant one way or the other, preferring conservative narratives of uplift, as in the case of *Chicago Defender* coverage of West.

Further, the black press has consistently, even when under extreme political pressure as in 1949, offered critiques of mainstream press constructions of celebrity, dissent, and racial politics on the whole. Black newsmakers, while making sense of particular moments of dissent with varying rhetoric and intensity, have insisted that a double standard exists in the treatment of African Americans who offer dissenting opinions in comparison to white members of society, and that often the very ideas deemed inappropriate in dominant frames are an accurate but ignored reflection of social hierarchies in America. These understandings hold mainstream journalists accountable for their contributions to the maintenance of ideologies that reinforce and legitimate inequality.

While the alternative frames presented by the black press have undoubtedly contributed invaluable understandings to members of the black public sphere, what remains troubling is that these understandings have never been widely consumed by white Americans, and that over time the traditional black press has lost more and more of its reach and readership.[7] At the same time, the goal of the founders of the black press, that eventual integration of the mainstream press would make the black press obsolete, appears to have only been partially fulfilled. Despite incontrovertible advancements in mainstream journalistic inclusion since 1827, one wonders how Samuel E. Cornish and John B. Russwurm, the editors of *Freedom's Journal*, would feel about the 2005 coverage of the victims of Hurricane Katrina and the countless other documented misrepresentations of African American communities that continue to occur.[8] Such misrepresentation, along with the stagnation of efforts to diversify mainstream newsrooms some 190 years after Cornish and Russwurm wrote, "Too long has the public been deceived by misrepresentations, in things that concern us dearly," is sobering to say the least.[9]

Thus, in the twenty-first century, those concerned with issues of equality and the public sphere must grapple with a society in which the historical space for the production of black counternarratives struggles to survive while mainstream narratives that continue to perpetuate problematic understandings of race and nation that marginalize entire populations make widespread claims of embodying racial inclusion.

Given the always-limited and shrinking reach of the traditional black press, a celebrity whose goal is to draw widespread attention to a particular issue must engage with the mainstream public sphere no matter how problematic subsequent understandings may be. While expressions of frustration and racial fatigue have never been treated as particularly surprising or new by black journalists (who struggle to contribute to anti-racist discourses in multiple public spheres every day), in mainstream culture these expressions continue to be deemed newsworthy because of the challenges they present to the otherwise seamless ideologies that continue to privilege whiteness in our society. While such moments of dissent may be treated as relevant purely on the basis of celebrity involvement and controversy, they nevertheless reach audiences and generate discussions that might otherwise be altogether invisible.

In the remainder of this chapter I discuss debates about black celebrity dissent moving forward from the second decade of the twenty-first century and consider the new spaces, facilitated by technology and the continuing consumption of black culture, that allow for engagement between the black public sphere and mainstream narratives of race and nation.

BLACK CELEBRITY DISSENT IN THE OBAMA ERA

The second decade of the twenty-first century continues to raise nuanced questions about the intersection of black celebrity and racial politics in America. While African American visibility in media coverage of sports and entertainment remains high, the 2008 election of Barack Obama as the forty-fourth President of the United States raised increasingly visible questions about American identity and race.[10]

While—as evidenced by contemporary coverage of Kanye West discussed in the conclusion of Chapter 6—mainstream media narratives in the Obama era continue to undermine and marginalize the potential of black celebrity dissent, public debates about this dissent and alternative media narratives and spaces are contributing to national conversations about race and politics in very real ways. In the wake of the 2012 profiling and shooting of black teenager Trayvon Martin, for example, some black celebrities used their access to media to contribute to conversations about black experiences with racial profiling and the justice system that activists pushing for the trial of Martin's shooter had worked tirelessly to introduce to the mainstream.

Millennial LeBron James, a figure who like predecessor Michael Jordan has been constructed in mainstream discourse as evidence of both the supposedly idealistically open nature of the "American Dream" and the exceptionalism that justifies continued lack of access to it, posted a photograph tribute to Martin to his over 10.5 million Twitter followers several weeks after the teenager's death.[11] The photo, an image of the entire Miami Heat squad, eyes downcast, faces hidden beneath hoodies like the one Martin wore the night he was deemed "suspicious," quickly circulated on social media, and this image along with stories about James, his teammate Dwayne Wade, and other Heat players writing "R.I.P Trayvon" and "We Want Justice" on their basketball shoes, were picked up as brief news, entertainment, and sports snippets by mainstream outlets nationwide.[12]

Likewise, in the wake of the July 2013 not-guilty verdict reached in the trial of Trayvon Martin's shooter, George Zimmerman, Ahmir "Questlove" Thompson of the Roots took to his Facebook page to write an impassioned post about how Martin's profiling, and its normalization in the trial and broader society, reminded him of the many times he was treated as a racialized threat in his own life.[13] This post was picked up and re-run online by a range of outlets amid other coverage of the trial verdict, drawing readers who might have the privilege of having never been racially profiled into a conversation about how even their favorite black celebrities were not immune from this bigotry.

Thus technology, which allows black celebrities to speak directly to their fans and followers, presents unique twenty-first-century opportunities for dissent and for non-black audiences to consume black perspectives unaltered by traditional media institutions. While this phenomenon points to an important opening in the expansion of dissenting conversations that have traditionally only been legitimized within the black public sphere, research on social media–based stories suggests that while online spaces are more likely to treat dissent with legitimacy than traditional news outlets, stories in these spaces also have significantly shorter life spans and are regarded as less consequential by political elites than stories covered by traditional news outlets.[14] Further, it is notable that neither James nor Thompson chose more traditional spaces—like a widely covered NBA press conference or highly rated late-night television show—to broadcast their experiences, suggesting that, while contemporary black celebrities may feel safe using niche media to introduce narratives about inequality, dominant spaces are still understood as off-limits for such conversations.

Likewise, the continuing mainstreaming and commercialization of black expressive forms in the twenty-first century has allowed for some publicization of African American community-based debates about dissent in mainstream spaces. At the 2013 NAACP Image Awards, an event that has been held as a reflection of the black public sphere's attempts to shift mainstream representations of African Americans since 1967 but has only been included in mainstream primetime broadcasts since 1996, always-activist Harry Belafonte took to the stage to plead with younger generations of black celebrities to more forcefully engage in political dissent in "these troubled times."[15]

Belafonte listed the overrepresentation of black Americans in prisons and the prevalence of black deaths from gun violence as evidence of continued "racial carnage" in America.

Belafonte named Paul Robeson among activists and politicians as an example of those "committed to radical thought" who "spoke up to remedy the ills of the nation," saying:

> He was the sparrow. He was an artist who made us understand the depth of that calling when he said, "Artists are the gatekeepers of truth, we are civilizations radical voice." Never in the history of black America has there ever been such a harvest of truly gifted and powerful artists as we witness today. Yet, our nation hungers for their radical song. Let us not sit back silently. Let us not be charged with patriotic treason ... I will tell you that our kids, those who languish in the prisons of America, are waiting for us to change the system.[16]

These comments from Belafonte, broadcast during primetime on NBC, serve as an example of how traditional debates within the black public sphere about the role African American celebrities should play in shaping national conversation about race and politics have become more (though by no means widely) accessible to mainstream audiences. While the presence of this unedited narrative of black dissent on a mainstream television network is undoubtedly significant, it is worth considering if such narratives are in anyway legitimized by mainstream media makers, and if their mere presence results in any mass engagement.[17] It seems the answer is "No."[18] A search of the mainstream newspapers included throughout this volume reveal that only the *Chicago Tribune* ran a (online) story on Belafonte's comments at the Image Awards—but left out the quote and discussion of celebrity radicalism to solely focus on his line regarding gun violence.[19] Further not even NBC, the network on which Belafonte levied this dissent, made space in their news programming to cover or consider it.

Thus, Belafonte's public plea for more black celebrity intervention in politics and the discussion of inequality by black stars online suggest that even as spaces increase for the expression of black celebrity dissent, traditional news media remains necessary for introducing and legitimizing this dissent in the mainstream public sphere. Given the proliferation of media spaces and types that serve very niche audiences and the attention scarcity that has intensified with it, we must consider if in fact instances of black celebrity dissent in the future will reach the wide audiences it did in the twentieth century or if nuanced conversations about this dissent will be segregated into spaces with even smaller self-selected audiences than the traditional black press once served.

Considering that Kanye West's 2005 dissent received less than half the mainstream coverage of most other cases examined in this volume, and considering the lack of attention paid by traditional, and still powerful, media to celebrity interventions into highly contentious political and social debates in the decade since then, future scholarship must consider if the "post-racial" America celebrated in the second decade of the twenty-first century has perhaps adapted the most successful, and implicit, limitation on celebrity dissent yet—inattention. Journalists and celebrities wishing to continue the counterdiscursive tradition of the black public sphere must develop methods for not only using the new spaces available to them in the twenty-first century but also demanding mainstream recognition.

NOTES

1. James Baldwin, *Autobiographical Notes* (New York: AA Knopf, 1953).
2. Theodore G. Vincent, *Voices of a Black Nation: Political Journalism in the Harlem Renaissance* (Palo Alto, CA: Ramparts Press, 1973): 15.
3. Shanto Iyengar, *Is Anyone Responsible?: How Television Frames Political Issues* (Chicago: University of Chicago Press, 2001); William A. Gamson and Andre Modigliani, "The Changing Culture of Affirmative Action," in *Equal Employment Opportunity: Labor Market Discrimination and Public Policy*, ed. Paul Burstein (New York: Walter D. Gruyter, Inc., 1994); Tali Mendelberg, *The Race Card: Campaign Strategy, Implicit Messages and the Norm of Equality* (Princeton, NJ: Princeton University Press, 2001); Thomas Nelson, Rosalee Clawson, and Zoe Oxley, "Media Framing of a Civil Liberties Conflict and Its Effect on Tolerance," *American Political Science Review* 91, no. 3 (Sep. 1997): 567–583; Donald Kinder and Lynn Sanders, *Divided by Color* (Chicago: University of Chicago Press, 1996); Robert Entman and Andrew Rojecki, *The Black Image in the White Mind: Media and Race in America* (Chicago: University of Chicago Press, 2000).
4. As previously noted, many of these frames overlapped in their appearance within each press as is most apparent in the primary frames offered in black press coverage of Tommie Smith and John Carlos, as well as the coverage of Sister Souljah.
5. Amy Bass, *Not the Triumph but the Struggle: The 1968 Olympics and the Making of the Black Athlete* (Minneapolis: University of Minnesota Press, 2002): 314.
6. Catherine Squires, "Rethinking the Black Public Sphere: An Alternative Vocabulary for Multiple Spheres," *Communication Theory* 12, no. 4 (Nov. 2002): 446–468; Robert Asen and Daniel C. Brouwer, "Reconfigurations of the Public Sphere," in *Counterpublics and the State* (New York: State University of New York Press, 2001): 1–32; Houston A. Baker Jr., "Critical Memory and the Black Public Sphere," *Public Culture* 7, no. 3 (1994): 3–33.
7. Ronald Jacobs, *Race, Media and the Crisis of Civil Society: From Watts to Rodney King* (Cambridge: University Press Cambridge, 2000); Todd Vogel, ed., *The Black Press: New Literary and Historical Essays* (New Brunswick, NJ: Rutgers University Press, 2001).
8. Dan Berger, "Constructing Crime, Framing Disaster," *Punishment & Society* 11, no. 4 (2009): 491–520; Stephen Caliendo and Charlton McIlwain, "Minority Candidates, Media Frames and Racial Cues in the 2004 Election," *The Harvard International Journal of Press Politics* 11, no. 4 (2006): 1–25; Ronald Jackson II, *Scripting the Black Masculine Body: Identity, Discourse, and Racial Politics in Popular Media*. (Albany: The State University of New York Press, 2006); Entman and Rojecki, *The Black Image;* Mendelberg, *The Race Card.*

9. Pamela Newkirk, *Within the Veil: Black Journalists, White Media* (New York: New York University Press, 2000).
10. In an incredibly telling illustration of how celebrities, and raced celebrities in particular, continue to be delegitimized in some political narratives, John McCain's 2008 presidential campaign launched a series of attack ads and talking points labeling Obama a celebrity and positing very clearly that being a celebrity *and* a political leader were antithetical to one another. It is of course no coincidence that in the ongoing era of enlightened racism, which with Obama's election became frequently hailed as "post-racial," many critics of a black presidential candidate felt the best way to undermine his legitimacy was to locate him as part of popular culture trends that have, for decades, been one of the only spaces in the U.S. where blackness is visible, black culture is profitable, and black bodies can be safely consumed. Yet, as Douglas Kellner points out, it was exactly the opportunities that Obama's mainstream construction as a celebrity opened up that helped him toward a decisive victory over McCain. Douglas Kellner, "Barack Obama and Celebrity Spectacle," *International Journal of Communication* 3 (2009): 715–741; Robert Draper, "The Making (and Remaking) of McCain," *The New York Times*, Oct. 22, 2008, www.nytimes.com/2008/10/26/magazine/26mccain-t.html (accessed Dec. 12, 2013).
11. Lisa Guerrero, "One nation under a Hoop: Race, Meritocracy, and Messiahs in the NBA," in *Commodified and Criminalized: New Racism and African Americans in Contemporary Sports*, ed. David J. Leonard and C. Richard King (Lanham, MD: Rowman & Littlefield Publishers, Inc. 2011): 121–146.
12. Jamelle Hill, "The Heat's Hoodies as Change Agent," *ESPN*, Mar. 26, 2012, http://espn.go.com/nba/truehoop/miamiheat/story/_/id/7728618/miami-heat-don-hoodies-response-death-teen-trayvon-martin (accessed Dec. 12, 2013).
13. Ahmir "Questlove" Thompson, "Questlove: Trayvon Martin and I Ain't Shit," *New York Magazine,* Jul. 16, 2013, http://nymag.com/daily/intelligencer/2013/07/questlove-trayvon-martin-and-i-aint-shit.html (accessed Dec. 12, 2013).
14. Dhiraj Murthy, "Twitter: Microphone for the Masses?" *Media Culture and Society* 33, no. 5 (2011): 779; Summer Harlow and Thomas J. Johnson, "Overthrowing the Protest Paradigm? How The New York Times, Global Voices and Twitter Covered the Egyptian Revolution," *International Journal of Communication* 5 (2011): 1359–1374.
15. "The 44th NAACP Image Awards," NAACP Hollywood Bureau and NBC Studios, Feb. 1, 2013.
16. Ibid.
17. James E. Wright, "NAACP Image Awards: Harry Belafonte Speaks on Gun Control in Acceptance Speech," YouTube, Feb. 1, 2013, www.youtube.com/watch?v = T-ZRo5ws44I (accessed Dec. 12, 2013).
18. In a telling comparison of the public's engagement with YouTube alone, the video of Belafonte's comments at the Image Awards stands at just over thirty-eight thousand views at the writing of this volume, while the much more recent (and racially problematic) performance of pop star Miley Cyrus at the 2013 Video Music Awards has been viewed over sixteen million times.
19. Nicola Groom, "Actress Kerry Washington Wins Big at NAACP Image Awards," *Chicago Tribune,* Feb. 1, 2013, http://articles.chicagotribune.com/2013–02–01/entertainment/sns-rt-us-usa-naacp-awardsbre911034–20130201_1_special-award-naacp-image-awards-movie-award (accessed Dec. 11, 2013). The *Los Angeles Times*' entertainment blog included a short photo essay on the event that pictured Belafonte but made no mention of his comments ("44th NAACP Image Awards Photo Booth," Feb. 1, 2013, www.latimes.com/entertainment/news/la-et-en-44th-naacp-image-awards-photo-booth-024,0,6442018.photo#axzz2nD1i30a7 [accessed Dec. 12, 2013]).

Appendix

Appendix Table 1 Sources, Dates, and Number of Stories Examined by Subject

	Paul Robeson 8/27/49 – 10/13/49*	Eartha Kitt 1/19/68 – 3/19/68	Smith & Carlos 10/16/68 – 12/16/68	Sister Souljah 5/13/92 – 7/13/92	Abdul-Rauf 3/12/96 – 5/12/96	Kanye West 9/2/05 – 11/2/05
Mainstream Press	The New York Times, Chicago Tribune, Los Angeles Times, Time, Newsweek n = 102	The New York Times, The Washington Post, Chicago Tribune, Los Angeles Times, Time, Newsweek n = 72	The New York Times, Chicago Tribune, Los Angeles Times, Time, Newsweek n = 84	The New York Times, The Washington Post, Los Angeles Times, Time, Newsweek n = 143	The New York Times, Los Angeles Times, Denver Post, Time, Newsweek n = 126	The New York Times, Chicago Tribune, Los Angeles Times, Time, Newsweek n = 42
Black Press	New York Amsterdam News, Chicago Defender, Los Angeles Sentinel, Negro Digest, Ebony n = 34	New York Amsterdam News, Washington Informer, Chicago Defender, Los Angeles Sentinel, Pittsburgh Courier, Negro Digest, Ebony n = 29	New York Amsterdam News, Chicago Defender, Los Angeles, Sentinel, Negro Digest, Ebony n = 26	New York Amsterdam News, Washington Informer, Los Angeles Sentinel, Jet, Essence, Ebony n = 29	New York Amsterdam News, Los Angeles Sentinel, Denver Urban Spectrum, Jet, Ebony n = 7	New York Amsterdam News, Chicago Defender, Los Angeles Sentinel, Jet, Ebony n = 10
Total Stories	N = 136	N = 101	N = 110	N = 172	N = 133	N = 52

Note: Sources were selected for each case based on both the importance of including flagship publications from each press and publications based in the locations most relevant to understandings of the celebrity in question and the topic of her/his dissent.

*Because there were two riots at Peekskill, and Robeson's dissent about them took place both after the first and second, I have included a date range that incorporates the beginning of these events through two months after the second riot.

Bibliography

"17 Protestors Back Eartha in LBJ's Church." *Chicago Tribune*, Jan. 22, 1968: 11.
"The 44th NAACP Image Awards." *NAACP Hollywood Bureau and NBC Studios*, Feb. 1, 2013.
"44th NAACP Image Awards Photo Booth." *Los Angeles Times*, Feb 1, 2013. www.latimes.com/entertainment/news/la-et-en-44th-naacp-image-awards-photo-booth-024,0,6442018.photo#axzz2nD1i30a7 (accessed Dec. 11, 2013).
"50 Women in a Room." *New Pittsburgh Courier (1966–1981)*, Feb. 3, 1968. ProQuest (accessed Dec. 1, 2013).
"100 Most Memorable Moments in TV History." *TV Guide*, Jun. 29, 1996.
"5000 Riot as Veterans Protest Robeson Concert." *Los Angeles Times*, Aug. 28, 1949.
"Abdul-Rauf Tells Why He'll Stand." *USA Today*, March 15, 1996. LexisNexis Academic (accessed Nov. 26, 2010).
"Ask Dewey Quiz of Robeson Riot." *The Chicago Defender (National Edition) (1921–1967)*, Sep. 3, 1949: 1. ProQuest (accessed Dec. 1, 2013).
"At White House Luncheon: Eartha Kitt's Tirade on War Leaves First Lady in Tears." *Los Angeles Times*, Jan. 19, 1968.
"Bill Clinton's Dilemma." *Los Angeles Sentinel*, Jul. 9, 1992: A6. ProQuest (accessed March 7, 2014).
"'Black Athlete—' A Book." *New York Amsterdam News (1962–1993)*, Oct. 26, 1968. ProQuest (accessed Dec. 1, 2013).
"Black-Fist Display Gets Varied Reaction in Olympic Village." *Los Angeles Times*, Oct.18, 1968.
"Blame Cops in Riot." *New York Amsterdam News (1943–1961)*, Sep. 10, 1949. ProQuest (accessed Dec. 1, 2013).
"Boston Gets into the Act Again." *The Modesto Bee and News-Herald*, Sep. 26, 1967: A15.
"Communists: Picnic at Peekskill." *Time*, Sep. 5, 1949. http://content.time.com/time/magazine/article/0,9171,933865,00.html (accessed Mar. 5, 2010).
"A Concert for Hurricane Relief." NBC, Sep. 2, 2005.
"Confusion, Shock Grip U.S. Squad after Pair Ousted." *Los Angeles Times*, Oct. 19, 1968.
"Council Advises Public to Avoid Robeson Show." *Los Angeles Times*, Sep. 20, 1949: 1
"Cross-Burnings Planned by Klan in Red Crusade." *Los Angeles Times*, Sep. 4, 1949: 7.
"Desecration of Mosque Defiles All Faiths." *Denver Post*, Mar. 22, 1996: B6. LexisNexis (accessed March 7, 2014).
"Dewey Orders Grand Jury Probe of Riot at Robeson Concert." *Chicago Daily Tribune (1923–1963)*, Sep. 15, 1949. ProQuest (accessed Dec. 1, 2013).

180 Bibliography

"Disc Jockeys Will Apologize for Mosque Incident." *The New York Times,* Mar. 30, 1996. *LexisNexis Academic* (accessed March 7, 2014).
"Double Standard?" *Chicago Tribune (1963–Current File),* Nov. 15, 1968. *ProQuest* (accessed Dec. 1, 2013).
"Down to Eartha." *The Washington Post,* Jan. 20 1968, A10.
"Eartha Kitt Denounces War Policy to Mrs. Johnson." *The New York Times (1923–Current File),* Jan. 19, 1968. *ProQuest* (accessed Dec. 1, 2013).
"Eartha Kitt's Outburst." *Chicago Daily Defender,* Jan. 23, 1968: 13. *ProQuest* (accessed March 7, 2014).
"Eartha's Shouts Stun Lady Bird into Tears." *Chicago Tribune (1963–Current File),* Jan. 19, 1968. *ProQuest* (accessed Dec. 1, 2013).
"Eartha Was Right, Dr. King Contends." *Chicago Daily Defender,* Jan. 22, 1968: 2. *ProQuest* (accessed March 7, 2014).
"Editorial Cartoon 1—No Title." *Chicago Daily Defender (Big Weekend Edition) (1966–1973),* Oct. 26, 1968. *ProQuest* (accessed Dec. 1, 2013).
"Editorials." *New York Amsterdam News (1962–1993),* Jan. 27, 1968. *ProQuest* (accessed Dec. 1, 2013).
"Editorials: Abdul-Rauf's Selective Objection Doesn't Meet Religious Tests." *Denver Post,* Mar. 14, 1996: B10. *LexisNexis Academic* (accessed March 7, 2014).
"From the Heart of Eartha Kitt." *The New York Times (1923–Current File),* Jan. 20, 1968. *ProQuest* (accessed Dec. 1, 2013).
"Gov. Clinton's Remarks." *The Washington Post,* Jun. 16, 1992: A20.
"Grand Jury Probes Robeson Riot." *New York Amsterdam News (1943–1961),* Sep. 17, 1949. *ProQuest* (accessed Dec. 1, 2013).
"Hold the Beef." *Chicago Tribune,* Sep. 14, 2005. http://articles.chicagotribune.com/2005-09-14/news/0509140348_1_usher-false-claims-relief-efforts (accessed March 7, 2014).
"I Didn't Plan to Rap U.S." *Chicago Daily Defender (Daily Edition) (1960–1973),* Jan. 23, 1968. *ProQuest* (accessed Dec. 1, 2013).
"In Her Own Disputed Words: Transcript of Interview That Spawned Souljah's Story." *The Washington Post,* Jun. 16, 1992: A7. *LexisNexis Academic* (accessed March 7, 2014).
"Inquiring Photographer." *Chicago Daily Defender (Daily Edition) (1960–1973),* Jan. 31, 1968. *ProQuest* (accessed Dec. 1, 2013).
"Islamic Leaders: Standing for Anthem a Matter of Conscience." *Los Angeles Sentinel,* Mar. 21, 1996: B2. *ProQuest* (accessed March 14, 2014).
"The Issue Is Respect; And Elsewhere?" *The New York Times,* Mar. 24, 1996. www.lexisnexis.com/hottopics/lnacademic (accessed Nov. 26, 2013).
"The Issue Is Respect; Lest We Forget." *The New York Times,* Mar. 24, 1996. www.lexisnexis.com/hottopics/lnacademic (accessed Nov. 26, 2013).
"The Issue Is Respect; Respect, Part 2." *The New York Times,* Mar. 24, 1996. www.lexisnexis.com/hottopics/lnacademic (accessed Nov. 26, 2013).
"The Issue Is Respect; Respect, Part 3." *The New York Times,* Mar. 24, 1996. www.lexisnexis.com/hottopics/lnacademic (accessed Nov. 26, 2013).
"The Issue Is Respect; Why Not Sit?" *The New York Times,* Mar. 24, 1996. www.lexisnexis.com/hottopics/lnacademic (accessed Nov. 26, 2013).
"Johnson Church Ousts War Foes." *The New York Times,* Jan. 22, 1968: 3. *ProQuest* (accessed March 14, 2014).
"Johnson's Pastor Sends Apology for Eartha Kitt Tirade." *Los Angeles Tribune,* Jan. 20, 1968.
"KABC's Allin Slate: White Man Backs Smith and Carlos." *Los Angeles Sentinel,* Nov. 7, 1968.
"Kanye Sticks to the Script." *Chicago Tribune,* Sep. 8, 2005. http://articles.chicagotribune.com/2005-09-08/news/0509080387_1_george-bush-doesn-t-care-concert-sticks (accessed Nov. 23, 2013).

"Kanye West Gives the Most Humble and Self-Effacing Interview of His Career: JK! 'Ye Is Still Gloriously Arrogant in 'New York Times' Q&A." *Spin*, Jun. 12, 2013. www.spin.com/articles/kanye-west-new-york-times-interview-caramanica-yeezus/ (accessed Dec. 9, 2013).
"Keino Faints at Jubilant Nairobi Fete." *Los Angeles Times*, Oct. 31, 1968.
" 'The Land of the Free?' " *Newsweek*, April 15, 1996. www.lexisnexis.com/hottopics/lnacademic (accessed Nov. 26, 2013).
"Legion, V.F.W. Urge Members to Ignore Robeson's Concerts." *Chicago Daily Tribune (1923–1963)*, Sep. 14, 1949. *ProQuest* (accessed Dec. 1, 2013).
"Letters to the Post." *Denver Post*, Mar. 31, 1996: F2. *LexisNexis Academic* (accessed March 7, 2014).
"Letters: Sep. 19, 2005." *Time*, Sep. 19, 2005. http://content.time.com/time/magazine/article/0,9171,1103596,00.html (accessed Nov. 25, 2013).
"Life on Roller Coaster." *Los Angeles Sentinel*, Oct. 24, 1968.
"Mahmoud Abdul-Rauf: A Very Private Person in the Spotlight." *Los Angeles Sentinel*, Mar. 21, 1996: B2. *ProQuest* (accessed March 7, 2014).
"Matt Lauer Reports." NBC, Nov. 8, 2010.
"Mills Proud of Carlos and Smith." *Los Angeles Sentinel*, Oct. 24, 1968.
"Mrs. Johnson Sorry Furor Obscured Other Ideas." *The New York Times (1923–Current File)*, Jan. 20, 1968. *ProQuest (*accessed Dec. 1, 2013).
"National Hotline: Capital Divided on Eartha Kitt Rhubarb." *Los Angeles Sentinel*, Feb. 1, 1968.
"National Newspaper Publishers Association." NNPA. www.nnpa.org (accessed Jul. 8, 2010).
"The Natural Right of Being a Slob." *Chicago Tribune*, Oct. 19, 1968: 10. *ProQuest* (accessed March 7, 2014).
"New Group Organizes to Fight Reds." *Los Angeles Times*, Sep. 23, 1949.
"Newspapers: The Chicago Defender." PBS. www.pbs.org/blackpress/news_bios/defender.html (accessed Sep. 29, 2010).
"New York." *The New York Times (1923–Current File)*, Sep. 11, 1949. *ProQuest* (accessed Dec. 1, 2013).
"Nuggets Not in the Mahmoud: Abdul-Rauf Can Lead Team in a Silent Prayer." Pike's Peek, *Denver Post*, Mar. 17, 1996.
"The Olympics: Black Complaint." *Time*, Oct. 25, 1968. http://content.time.com/time/magazine/article/0,9171,900397,00.html (accessed Apr. 15, 2010).
"The Olympics' Extra Heat." *Newsweek*, Oct. 28, 1968: 74–80.
"Olympic Show—Press Interview." *Chicago Tribune (1963–Current File)*, Oct. 23, 1968.*ProQuest* (accessed March 7, 2014).
"Party Affiliation." Gallup. http://www.gallup.com/poll/15370/party-affiliation.aspx (accessed Oct. 18, 2010).
"Passion and Politesse." *Newsweek*. Feb. 12, 1968.
"The Peekskill Riot." *New York Amsterdam News (1943–1961)*, Sep. 17, 1949. *ProQuest* (accessed Dec. 1, 2013).
"Photo-Editorial: Olympic Retrospective." *Ebony*, Dec. 1968: 160–161.
"Presidential Approval Ratings—George W. Bush." Gallup. www.gallup.com/poll/116500/presidential-approval-ratings-george-bush.aspx (accessed Oct. 18, 2010).
"A Puzzled Olajuwon Speaks Out on Citizenship." *The New York Times (1923–Current File)*, Mar. 14, 1996: B19. *ProQuest* (accessed March 7, 2014).
"Racial Display at the Olympics." *Los Angeles Times*, Oct. 24, 1968.
"The Right to Assemble." *The New York Times*, Sep. 4, 1949: 74. *ProQuest* (accessed March 7, 2014).
"Riots: Robeson Ruckus." *Newsweek*, Sep. 12, 1949: 23.
"The Riot That Interests Gov. Dewey." *Chicago Daily Tribune (1923–1963)*, Sep. 3, 1949. *ProQuest* (accessed Dec. 1, 2013).

182 Bibliography

"Robeson Forces Well Organized for Outbreaks." *Chicago Daily Tribune (1923–1963)*, Sep. 6, 1949. ProQuest (accessed Dec. 1, 2013).

"Robeson Launches Boycott." *New York Amsterdam News (1943–1961)*, Sep. 3, 1949. ProQuest (accessed Dec. 1, 2013).

"Robeson Wife Rips Bias at Mexican Meet." *New York Amsterdam News (1943–1961)*, Sep. 17, 1949. ProQuest (accessed Dec. 1, 2013).

"Robeson's Talks—Not Songs—Annoy Eleanor." *Los Angeles Times*, Sep. 1, 1949.

"Roundup Interview on the Subject of Peekskill . . ." *New York Amsterdam News (1943–1961)*, Sep. 3, 1949. ProQuest (accessed Dec. 1, 2013).

"Scores Hurt in Robeson Riot; Battle Halted by State Police." *Los Angeles Times*, Sep. 5, 1949.

"The Second Coming of Reverend Run." *The New York Times (1923–Current File)*, Oct. 9, 2005. ProQuest (accessed Dec. 1, 2013).

"'Silent Protest' at Olympics." *Chicago Tribune (1963–Current File)*, Oct. 23, 1968. ProQuest (accessed March 7, 2014).

"Sister Souljah Is No Willie Horton." *The New York Times (1923–Current File)*, Jun. 17, 1992. ProQuest (accessed Dec. 1, 2013).

"Sister Souljah to Keynote Malcolm X Celebration." *Washington Informer*, May 20, 1992: 1.

"Sister Souljah's Call to Arms." *The Washington Post*, May 23, 1992: A29. Lexis-Nexis Academic (accessed March 7, 2014).

"Six Indicted in Robeson Rioting." *New York Amsterdam News (1943–1961)*, Sep. 24, 1949. ProQuest (accessed Dec. 1, 2013).

"Smith, Carlos in Flight from 'Mean' Reporters." *Los Angeles Times*, Oct. 22, 1968.

"Sport: Records All Around." *Time*, Oct. 25, 1968. http://content.time.com/time/magazine/article/0,9171,900399,00.html (accessed Apr. 15, 2010).

"Spreading the U.S. Gospel Elsewhere." *New York Amsterdam News (1962–1993)*, Oct. 26, 1968. ProQuest (accessed Dec. 1, 2013).

"State Police Data on Robeson Drawn." *The New York Times (1923–Current File)*, Sep. 11, 1949. ProQuest (accessed Dec. 1, 2013).

"Star-Spangled Coercion." *The New York Times*, Mar. 15, 1996. www.lexisnexis.com/hottopics/lnacademic (accessed Nov. 26, 2013).

"Taxpayers Get the Bill for Robeson's Concert, Plus Riot." *Chicago Daily Tribune (1923–1963)*, Sep. 14, 1949. ProQuest (accessed Dec. 1, 2013).

"That Robeson Riot." *The Chicago Defender (National Edition) (1921–1967)*, Sep. 10, 1949. ProQuest (accessed Dec. 1, 2013).

"A Travelling Riot?" *Los Angeles Times*, Sep. 13, 1949: A4.

"Truman, Mrs. FDR Hit Robeson Riot." *The Chicago Defender (National Edition) (1921–1967)*, Sep. 17, 1949. ProQuest (accessed Dec. 1, 2013).

"Two Vets in Critical Condition Following Paul Robeson Rioting." *Los Angeles Sentinel*, Sep. 8, 1949: A8.

"U.S. Apologizes for Athletes 'Discourtesy.'" *Los Angeles Times*, Oct. 18, 1968.

"U.S. Women Dedicate Victory to Smith, Carlos." *The New York Times (1923–Current File)*, Oct. 21, 1968. ProQuest (accessed Dec. 1, 2013).

"Vantage Point: Clinton's Attack on Sister Souljah, Insult to Jackson, Is an Affront to Black Voters and Progressives." *Los Angeles Sentinel*, Jun. 25, 1992.

"We All Live in Glass Houses." *Los Angeles Sentinel*, Sep. 15, 2005. ProQuest (accessed Nov. 28, 2013).

"Yo! MTV Unwrapped." *Spin*, Sep. 1991.

Aldridge, Cathy W. "The Ladies and Eartha: Pro-Con." *New York Amsterdam News (1962–1993)*, Jan. 27, 1968. ProQuest (accessed Dec. 1, 2013).

———. "PS." *New York Amsterdam News*, Jan. 27, 1968: 7. ProQuest (accessed March 7, 2014).

Alsultany, Evelyn. "Selling American Diversity and Muslim American Identity through Nonprofit Advertising Post-9/11." *American Quarterly* 59, no. 3 (2007): 593–622.
Alter, Jonathan. "The Other America." *Newsweek*, Sep. 19, 2005: 42. *LexisNexis Academic* (accessed March 7, 2014).
Amdur, Neil. "Davenport Gains Seventh Track Gold Medal for U.S. in Winning Hurdles." *The New York Times*, Oct. 18, 1968: 54. *ProQuest* (accessed March 7, 2014).
Apple, R. W. Jr. "The 1992 Campaign: Democrats; Jackson Sees a 'Character Flaw' in Clinton's Remarks on Racism." *The New York Times (1923–Current File)*, Jun. 19, 1992. *ProQuest* (accessed Dec. 1, 2013).
Araton, Harvey. "Sports of the Times; An Issue of Religion and Respect." *The New York Times*, Mar. 14, 1996. www.nytimes.com/1996/03/14/sports/sports-of-the-times-an-issue-of-religion-and-respect.html (accessed Feb. 25, 2014).
Asen, Robert, and Daniel C. Brouwer, eds. "Reconfigurations of the Public Sphere." In *Counterpublics and the State*. New York: State University of New York Press, 2001: 1–34.
Associated Press. "80,000 Watch Olympics End on Happy Note." *Los Angeles Times*, Oct. 28, 1968.
———. "Black-Fist Display Gets Varied Reaction in Olympic Village." *Los Angeles Times*, Oct.18, 1968.
———. "Pro Basketball: NBA Suspends Rauf." *The New York Times*, Mar. 13, 1996: 15. *LexisNexis Academic* (accessed March 7, 2014).
Aurthur, Kate. ". . . But No More Politics." *New York Times (1923–Current File)*, Sep. 8, 2005. *ProQuest* (accessed Nov. 23, 2013).
Baker, Aaron. *Contesting Identities: Sports in American Film*. Champaign: University of Illinois Press, 2003.
Baker, Houston A. Jr. "Critical Memory and the Black Public Sphere." *Public Culture* 7, no. 3 (1994): 3–33.
Baker, Russell. "Back from the Dead." *The New York Times (1923–Current File)*, Jun. 23, 1992. *ProQuest* (accessed Dec. 1, 2013).
Baker, William A. "Hard-Core Haters." *The New York Times (1923–Current File)*, Jul. 1, 1992. *ProQuest* (accessed Dec. 1, 2013).
Baldwin, James. *Autobiographical Notes*. New York: AA Knopf, 1953.
Balz, Dan. "Clinton Says Jackson Is Rewriting History; Candidate Reacts to Remarks in Controversy Concerning Rap Singer Sister Souljah." *The Washington Post*, Jun. 20, 1992: A11. *LexisNexis Academic* (accessed March 7, 2014).
Bass, Amy. *Not the Triumph but the Struggle: The 1968 Olympics and the Making of the Black Athlete*. Minneapolis: University of Minnesota Press, 2002.
Beeching, Barbara J. "Paul Robeson and the Black Press: The 1950 Passport Controversy." *The Journal of African American History* 87 (2002): 339–354.
Bernstein, Alina, and Neil Blain, eds. *Sport, Media, Culture: Global and Local Dimensions*. New York: Routledge, 2003.
Black, J. R. "Clinton's Attacks on Sister Souljah Are Misleading." *New York Amsterdam News (1962–1993)*, Jul. 4, 1992. *ProQuest* (accessed Dec. 1, 2013).
Black, Joseph. "Letter to the Editor 1—No Title." *Los Angeles Sentinel*, Sep. 15, 1949.
Blackwell, Joyce. *No Peace Without Freedom: Race and the Women's International League for Peace and Freedom, 1915-1975*. Carbondale: Southern Illinois University Press, 2004.
Bloice, Carl. "Big Demonstration Planned for Democratic Convention." *New York Amsterdam News (1962–1993)*, Jun. 27, 1992. *ProQuest* (accessed Dec. 1, 2013).

———. "Clinton Drops a Bomb beneath the Rainbow Sign." *New York Amsterdam News (1962–1993)*, Jun. 20, 1992. *ProQuest* (accessed Dec. 1, 2013).
Bohler, Father Lewis P. Jr. "Readers Comment on Issues." *Los Angeles Sentinel*, Jan 25, 1968.
Bonilla-Silva, Eduardo. *Racism without Racists: Colorblind Racism and the Persistence of Racial Inequality in America*. Lanham, MD: Rowman and Littlefield, 2006.
———. *White Supremacy and Racism in the Post-Civil Rights Era*. Boulder, CO: Lynne Reinner Publishers, Inc., 2001.
Booth, Michael. "Is Loyalty Dead?" *Denver Post*, Mar. 17, 1996: A1. *LexisNexis Academic* (accessed March 7, 2014).
Boucher, Geoff. "Celebs or Saviors: Kanye West a Critic with Cred." *Los Angeles Times*, Sep. 9, 2005.
Boyd, Todd. *The New H.N.I.C. (Head Nigga in Charge): The Death of Civil Rights and the Reign of Hip Hop*. New York: New York University Press, 2003.
Braxton, Greg. "Cover Story: The Voices of Rap—Politics or Just Music?" *Los Angeles Times*, Jun. 19, 1992. http://articles.latimes.com/1992-07-19/entertainment/ca-4407_1_rap-music (accessed March 7, 2014).
Brinkley, Douglas. *The Great Deluge: Hurricane Katrina, New Orleans, and the Mississippi Gulf Coast*. New York: Morrow, 2006.
Broder, David S. "Clinton's Gamble with Jesse Jackson." *The Washington Post*, Jun. 17, 1992: A25. *LexisNexis Academic* (accessed March 7, 2014).
Broder, David S., and Thomas B. Edsall. "Clinton Finds Biracial Support for Criticism of Rap Singer." *The Washington Post*, Jun. 16, 1992: A7. *LexisNexis Academic* (accessed March 7, 2014).
Brown, Al. "Autopsy Not Pretty." *Los Angeles Sentinel*, Apr. 4, 1996. *ProQuest* (accessed Dec. 1, 2013).
Brown, Earl. "Press Propaganda." *New York Amsterdam News (1943–1961)*, Sep. 10, 1949. *ProQuest* (accessed Dec. 1, 2013).
———. "Violence American Style." *New York Amsterdam News (1943–1961)*, Sep. 17, 1949. *ProQuest* (accessed Dec. 1, 2013).
Brown, Eleanor. "Clinton and Sister Souljah." *Los Angeles Sentinel*, Jul. 2, 1992.
Browne, J. Zamgba. "Rangel, Rivera Say Clinton Insulted Jesse and the Rainbow." *New York Amsterdam News (1962–1993)*, Jun. 20, 1992. *ProQuest* (accessed Dec. 1, 2013).
Burnett, John. "What Happened on New Orleans' Danziger Bridge?" *All Things Considered*, NPR, Sep. 12, 2006. www.npr.org/templates/story/story.php?storyId=6063982 (accessed Feb. 25, 2014).
Busby, Helen L. "Seagren Example Cited." *The New York Times*, Oct. 27, 1968: S2. *ProQuest* (accessed March 7, 2014).
Berger, Dan. "Constructing crime, framing disaster." *Punishment & Society* 11, no. 4 (2009): 491–520.
Butler, Judith. "Endangered/Endangering: Schematic Racism and White Paranoia." In *Reading Rodney King/Reading Urban Uprising*, edited by Robert Gooding-Williams, 15–22. New York: Routledge, 1993.
Caliendo, Stephen, and Charlton McIlwain. "Minority Candidates, Media Frames and Racial Cues in the 2004 Election." *The Harvard International Journal of Press Politics* 11, no. 4 (2006): 1–25.
Caramanica, Joe. "The Visionaries: Behind Kanye's Mask." *The New York Times*, Jun. 11, 2013.
Carlos, John, and Dave Zirin. *The John Carlos Story: The Sports Moment That Changed the World*. Chicago: Haymarket Books, 2011.
Carpenter, Liz. *First Lady's Luncheon for Women Doers*. White House Social Files, Jan. 18, 1968: 5–6.

Carsley, William E. "Athletes Who Care and Those Who Don't." *Chicago Tribune (1963–Current File)*, Oct. 25, 1968. *ProQuest* (accessed Dec. 1, 2013).
CBS Morning News. "Sports Report." Mar. 13, 1996.
Chang, Jeff. *Can't Stop Won't Stop: A History of the Hip-Hop Generation*. New York: Picador, St. Martin's Press, 2005.
Cherokee, Charley. "National Grapevine." *The Chicago Defender (National Edition) (1921–1967)*, Sep. 24, 1949. *ProQuest* (accessed Dec. 1, 2013).
Christian, Margena A. "Black Leaders Sound Off: Did Race Delay Relief to Disaster Areas?" *Jet*, Sep. 26, 2005. www.lexisnexis.com/hottopics/lnacademic (accessed Nov. 28, 2013).
Cleaver, Jim. "Kleaver's Klippings: Far Too Much Ado about Nothing." *Los Angeles Sentinel*, Jul. 2, 1992.
Clemmons, Montoya. "Denver Nugget Finds Solace in Islam." *The Urban Spectrum*, Mar. 1996.
———. "Religious Diversity Unifies Team." *The Urban Spectrum*, Mar. 1996.
Coates, Ta-nehisi. "Fear of a Black President." *Atlantic Monthly (10727825)* 310, no. 2 (Sep. 2012): 76–90.
Cockburn, Alexander. "All Hail the Party of Total Decay: It's Not Too Late for the Left to Run a Fourth Candidate against Clinton's Hollow Platform." *Los Angeles Times*, Jul. 12, 1992. http://articles.latimes.com/1992-07-12/opinion/op-4069_1_democratic-party (accessed Dec. 1, 2013).
———. "The Stupidity of Believing in Nothing: Clinton's Utterly Calculated Slap at Jesse Jackson Cost Him Many Votes and Gained None." *Los Angeles Times*, Jun. 22, 1992. http://articles.latimes.com/1992-06-22/local/me-512_1_jesse-jackson (accessed Dec. 1, 2013).
Cohen, Richard. "Racist Rappings of Sister Souljah." *The Washington Post*, May 15, 1992. www.lexisnexis.com/hottopics/lnacademic (accessed Nov. 26, 2013).
———. "The Rap on Jesse Jackson." *The Washington Post*, Jun. 23, 1992: A21. *LexisNexis Academic* (accessed Nov. 26, 2013).
———. "Sister Souljah: Clinton's Gumption . . ." *The Washington Post*, Jun. 16, 1992: A21. *LexisNexis Academic* (accessed Nov. 26, 2013).
Collins, Patricia Hill. *Black Feminist Thought: Knowledge, Consciousness, and the Politics of Empowerment*. New York: Routledge, 2000.
Condon, David. "In the Wake of the News." *Chicago Tribune*, Oct. 28, 1968: C1. *ProQuest* (accessed March 7, 2014).
Crenshaw, Kimberlé, and Gary Peller. "Real Time/Real Justice." In *Reading Rodney King/Reading Urban Uprising*, edited by Robert Gooding-Williams, 56–70. New York: Routledge, 1993.
Cromelin, Richard. "TV Fundraisers Focus on Storm Victims Instead of Politics." *Los Angeles Times*, Sep. 10, 2005. http://articles.latimes.com/2005/sep/10/entertainment/et-pop10 (accessed Nov. 23, 2013).
Culver, Virginia. "Faiths Unite in Outrage over Mosque Defilement." *Denver Post*, Mar. 22, 1996: A1. *LexisNexis Academic* (accessed March 7, 2014).
Dagbovie, Sika A. "Star-Light, Star-Bright, Star Damn Near White: Mixed Race Superstars." *Journal of Popular Culture* 40, no. 2 (2001): 217–237.
Daley, Arthur. "The Incident." *The New York Times (1923–Current File)*, Oct. 20, 1968. *ProQuest* (accessed Dec. 1, 2013).
Datrooth, Diggs. "National Hotline." *Chicago Daily Defender (Big Weekend Edition) (1966–1973)*, Feb. 3, 1968. *ProQuest* (accessed Dec. 1, 2013).
Deford, Frank. "Of Stars and Stripes." *Newsweek*, Mar. 25, 1996: 64.
Denisoff, R. Serge. "Folk Music and the American Left: A Generational Ideological Comparison." *The British Journal of Sociology* 20, no. 4 (Dec. 1969): 427–442.
———. "The Religious Roots of the American Song of Persuasion." *Western Folklore* 29, no. 3 (Jul. 1970): 175–84.

Diamos, Jason. "Abdul-Rauf Is Calm in Face of Controversy." *The New York Times,* Mar. 21, 1996: B9. *LexisNexis Academic* (accessed March 7, 2014).
———. "Abdul-Rauf Vows Not to Back Down from the N.B.A." *The New York Times,* Mar. 14, 1996: B13. *LexisNexis Academic* (accessed March 7, 2014).
———. "Basketball; Abdul-Rauf's Plan: Stand, Pray and Play." *The New York Times,* Mar. 15, 1996. www.lexisnexis.com/hottopics/lnacademic (accessed Nov. 26, 2013.)
Dickinson, Hunt T., G. R. McLaughlin, D. A. L., Larry Wanamaker, et al. "White House Luncheon." Voice of the People. *Chicago Tribune (1963–Current File),* Jan. 24, 1968. *ProQuest* (accessed Dec. 1, 2013).
Dorinson, Joseph, and William A. Pencak, eds. *Paul Robeson: Essays on His Life and Legacy.* Jefferson, NC: McFarland & Company, Inc., 2002.
Draper, Robert. "The Making (and Remaking) of McCain." *The New York Times,* Oct. 22, 2008. www.nytimes.com/2008/10/26/magazine/26mccain-t.html (accessed Feb. 25, 2014).
Druckman, James. "On the Limits of Framing Effects: Who Can Frame?" *The Journal of Politics* 63, no. 4 (2001): 1041–1066.
Duberman, Martin B. *Paul Robeson: A Biography.* New York: Ballantine Books, 1988.
Dudziak, Mary L. *Cold War Civil Rights: Race and the Image of American Democracy.* Princeton, NJ: Princeton University Press, 2002.
Duke, Lynne. "Souljah's Meaning, Refracted through Racial Prism: Rapper's Post-Riot Words on Killing Whites Are Subject of Wildly Different Interpretations." *The Washington Post,* Jun. 22, 1992.
Dyson, Michael Eric. *Come Hell or High Water: Hurricane Katrina and the Color of Disaster.* New York: Basic Books, 2007.
Early, Gerald. "The Black Intellectual and the Sport of Prizefighting." *Kenyon Review* 10, no. 3 (1988): 102.
Edsall, Thomas B. "Clinton Stuns Rainbow Coalition; Candidate Criticizes Rap Singer's Message." *The Washington Post,* Jun. 14, 1992: A1. *LexisNexis Academic* (accessed March 7, 2014).
Edwards, Harry. *The Revolt of the Black Athlete.* New York: Free Press, 1969.
Egan, Leo. "Dewey Asks Report on Robeson Battle." *The New York Times (1923–Current File)* Aug. 30, 1949. *ProQuest* (accessed Dec. 1, 2013).
———."Governor Orders Grand Jury Study of Robeson Rioting." *The New York Times (1923–Current File),* Sep. 15, 1949. *ProQuest* (accessed Dec. 1, 2013).
Entman, Robert. "Framing: Toward Clarification of a Fractured Paradigm." *Journal of Communication* 43, no. 4 (1993): 51–58.
———. "Modern Racism and the Images of Blacks in Local Television News." *Critical Studies in Media Communication* 7, no. 4 (1990): 332–345.
Entman, Robert M., and Andrew Rojecki. *The Black Image in the White Mind: Media and Race in America.* Chicago: University of Chicago Press, 2000.
Essed, Philomena, and David Theo Goldberg, eds. *Race Critical Theories.* Malden, MA: Wiley-Blackwell, 2000.
Estes, William. "U.S. Olympic Star Tardy but Get's Hero's Welcome." *Los Angeles Times,* Nov. 5, 1968.
Farred, Grant. *What's My Name?: Black Vernacular Intellectuals.* Minneapolis: University of Minnesota Press, 2003.
Fast, Howard. "Remembering Peekskill USA, 1949." In *Paul Robeson: Essays on His Life and Legacy,* edited by Joseph Dorinson and William A. Pencak, 130–144. Jefferson, NC: McFarland & Company, Inc., 2002.
Feagin, Joe, Vera, Hernán, and Batur, Pinar. *White Racism.* New York: Routledge, 2001.

Fields, A. N. "Akers and Fields See Eye to Eye on Robeson." *The Chicago Defender (National Edition) (1921–1967)*, Sep. 24, 1949. ProQuest (accessed Dec. 1, 2013).

Foster, Chris. "Pros Can't Escape the Glare." *Los Angeles Times*, Mar. 19, 1996.

Fraser, Nancy. "Rethinking the Public Sphere: A Contribution to the Critique of Actually Existing Democracy." In *Habermas and the Public Sphere*, edited by Craig Calhoun. Cambridge, MA: Massachusetts Institute of Technology Press, 1992.

Frei, Terry. "Mahmoud Abdul-Rauf's Short-Lived Stand against Standing for the Anthem Cause for a . . . Flashback." *Denver Post*, Mar. 24, 1996: C4. LexisNexis Academic (accessed March 7, 2014).

Fulwood, Sam III. "92 Democratic Convention: Jordan's Words Seen as a Shock to Blacks." *Los Angeles Times*, Jul. 16, 1992.

———. "Clinton Carves New Strategy with Double-Edged Sword." *Los Angeles Times*, Jun. 16, 1992.

———. "Clinton Chides Rap Singer, Stuns Jackson." *Los Angeles Times*, Jun. 14, 1992.

———. "New Barbs Fly in Clinton-Jackson Feud: Democrats: Risk Arises That Squabble, Which Began with Remarks about Rap Singer, Will Intrude on Party Convention." *Los Angeles Times*, Jun. 20 1992.

Gamson, William A., and Andre Modigliani, "The Changing Culture of Affirmative Action." In *Equal Employment Opportunity: Labor Market Discrimination and Public Policy*, edited by Paul Burstein. New York: Walter D. Gruyter, Inc., 1994.

Gans, Herbert, J. *Democracy and the News*. New York: Oxford University Press, 2003.

Gavin, Alice. "Reading Katrina: Race, Space and an Unnatural Disaster." *New Political Science*, 30, no. 3 (2008): 325–346.

George, Bill. "Oh, Say Can You See the Argument Here?" *Los Angeles Times*, Mar. 16, 1996.

George, Nelson. *Post-Soul Nation: The Explosive, Contradictory, Triumphant and Tragic 1980s as Experienced by African Americans*. New York: Penguin Books, 2004.

Gilliam, Dorothy. "Clinton's Low Blow to Black Aspirations." *The Washington Post*, Jun. 17, 1992.

Gilroy, Paul. "The End of Antiracism." In *Race Critical Theories*, edited by Philomena Essed and David Theo Goldberg. Malden, MA: Wiley-Blackwell, 2001: 249–264.

Gitlin, Todd. *The Whole World Is Watching: Mass Media in the Making & Unmaking of the New Left*. Berkeley: University of California Press, 1980.

Godonoo, Prosper. "Paul Robeson: Honor & the Politics of Dignity." In *Reconstructing Fame*, edited by David C. Ogden and Joel Nathan Rosen, 48–66. Jackson: University Press of Mississippi, 2008.

Gold, Matea, and Chris Lee. "Kibosh on Telethon Artist Comments?" *Los Angeles Times*, Sep. 9, 2005. http://articles.latimes.com/2005/sep/09/entertainment/et-telethon9 (accessed Nov. 23, 2013).

Gold, Matea, and Scott Collins. "NBC Deletes Rap Star's Remarks on Telethon." *Los Angeles Times*, Sep. 4, 2005. http://articles.latimes.com/2005/sep/04/nation/na-telethon4 (accessed Nov. 23, 2013).

Gooding-Williams, Robert. *Reading Rodney King/Reading Urban Uprising*. New York: Routledge, 1993.

Gray, Herman. *Cultural Moves: African Americans and the Politics of Representation*. Berkeley: University of California Press, 2005.

Griffin, Booker. "Olympic Exclusive: Some Untold Tales of Mexico City." *Los Angeles Sentinel*, Oct. 24, 1968.

Griffin, John G. "Black Power Bows at the Olympics." *Chicago Daily Defender (Big Weekend Edition) (1966–1973)*, Oct. 19, 1968. ProQuest (accessed Dec. 1, 2013).

Groom, Nicola. "Actress Kerry Washington Wins Big at NAACP Image Awards." *Chicago Tribune*, Feb. 1, 2013. http://articles.chicagotribune.com/2013-02-01/entertainment/sns-rt-us-usa-naacp-awardsbre911034-20130201_1_special-award-naacp-image-awards-movie-award (accessed Dec. 11, 2013).

Guerrero, Lisa. "One Nation under a Hoop: Race, Meritocracy, and Messiahs in the NBA." In *Commodified and Criminalized: New Racism and African Americans in Contemporary Sports*, edited by David J. Leonard and C. Richard King. Lanham, MD: Rowman & Littlefield Publishers, Inc. 2011: 121–146.

Gunewardena, Nandini, and Mark Schuller, eds. *Capitalizing on Catastrophe: Neoliberal Strategies in Disaster Reconstruction*. Walnut Creek, CA: AltaMira Press, 2008.

Haber, Joyce. "Los Angeles Fete for Vidal Sassoon." *Los Angeles Times*, Jan. 22, 1968: C21.

Habermas, Jürgen. *The Structural Transformation of the Public Sphere: An Inquiry into a Category of Bourgeois Society*. Translated by Thomas Burger and Frederick Lawrence. Cambridge: Massachusetts Institute of Technology Press, 1989.

Haggins, Bambi. *Laughing Mad: The Black Comic Persona in Post-Soul America*. New Brunswick, NJ: Rutgers University Press, 2007.

Hall, John. "Foreman's Fan Club." *Los Angeles Times*, Nov. 6, 1968.

Hall, Stuart. "Encoding/Decoding." In *Culture, Media, Language*, edited by Stuart Hall, Dorothy Hobson, Andrew Lowe, and Paul Willis. London: Hutchinson & Co. Ltd, 1980: 128–138.

———. *Representation: Cultural Representations and Signifying Practices*. London: Sage Publications, Inc., 1997.

———. "The Whites of Their Eyes: Racist Ideologies and the Media." In *Gender, Race, and Class in Media*, edited by Gail Dines and Jean M. Humez, 89–93. Thousand Oaks, CA: Sage Publications, Inc., 1981.

Hancock, Dean Gordon B. "Between the Lines." *Los Angeles Sentinel*, Sep. 29, 1949: A8.

Hargreaves, John. "Globalisation Theory, Global Sport, and Nations and Nationalism." In *Power Games*, edited by John Sugden and Alan Tomlinson, 25–43. New York: Routledge, 2002.

Harlow, Summer, and Thomas J. Johnson. "Overthrowing the Protest Paradigm? How The New York Times, Global Voices and Twitter Covered the Egyptian Revolution." *International Journal of Communication* 5 (2011): 1359–1374.

Harris-Lacewell, Melissa. *Barbershops, Bibles, and BET: Everyday Thought and Black Political Thought*. Princeton, NJ: Princeton University Press, 2004.

Hartmann, Douglas. "Bound by Blackness or Above It?: Michael Jordan and the Paradoxes of Post-Civil Rights American Race Relations." In *Out of the Shadows: A Biographical History of African American Athletes*, edited by David K. Wiggins, 301–323. Fayetteville: University of Arkansas Press, 2006.

———. *Race, Culture, and the Revolt of the Black Athlete: The 1968 Olympic Protests and Their Aftermath*. Chicago: The University of Chicago Press, 2003.

Hathaway, Maggie. "Tee Time." *Los Angeles Sentinel*, Jan. 25, 1968: B4

Hauser, Thomas. *Muhammad Ali: His Life and Times*. New York: Touchstone, 1999.

Heisler, Mark. "Top Pro Prospects Run Hot, Cool." *Los Angeles Times*, Mar. 17, 1996.

Helem, John A. "Take Ten." *Chicago Daily Defender (Big Weekend Edition) (1966–1973)*, Oct. 26, 1968. ProQuest (accessed Dec. 1, 2013).

Hersh, Seymour. "C.I.A. in '68 Gave Secret Service a Report Containing Gossip about Eartha Kitt after White House Incident." *The New York Times (1923–Current File)*, Jan. 3, 1975. *ProQuest* (accessed Dec. 1, 2013).
Higgs, Robert. *God in the Stadium: Sports and Religion in America*. Lexington: The University Press of Kentucky, 1995.
Higgs, Robert., and Michael, Braswell. *An Unholy Alliance: The Sacred and Modern Sports*. Macon, GA: Mercer University Press, 2004.
Hilburn, Robert. "He's Energizing and Enthralling: Kanye West Puts the 'New' Back in Concerts as He Opens His U.S. Tour in Florida." *Los Angeles Times*, Oct. 13, 2005.
———. "Too Much of a Good Thing?" *Los Angeles Times*, Sep. 12, 2005. http://articles.latimes.com/2005/sep/12/entertainment/et-critics12 (accessed Nov. 24, 2013).
Hill, Jamelle. "The Heat's Hoodies as Change Agent," *ESPN*, Mar. 26, 2012, http://espn.go.com/nba/truehoop/miamiheat/story/_/id/7728618/miami-heat-don-hoodies-response-death-teen-trayvon-martin (accessed Feb. 26, 2014).
Hill, Urla. "Racing after Smith and Carlos: Revisiting Those Fists Some Forty Years Hence." In *Reconstructing Fame: Sport, Race, and Evolving Reputations*, edited by David C. Ogden and Joel Nathan Rosen, 102–126. Jackson: University Press of Mississippi, 2008.
Hoberman, John. *Darwin's Athletes: How Sport Has Damaged Black America and Preserved the Myth of Race*. New York: Houghton Mifflin Company, 1997.
Hochman, Steve. "Kanye West Continues His Rap on Bush." *Los Angeles Times*, Sep. 12, 2005.
Hodges, Jim. "N.B.A. Sits Abdul-Rauf for Stance on Anthem." *Los Angeles Times*, Mar. 13, 1996.
Hodges, Jim, and Larry B. Stammer. "NBA and Abdul-Rauf Are Standing Firm; Pro Basketball: Area Islamic Leaders Disagree with Nuggets' Guard for Decision on Anthem." *Los Angeles Times*, Mar. 14, 1996.
Hoffer, Richard. *Something in the Air: American Passion and Defiance in the 1968 Mexico City Olympics*. New York: Free Press, 2009.
Hopper, Hedda. "Looking at Hollywood." *Chicago Daily Tribune (1923–1963)*, Sep. 8, 1949. *ProQuest* (accessed Dec. 1, 2013).
Horne, Gerald. "Comrades and Friends: The Personal/Political World of Paul Robeson." In *Paul Robeson: Artist and Citizen*, edited by Jeffrey C. Stewart. New Brunswick, NJ: Rutgers University Press, 1998.
Hughes, Langston. "World's Most Exciting Singer Poses Questions of Art, Politics, Race." *The Chicago Defender (National Edition) (1921–1967)*, Sep. 24, 1949. *ProQuest* (accessed Dec. 1, 2013).
Ifill, Gwen. "Clinton Stands by Remark on Rapper." *The New York Times (1923–Current File)*, Jun. 15, 1992. *ProQuest* (accessed Dec. 1, 2013).
———. "Clinton at Jackson Meeting: Warmth, and Some Friction." *The New York Times (1923–Current File)*, Jun. 14, 1992. *ProQuest* (accessed Dec. 1, 2013).
———. "For Clinton, Attention Grows, Problems Remain." *The New York Times (1923–Current file)*, Jun. 21, 1992. ProQuest (accessed Dec. 1, 2013).
Irwin, Donald M. "Smith, Carlos Receive Praise and Blame for Stance at Olympic Fete." *Los Angeles Times*, Oct. 24, 1968.
Ishiwata, Eric. "'We Are Seeing People We Didn't Know Exist': Katrina and the Neoliberal Erasure of Race." In *The Neoliberal Deluge: Hurricane Katrina, Late Capitalism, and the Remaking of New Orleans*, edited by Cedric Johnson, 32–59. Minneapolis: University of Minnesota Press, 2011.
Iyengar, Shanto. *Is Anyone Responsible? How Television Frames Political Issues*. Chicago: University of Chicago Press, 2001.

Jackson, Ronald II. *Scripting the Black Masculine Body: Identity, Discourse, and Racial Politics in Popular Media*. Albany: The State University of New York Press, 2006.

Jackson, Sarah J. "Hurricanes Don't Care about Black People: Hurricane Katrina, Racial Inequality and News Media Response." MA thesis, University of Michigan, 2007.

Jacobs, Ronald. *Race, Media and the Crisis of Civil Society: From Watts to Rodney King*. Cambridge: University Press Cambridge, 2000.

Jensen, Klaus Bruhn., ed. *A Handbook of Media and Communication Research: Qualitative and Quantitative Methodologies*. London: Routledge, 2002.

Jhally, Sut, and Justin Lewis. *Enlightened Racism: The Cosby Show, Audiences and the Myth of the American Dream*. Boulder, CO: Westview Press, Inc., 1992.

Johnson, Cedric, ed. *The Neoliberal Deluge: Hurricane Katrina, Late Capitalism, and the Remaking of New Orleans*. Minneapolis: University of Minnesota Press, 2011.

Johnson, Kirk, Dolan, Mark, and Sonnett, John. "Speaking of Looting: An Analysis of Racial Propaganda in National Television Coverage of Hurricane Katrina." *The Howard Journal of Communications* 22 (2011): 302–318.

Johnson, John B. "More Comment on Trouble over Robeson in Peekskill." *New York Amsterdam News (1943–1961)*, Sep. 10, 1949. ProQuest (accessed Dec. 1, 2013).

Johnson, Scott T. Jr. "Indomitable John Akhwari Cited as Symbol of Sports' True Purpose." *Los Angeles Times*, Oct. 28, 1968.

Jones, Charles E. *The Black Panther Party (Reconsidered)*. Baltimore: Black Classic Press, 1998.

Jones, David R. "The Urban Agenda." *New York Amsterdam News (1962–1993)*, Jun. 27, 1992. ProQuest (accessed Dec. 1, 2013).

Jordan, Elfrida. "Moved to Write." *New York Amsterdam News (1962–1993)*, Feb. 10, 1968. ProQuest (accessed Dec. 1, 2013).

Kang, K. Connie. "A Rotating Panel of Experts from the Worlds of Philosophy, Psychology and Religion Offer Their Perspective on the Dilemmas That Come with Living in Southern California." *Los Angeles Times*, Mar. 20, 1996.

Kellner, Douglas. "Barack Obama and Celebrity Spectacle." *International Journal of Communication* 3, (2009): 715–741

Kertzer, David. *Ritual, Politics, & Power*. New Haven: Yale University Press, 1988.

Kim, Claire Jean. "Managing the Racial Breach: Clinton, Black-White Polarization, and the Race Initiative." *Political Science Quarterly* 117, no. 1 (2002): 55–79.

Kinder, Douglas, and Lynn Sanders. *Divided by Color*. Chicago: University of Chicago Press, 1996.

Kish, Zenia. " 'My FEMA People': Hip-Hop as Disaster Recovery in the Katrina Diaspora." *American Quarterly* 61, no. 3 (Sep. 2009): 671–692.

Kiszla, Mark. "Abdul-Rauf: Nuggets' Rebel without a Clue." *Denver Post*, Mar. 14, 1996: D1. *LexisNexis Academic* (accessed March 7, 2014).

———. "Final Verse Near on Nugget." *Denver Post*, Mar. 26, 1996: D1. *LexisNexis Academic* (accessed March 7, 2014).

———. "They Don't Listen to Bickerstaff." *Denver Post*, Apr. 6, 1996: C1. *LexisNexis Academic* (accessed March 7, 2014).

Kitwana, Bakari. *Why White Kids Love Hip Hop: Wankstas, Wiggers, Wannabes, and the New Reality of Race in America*. New York: Basic Books, 2005.

Klein, Joe. "The Jesse Primary." *Newsweek*, Jun. 22, 1992.

Klinkner, Philip A., with Rogers M. Smith. *The Unsteady March: The Rise and Decline of Racial Equality in America*. Chicago: The University of Chicago Press, 1999.

Kneipp, Paul. "Oh, Say Can You See the Argument Here?" *Los Angeles Times*, Mar. 16, 1996.

Knight, Jennifer L., Traci A. Giuliano, and Monica G. Sanchez-Ross. "Famous or Infamous? The Influence of Celebrity Status and Race on Perceptions of Responsibility for Rape." *Basic & Applied Social Psychology* 23, no. 3 (2001): 183–190.

Kramer, Michael. "The Political Interest: The Green-Eyed Monster." *Time*, Jun. 29, 1992. www.time.com/time/printout/0,8816,975892,00.html (accessed Apr. 20, 2010).

Lane, Bill. "The Inside Story." *Los Angeles Sentinel*, Jan. 25, 1968: D2.

Lauter, David. "Clinton Endorsement Avoided by Jackson." *Los Angeles Times*, Jun. 22, 1992.

Leland, John. "Art Born of Outrage in the Internet Age." *The New York Times*, Sep. 25, 2005. www.nytimes.com/2005/09/25/weekinreview/25leland.html?_r=0 (accessed March 7, 2014).

Lewis, Anthony. "Black and White: Perceptions and the Politics of Race." *The New York Times (1923–Current File)*, Jun. 18, 1992. *ProQuest* (accessed Dec. 1, 2013).

Lewis, Carolyn. "Mrs. Johnson Chides Eartha Kitt: 'Shrill Voice' Jars First Lady." *The Washington Post*, Jan. 20, 1968.

Lewis, S. C. "Finger-Point Later." *Chicago Tribune*, Sep. 9, 2005. http://articles.chicagotribune.com/2005-09-09/news/0509090325_1_finger-gulf-coast-cities-wait (accessed Nov. 23, 2013).

Lipsitz, George. *The Possessive Investment in Whiteness: How White People Profit from Identity Politics*. Philadelphia: Temple University Press, 2006.

Lipsyte, Robert. "Athletes Standing Up as They Did Before." *The New York Times*, Mar. 17, 1996: 8. *LexisNexis Academic* (accessed March 7, 2014).

———. "Clay Discusses His Future, Liston and Black Muslims." *The New York Times*, Feb. 27, 1964.

———. "The Morning After." *The New York Times*, Nov. 2, 1968.

———. "The Spirit of the Olympics." *The New York Times*, Aug. 1, 1968.

Love, David Andrew. "When Black Men Try to Leave the Plantation." *New York Amsterdam News*, May 11, 1996. *ProQuest* (accessed Dec. 1, 2013).

Lowry, Brian. "Jimmy Kimmel, Kanye West Parley Twitter 'Feud' into PR." *Variety*, Oct. 10, 2013. http://variety.com/2013/voices/columns/jimmy-kimmel-kanye-west-parlay-twitter-feud-into-pr-1200709142/ (accessed Dec. 9, 2013).

Lucas, Bob. "Tempest at a Tea Party." *Los Angeles Sentinel*, Jan. 25, 1968: A1.

Luck, Adam. "Eartha Kitt's Life Was Scarred by Her Failure to Learn the Identity of Her White Father, Says Daughter." *The Observer*, Oct. 19, 2013. www.theguardian.com/music/2013/oct/19/eartha-kitt-suffered-over-identity (accessed Dec. 11, 2013).

Lusane, Clarence. "Rhapsodic Aspirations: Rap, Race and Power Politics." *The Black Scholar* 23, no. 2 (1993): 37–51.

MacMullan, Jackie. "The NBA." *Sports Illustrated*, Jan. 22, 1996. http://vault.sportsillustrated.cnn.com/vault/article/magazine/MAG1007681/2/index.htm (accessed Dec. 2, 2008).

Maher, Charles. "Smith Case (Continued)." *Los Angeles Times*, Nov. 7, 1968.

———. "Tommie to the Rams?" *Los Angeles Times*, Oct. 31, 1968.

Malamud, Allan. "Notes on a Scorecard." *Los Angeles Times*, Mar. 14, 1996.

Mamdani, Mahmood. *Good Muslim, Bad Muslim, the Cold War, and the Roots of Terror*. New York: Pantheon Books, 2004.

Marable, Manning. *Black Leadership*. New York: Columbia University Press, 1998.

———. "Affirmative Action and the Politics of Race." In *Race Critical Theories*, edited by Philomena Essed and David Theo Goldberg, 344–354. Malden, MA: Wiley-Blackwell, 2001.

Markus, Robert. "Sports Trail: Future of Olympics Worries Wright." *Chicago Tribune,* Nov. 14, 1968.
———. "Sports Trail: WIU Track Coach Man of Principle." *Chicago Tribune,* Nov. 13, 1968.
Marqusee, Mike. *Redemption Song: Muhammad Ali and the Spirit of the Sixties.* New York: Verso, 1999.
Marshall, Gloria A. "Racial Classifications: Popular and Scientific." In *The "Racial" Economy of Science: Toward a Democratic Future,* edited by Sandra Harding, 116–125. Bloomington: Indiana University Press, 1993.
Martel, Ned. "On a Telethon Weekend, Restraint from an Unlikely Source." *The New York Times (1923–Current File),* Sep. 12, 2005. ProQuest (accessed Nov. 25, 2013).
McCallister, Melani. *Epic Encounters: Culture, Media, & U.S. Interests in the Middle East.* Berkeley: University of California Press, 2002.
McCardle, Dorothy. "Mrs. Johnson Cold-Shoulders Heated Protest." *The Washington Post,* Jan. 25, 1968: B1.
McCarthy, Colman. "For Grim Rapper, Hatred Is a Cash Crop." *The Washington Post,* June 23, 1992: C10. www.lexisnexis.com/hottopics/lnacademic (accessed Nov. 26, 2013).
McGrory, Mary. "Backing Jackson into a Corner." *The Washington Post,* Jun. 16, 1992: A2. *LexisNexis Academic* (accessed March 7, 2014).
Mendelberg, Tali. *The Race Card: Campaign Strategy, Implicit Messages and the Norm of Equality.* Princeton, NJ: Princeton University Press, 2001.
Meyer, David, and Joshua Gamson. "The Challenge of Cultural Elites: Celebrities and Social Movements." *Sociological Inquiry* 65, no. 2 (1995): 181–206.
Mezzack, Janet. " 'Without Manners You Are Nothing': Lady Bird Johnson, Eartha Kitt, and the Women Doers' Luncheon of January 18, 1968." *Presidential Studies Quarterly* 20, no. 4 (Fall 1990): 745–760.
Milloy, Courtland. "A Music Rapped in Insincerity." *The Washington Post,* June 28, 1992: B1. www.lexisnexis.com/hottopics/lnacademic (accessed Dec. 1, 2013).
Mills, David. "Sister Souljah's Call to Arms: The Rapper Says Riots Were Payback. Are You Paying Attention?" *The Washington Post,* May 13, 1992. www.washingtonpost.com/wp-dyn/content/article/2010/03/31/AR2010033101709.html (accessed Dec. 1, 2013).
Moore, Jacqueline M. *Booker T. Washington, W.E.B. Du Bois, and the Struggle for Racial Uplift.* Lanham, MD: Rowman & Littlefield Publishers, 2003.
Morgan, Edward P. "The Good, the Bad, and the Forgotten: Media Culture and Public Memory of the Civil Rights Movement." In *Civil Rights Movement in American Memory,* edited by Renee C. Romano and Leigh Raiford, 137–166. Athens: University of Georgia Press, 2006.
Motel, Seth. "Polling Flashback: Remembering RFK." Pew Research Center, Jun. 5, 2013. www.pewresearch.org/fact-tank/2013/06/05/polling-flashback-remembering-rfk (accessed Nov. 12, 2013).
Muhammad, James G. "Hurricane Katrina on Everybody's Mind at Football Classic." *Chicago Defender,* Sep. 5–6, 2005.
Mukherjee, Roopali. *The Racial Order of Things.* Minneapolis: University of Minnesota Press, 2006.
Murray, Jim. "Excuse My Glove." *Los Angeles Times,* Oct. 18, 1968.
———. "The Olympic Games—No Place for a Sportswriter." *Los Angeles Times,* Oct. 20, 1968.
Murthy, Dhiraj. "Twitter: Microphone for the masses?" *Media Culture and Society* 33, no. 5 (2011): 779.
Naber, Nadine. "Ambiguous Insiders: An Investigation of Arab American Invisibility." *Ethnic & Racial Studies* 23, no. 1 (2000): 37–61.

Naison, Mark. "Paul Robeson and the American Labor Movement." In *Paul Robeson: Artist and Citizen,* edited by Jeffrey C. Stewart, 179–194. New Brunswick, NJ: Rutgers University Press, 1998.

Nakayama, Thomas K., and Robert L. Krizek. "Whiteness: A Strategic Rhetoric." *Quarterly Journal of Speech* 81, no. 3 (1995): 291–309.

Name Withheld, "Eartha Kitt." *New York Amsterdam News,* Jan. 27, 1968.

Neal, Mark Anthony. *Soul Babies: Black Popular Culture and the Post-Soul Aesthetic.* New York: Routledge, 2002.

Nelson, Jack. "Democrats Call for National Renewal, Rip Bush, Perot." *Los Angeles Times,* Jul. 14, 1992.

Nelson, Thomas, Rosalee Clawson, and Zoe Oxley. "Media Framing of a Civil Liberties Conflict and Its Effect on Tolerance." *American Political Science Review* 91, no. 3 (Sep. 1997): 567–583.

Newkirk, Pamela. *Within the Veil: Black Journalists, White Media.* New York: New York University Press, 2000.

Nichols, John. "Eartha Kitt: An Anti-War Patriot." *The Nation,* Dec. 26, 2008. www.thenation.com/blog/eartha-kitt-anti-war-patriot (accessed Dec. 1, 2013).

———. "Eartha Kitt: The Patriot Who Was Right All Along." *Chicago Tribune,* Dec. 29, 2008. http://articles.chicagotribune.com/2008-12-29/news/0812280062_1_first-lady-eartha-kitt-lady-bird-johnson (accessed Dec. 1, 2013).

Nigatu, Heben. "In Defense of Kanye's Vanity: The Politics of Black Self-Love," *Buzzfeed,* Jun. 20, 2013. www.buzzfeed.com/hnigatu/in-defense-of-kanyes-vanity-the-politics-of-black-self-love (accessed Dec. 9, 2013).

Nostro, Lauren. "Two Kids Spoof Kanye West's Interview with Zane Lowe on 'Jimmy Kimmel Live.'" *Complex Music,* Sep. 25, 2013. www.complex.com/music/2013/09/kimmel-spoofs-kanye-interview (accessed Dec. 9, 2013).

O'Connell, Barry. "Whose Land and Music Shall Ours Be? Reflections on the History of Protest in the Southern Mountains." *Appalachian Journal* 12, no. 1 (Fall 1984): 18–30.

Ogden, David C., and Joel Nathan Rosen. *Reconstructing Fame: Sport, Race, and Evolving Reputations.* Jackson: The University Press of Mississippi, 2008.

Okrand, Fred. "NBA Rules and the National Anthem." *Los Angeles Times,* Mar. 24, 1996.

Omi, Michael, and Howard, Winant. "Racial Formation." In *Race Critical Theories,* edited by Philomena Essed and David Theo Goldberg, 123–145. Malden, MA: Wiley-Blackwell, 2001.

Ortiz, Edwin. "Here's Pt. 1 of Kanye West's Interview with Zane Lowe." *Complex Music,* Sep. 23, 2013. www.complex.com/music/2013/09/kanye-west-zane-lowe-interview-part-1 (accessed Dec. 11, 2013).

Paige, Woody. "Abdul-Rauf Has a Right Not to Stand." *Denver Post,* Mar. 13, 1996: D1. *LexisNexis Academic* (accessed March 7, 2014).

———. "Rauf Takes a Lame Exit." *Denver Post,* Mar. 29, 1996: C1. *LexisNexis Academic* (accessed March 7, 2014).

———. "Seven-Point Plan for Resurrection." *Denver Post,* Apr. 22, 1996: C1. *LexisNexis Academic* (accessed March 7, 2014).

Pareles, Jon. "Pop View: Dissing the Rappers Is Fodder for the Sound Bite." *The New York Times,* June 28, 1992. www.lexisnexis.com/hottopics/lnacademic (accessed Nov. 26, 2013).

Parker, William T. "Rap Artists and Racism." *Los Angeles Times,* Jul. 13, 1992.

Payne, Ethel L. "Eartha Kitt Turns It on at D.C. Luncheon." *New Pittsburgh Courier (1966–1981),* Jan. 27, 1968. *ProQuest* (accessed Dec. 1, 2013).

———. "The Inside Story of the 'Pussycat.'" *Chicago Daily Defender (Daily Edition) (1960–1973),* Jan. 22, 1968. *ProQuest (accessed December 9, 2013).*

Peabody, Alvin. "Clinton, Blacks Squaring off as Campaign Heats Up." *Washington Informer,* Jun. 24, 1992.

Peer, Limor, and James S. Ettema. "The Mayor's Race: Campaign Coverage and the Discourse of Race in America's Three Largest Cities." *Critical Studies in Media Communication* 15, no. 3 (1998): 255–278.

Perry, Imani. *Prophets of the Hood: Politics and Poetics in Hip Hop*. Durham: Duke University Press, 2004.

Phillips, Joseph C. "A Government That Cares." *Chicago Defender*, Sep. 16–18, 2005: 13.

———. "Government That Cares—Part Two." *Chicago Defender*, Sep. 22, 2005: 12.

Piliawsky, Monte. "Racism or Realpolitik? The Clinton Administration and African-Americans." *The Black Scholar* 24, no. 2 (1994): 2–10.

Porter, Chuck. "What Angeleno Women Think of Eartha Kitt's 'Outburst.'" *Los Angeles Sentinel*, Jan. 25, 1968: 7A.

Post Office. "Nuggets Need New Coach Not a Purge of Their Roster." *The Denver Post*, May 6, 1996: C3. *LexisNexis Academic* (accessed March 7, 2014).

Powell, Shaun. *Souled Out?: How Blacks Are Winning and Losing in Sports*. Champaign, IL: Human Kinetics, 2008.

Pryce, Vinette K. "Sister Souljah Raps Dems and Clinton." *New York Amsterdam News (1962–1993)*, Jun. 20, 1992. *ProQuest* (accessed Dec. 1, 2013).

———. "Sister Souljah Visits the AmNews." *New York Amsterdam News (1962–1993)*, Jul. 11, 1992. *ProQuest* (accessed Dec. 1, 2013).

Pye, Brad, Jr. "A Beautiful Black Demonstration." *Los Angeles Sentinel*, Oct. 24, 1968.

———. "Quiet and Loud Protests." *Los Angeles Times*, Oct. 24, 1968.

Quindlen, Anna. "Public & Private; All of These You Are." *The New York Times*, June 28, 1992. www.lexisnexis.com/hottopics/lnacademic (accessed Nov. 26, 2013).

Rayner, Hazel O. B. "Eartha Kitt." *New York Amsterdam News (1962–1993)*, Mar. 9, 1968. http://ezproxy.neu.edu/login?url=http://search.proquest.com?url=http://search.proquest.com/docview/226589585?accountid=12826 (accessed Dec. 1, 2013).

Reese, Stephen D. "The Framing Project: A Bridging Model for Media Research Revisited." *Journal of Communication* 57, no. 1 (2007): 148–154, doi: 10.1111/j.1460-2466.2006.00334.x.

Remnick, David. *King of the World: Muhammad Ali and the Rise of an American Hero*. New York: Random House, 1998.

Reyes, Damaso. "Hip-Hop Stars Speak Out on Katrina," *New York Amsterdam News*, Sep. 8–14, 2005

Rhodes, Jane. *Framing the Black Panthers: The Spectacular Rise of a Black Power Icon*. New York: New Press, 2007.

Richards, Ronald O. "Oh, Say Can You See the Argument Here?" *Los Angeles Times*, Mar. 16, 1996.

Robertson, Linda. "News Coverage of Post-Katrina New Orleans and the 2008 Midwest Floods." In *The Neoliberal Deluge: Hurricane Katrina, Late Capitalism, and the Remaking of New Orleans*, edited by Cedric Johnson, 269–299. Minneapolis: University of Minnesota Press, 2011.

Rolark, Calvin. "Clinton's Sister Souljah Rap." *Washington Informer*, Jun. 24, 1992.

Romano, Renee C., and Leigh Raiford, ed. *The Civil Rights Movement in American Memory*. Athens: University of Georgia Press, 2006.

Rose, Tricia. *The Hip Hop Wars: What We Talk about When We Talk about Hip Hop—and Why It Matters*. New York: Basic Books, 2008.

Rosen, Mike. "Dissing the Flag." *Denver Post*, Mar. 22, 1996.

Rosenthal, A. M. "Jesse Jackson's Enemy." *The New York Times (1923–Current File)*, Jun. 23, 1992. *ProQuest* (accessed Dec. 1, 2013).

Rule, Sheila. "Rapper, Chided by Clinton, Calls Him a Hypocrite." *The New York Times (1923–Current File)*, Jun. 17, 1992.*ProQuest* (accessed Dec. 1, 2013).
Rutten, Tim. "Politicians Sow Double Standards on Race." *Los Angeles Times*, Jul. 9, 1992.
Sage, George. *Power and Ideology in American Sport: A Critical Perspective*. Champaign, IL: Human Kinetics, 1998.
Samad, A. Asadullah. "Between the Lines; America Got Us Lookin Real Crazy Right Now." *Los Angeles Sentinel*, Sep. 2005. *ProQuest* (accessed Dec. 1, 2013).
Sanchez, Robert. "The Conversion of Chris Jackson." *5280 Magazine*, Oct. 2007. www.5280.com/magazine/2007/10/conversion-chris-jackson (accessed March 7, 2014).
Sanneh, Kelefa. "Pop/Jazz." *The New York Times (1923–Current File)*, Sep. 18, 2005. http://ezproxy.neu.edu/login?url=http://search.proquest.com?url=http://search.proquest.com/docview/93025006?accountid=12826 (accessed Dec. 1, 2013).
Schatzman, Dennis. "Motorcycle Cop Removed from Streets after Fatal Shooting." *Los Angeles Sentinel*, Jul. 9, 1992.
Scheufele, Dietram. "Framing as a Theory of Media Effects." *Journal of Communication* 49, no. 1 (1999): 103–122.
Schmalz, Jeffrey. "Midwest: Fertile Region for Politics of Disgust." *The New York Times (1923–Current File)*, Jul. 1, 1992. *ProQuest* (accessed Dec. 1, 2013).
Schroder, Kim C. "Discourses of Fact." In *Handbook of Media and Communication Research: Qualitative and Quantitative Methodologies*, edited by Klaus Bruhn Jensen, 116. London: Routledge, 2002.
Schwartz, Maralee, and E. J. Dionne Jr. "Clinton Tells Municipal Workers He'd Cut Federal Jobs, Not Theirs." *The Washington Post*, Jun. 18, 1992.
Semati, Mehdi. "Islamophobia, Culture and Race in the Age of Empire." *Cultural Studies* 24, no. 2 (2010): 256–275.
Sengstacke, John H. "Olympic Blacks' Nonsense." *Chicago Daily Defender (Big Weekend Edition) (1966–1973)*, Oct. 26, 1968. *ProQuest* (accessed Dec. 1, 2013).
Shah, Hemant. "Legitimizing Neglect: Race and Rationality in Conservative News Commentary about Hurricane Katrina." *The Howard Journal of Communications* 20 (2009): 1–17.
Shaheen, Jack. *Reel Bad Arabs: How Hollywood Vilifies a People*. New York: Olive Branch Press, 2001.
Sheehan, Joseph M. "2 Black Power Advocates Ousted from Olympics." *The New York Times*, Oct. 19, 1968.
Shelton, Elizabeth. "Miss Peden: 'Outburst a Disgrace.'" *The Washington Post*, Jan. 23, 1968.
Simmons, Sylvia. "Pulse of New York's Public." *New York Amsterdam News (1962–1993)*, Feb. 24, 1968. *ProQuest* (accessed Dec. 1, 2013).
Simpson, Kevin. "Oh, Say, Can You See . . . The Decline of Manners?" *The Denver Post*, Mar. 14, 1996.
Sinclair, Abiola. "Media Watch: Clinton, Jackson, Souljah and You." *New York Amsterdam News (1962–1993)*, Jul. 4, 1992. *ProQuest* (accessed Dec. 1, 2013).
Smith, Jackie, John McCarthy, Clark McPhail, and Boguslaw Augustyn. "From Protest to Agenda Building: Description Bias in Media Coverage of Protest Events in Washington, DC." *Social Forces* 79, no. 4 (2001): 1397–1423.
Smith, Marie. "Eartha Kitt Confronts the Johnsons: Startled First Lady Responds to Singer's Attack on War." *The Washington Post*, Jan. 19, 1968.
Smith, Robert C. *We Have No Leaders: African Americans in the Post–Civil Rights Era*. Albany: SUNY Press, 1996.

Smith, Tommie, and David Steele. *Silent Gesture: The Autobiography of Tommie Smith*. Philadelphia: Temple University Press, 2007.

Snel, Alan. "Students Speak Out on Issue." *The Denver Post*, Mar. 14, 1996.

Sommers, Samuel R., Evan P. Apfelbaum, Kristin N. Dukes, Negin Toosi, and Elsie J. Wang. "Race and Media Coverage of Hurricane Katrina: Analysis, Implications, and Future Research Questions." *Analysis of Social Issues and Public Policy* 6, no. 1 (2006): 39–55.

Souljah, Sister. "Killing Me Softly: Deadly Code of Silence." Recorded with Ice Cube. In *360 Degrees of Power*, Epic Records, 1992.

Span, Paula. "The Nine Lives of Eartha Kitt; At 71, the Singer Is Still Landing on Her Feet." *The Washington Post*, Dec. 31, 1998.

Spencer, Gil. "United We Stand, Sometimes." *Denver Post*, Mar. 24, 1996.

Spivey, Donald. *Sport in America: New Historical Perspectives*. Westport, CT: Greenwood Press, 1985.

Spohrer, Erika. "Becoming Extra-Textual: Celebrity Discourse and Paul Robeson's Political Transformation." *Critical Studies in Media Communication* 24, no. 2 (2007): 151–168.

Squires, Catherine. *African Americans in the Media*. Cambridge and New York: Polity Press, 2009.

———. "The Black Press and the State: Attracting Unwanted(?) Attention." In *Counterpublics and the State*, edited by Robert Asen and Daniel C. Brouwer, 11–136. New York: State University of New York Press, 2001.

———. "Coloring in the Bubble: Perspectives from Black-Oriented Media on the (Latest) Economic Disaster." *American Quarterly* 64, no. 3 (2012): 543–570.

———. *Dispatches from the Colorline: The Press and Multiracial America*. New York: State University of New York Press, 2007.

———. "Rethinking the Black Public Sphere: An Alternative Vocabulary for Multiple Spheres." *Communication Theory* 12, no. 4 (Nov. 2002): 446–468.

Squires, Catherine, and Sarah J. Jackson. "Reducing Race: News Frames in the 2008 Primaries." *The Harvard International Journal of Press Politics* 15, no. 4 (2010): 375–400.

Stabile, Carole. "No Shelter from the Storm." *South Atlantic Quarterly* 106, no. 4 (2007): 683–708.

———. *White Victims, Black Villains: Gender, Race and Crime News in US Culture*. New York: Routledge, 2006.

Stange, Maren. "Photographs Taken in Everyday Life: *Ebony*'s Photojournalistic Discourse." In *The Black Press: New Literary and Historical Essays*, edited by Todd Vogel, 188–206. Rutgers, NJ: The State University Press, 2001.

Stanley, Alessandra. "A Good-Natured Show in the Shadow of Turbulent Times." *The New York Times (1923–Current File)*, Sep. 19, 2005. ProQuest (accessed Dec. 1, 2013).

Steinfels, Peter. "March 10–16; Anthems, Islam and Basketball." *The New York Times*. www.lexisnexis.com/hottopics/lnacademic (accessed Nov. 26, 2013).

———. "Anthems, Islam and Basketball." *The New York Times*, Mar. 17, 1996.

Stewart, Jeffrey C., ed. *Paul Robeson: Artist and Citizen*. New Brunswick, NJ: Rutgers University Press 1998.

Stewart, Larry. "Angels Add Some Spark to Prime Team." *Los Angeles Times*, Mar. 22, 1996.

Streeter, Caroline A. *Tragic No More: Mixed-Race Women and the Nexus of Sex and Celebrity*. Amherst: University of Massachusetts Press, 2012.

Strickland, William. "After the Verdict." *Essence* (Jul. 1992): 46.

Sugden, John, and Alan Tomlinson, eds. *Power Games: A Critical Sociology of Sport*. New York: Routledge, 2002.

Tenner, Jack. "Let's Take a Look . . . at Quotes and Questions." *Los Angeles Sentinel*, Oct. 24, 1968.
Thompson, Ahmir "Questlove." "Questlove: Trayvon Martin and I Ain't Shit." *New York Magazine*, Jul. 16, 2013. http://nymag.com/daily/intelligencer/2013/07/questlove-trayvon-martin-and-i-aint-shit.html (accessed Feb. 28, 2014).
Tolnay, Stewart E., and E. M. Beck. *A Festival of Violence: An Analysis of Southern Lynchings, 1882–1930*. Champaign: University of Illinois Press, 1995.
Tomlinson, Alan, and Christopher Young. *National Identity and Global Sport Event: Culture, Politics and Spectacle in the Olympics and the Football World Cup*. New York: State University of New York Press, 2006.
Tonkovich, Andrew. "Oh, Say Can You See the Ironies Here?" *Los Angeles Times*, Mar. 24, 1996.
Tribune Wire Service. "Suspend 2 Negro Olympians." *Chicago Tribune*, Oct. 19, 1968.
Tyrangiel, Josh. "Why You Can't Ignore Kanye." *Time*, Aug. 21, 2005. http://content.time.com/time/magazine/article/0,9171,1096499,00.html (accessed Dec. 1, 2013).
Valentino, Nicolas, Vincent Hutchings, and Ismail White. "Cues That Matter: How Political Ads Prime Racial Attitudes During Campaigns." *American Political Science Review* 96, no. 1 (2002): 75–90.
Van Syckle, Katie. "Kanye West's 12 Best Tangents on 'Kimmel.'" *Rolling Stone*, Oct. 10, 2013., www.rollingstone.com/music/videos/kanye-west-and-jimmy-kimmel-make-up-after-spat-20131010 (accessed Dec. 9, 2013).
Vincent, Theodore, G. *Voices of a Black Nation: Political Journalism in the Harlem Renaissance*. Palo Alto, CA: Ramparts Press, 1973.
Vogel, Todd, ed. *The Black Press: New Literary and Historical Essays*. New Brunswick, NJ: Rutgers University Press, 2001.
Walker, Esther G. "Sister Souljah Electrifies Audience at Abyssinian." *New York Amsterdam News*, Jul. 11, 1992.
Walwik, Joseph. "Paul Robeson, Peekskill, and the Red Menace." In *Paul Robeson: Essays on His Life and Legacy*, edited by Joseph Dorinson and William A. Pencak, 120–129. Jefferson, NC: McFarland & Company, Inc., 2002.
Ward, Brian. *Media, Culture, and the Modern African American Freedom Struggle*. Gainesville: University of Florida Press, 2001.
Washburn, Patrick Scott. *The African American Newspaper: Voice of Freedom*. Evanston, IL: Northwestern University Press, 2006.
———. *A Question of Sedition: The Federal Government's Investigation of the Black Press During World War II*. New York: Oxford University Press, 1986.
Watkins, S. Craig. "Framing Protest: News Media Frames of the Million Man March." *Critical Studies in Media Communication* 18, no. 1 (2001): 83–101.
———. *Hip Hop Matters: Politics, Pop Culture, and the Struggle for the Soul of a Movement*. Boston: Beacon Press, 2005.
Weisman, Aly. "The Most Gag-Worthy Quotes from Kanye West's *New York Times* Interview." *Business Insider*, Jun. 12, 2013. www.businessinsider.com/quotes-from-kanye-wests-nyt-interview-2013-6 (accessed Dec. 12, 2013).
West, Cornel. "A Genealogy of Modern Racism." In *Race Critical Theories*, edited by Philomena Essed and David Theo Goldberg, 90–112. Malden, MA: Wiley-Blackwell, 2001. West, Kanye. "Black Skinhead." In *Yeezus*, Roc-a-Fella/Def Jam, 2013.
White, Jack E. "Sister Souljah: Capitalist Tool." *Time*, Jun. 29, 1992. http://content.time.com/time/magazine/article/0,9171,159990,00.html (accessed Nov. 17, 2013).
Whizzer. "Canine Lines." *Chicago Tribune*, Sep. 7, 2005.

Wiggins, Lillian. "A Case of Blatant Discrimination by the Navy." *Washington Informer,* Jul. 1 1992.

———. "Wake Up My Brothers and Sisters." *Washington Informer,* Jun. 24, 1992.

Wilkins, Stan. "The Big Olympic Mistake." *Los Angeles Times,* Nov. 4, 1968.

Wilson, Clint Jr. "No Title." *Los Angeles Sentinel,* Oct. 31, 1968.

———. "Olympic Games' Events Most Disturbing." *Los Angeles Sentinel,* Oct. 24, 1968.

Wilson, Gertrude. "UFT Egos-and Black Athletes." *New York Amsterdam News (1962–1993),* Nov. 2, 1968. http://ezproxy.neu.edu/login?url=http://search.proquest.com?url=http://search.proquest.com/docview/226770839?accountid=12826 (accessed Dec. 1, 2013).

Winant, Howard. *The New Politics of Race: Globalism, Difference, Justice.* Minneapolis: University of Minnesota Press, 2004.

Woodard, Komozi. *A Nation within a Nation: Amiri Baraka (LeRoi Jones) and Black Power Politics.* Chapel-Hill: University of North Carolina Press, 1999.

Wright, James E. "NAACP Image Awards: Harry Belafonte Speaks on Gun Control in Acceptance Speech." YouTube, Feb. 1, 2013. www.youtube.com/watch?v=T-ZRo5ws44I (accessed Dec. 11, 2013).

Yaniz, Tony. "Wrong Priorities." *Chicago Tribune,* Sep. 9, 2005. http://articles.chicagotribune.com/2005–09–09/news/0509100019_1_wrong-priorities-hillary-clinton-wicker-park (accessed Nov. 25, 2013).

Yoshino, Kenji. *Covering: The Hidden Assault on Our Civil Rights.* New York: Random House, 2006.

Young, John. "Who Stands for the Right to Sit?" *The Denver Post,* Mar. 17, 1996.

Yuenger, James. "Lady Bird Calls Eartha's Blast 'Shrill Discord.'" *Chicago Tribune (1963–Current File),* Jan. 20, 1968. ProQuest (accessed Dec. 1, 2013).

Zang, David W. *Sports Wars: Athletes in the Age of Aquarius.* Fayetteville: The University of Arkansas Press, 2001.

Zibart, Eve. "Defending Rap Rights." *The Washington Post,* Jul. 3, 1992. www.lexisnexis.com/hottopics/lnacademic (accessed Dec. 1, 2013).

Index

2 Live Crew 111n19

ABC 150
Abdul-Rauf, Mahmoud 13, 116, 150, 158; in African American press 129–33, 167; backlash against 117–18, 134; comparisons to other dissenters 120–2; and Denver Nuggets 116–17; and Islam 116, 119–120, 125, 127–8, 129–31, 133, 168; in mainstream press 120–9, 133–4, 166–7; post-Nuggets career 117–18; and Tourette's syndrome 122
ACLU (American Civil Liberties Union) 128
Adams, Carol 152
affirmative action 91
African American Freedom Struggle 12–13, 19n65, 58
African American press 1, 7–8; censorship of 8, 22, 134; and Bill Clinton 104–6; conservatism in 8, 152–4, 158, 164n77; as counterpublic 6–8, 169–70; coverage of inequality in 132, 156–7, 166–7, 170; debates within 8, 40, 79, 82, 95, 152, 163n53, 166, 173; decline of 96, 111n28, 118, 135, 170; framing trends regarding black celebrity dissent 166–71; history of 7–8, 22; ideological diversity within 34, 79, 95, 157; media criticism by 7, 39, 60, 78, 103, 156, 170; and religious discourse 58, 83–4, 129–31; and respectability politics 55, 95, 152, 154; and truth-telling ethic 56–8, 82–4, 131, 133, 154; and uplift ideologies 79–82, 152–6; white journalists in 85–6
African American veterans 21; as Paul Robeson security 23, 30
Aldridge, Cathy 58, 61
Ali, Muhammad 5, 9–12, 59, 68, 121; and 1996 Atlanta Olympic Games 120; African American press coverage of 11; backlash against 10–11, 121; mainstream framing of 10–11; and Nation of Islam 10–11, 120; and Sonny Liston 10; and Vietnam War 10
Alter, Jonathan 146
alternative public sphere *see* counterpublics
Amateur Athlete 72
Amdur, Neil 73
American Dream 3, 40, 116, 171
American Legion 36
anti-Semitism 22, 23, 27, 37, 107
Araton, Harvey 128
Associated Press 21, 72, 75

Baker, Houston: critical memory of black public sphere 133
Baker, Russell 101
Balz, Dan 101
Banner, David 148
Bass, Amy 67, 119, 124, 169
Batman (television series) 49
Beamon, Bob 73, 80
Belafonte, Harry 53, 172–3
Billboard charts 91, 140–1
Bill of Rights *see* U.S. Constitution

Birth of a Nation 99
black celebrities 1, 4–5, 9, 12, 165, 168–70; agency of 5, 9, 12–14, 36, 102, 108, 130, 146, 148, 159–60, 165; commodification of 20, 123–4, 126, 144–7, 159; conditions for acceptance 1, 21, 50, 146, 168–9; and crossing over 20; economic and cultural capital of 48, 140, 169; role in public debates 5, 8–9, 12, 95, 171; use of social media 171–2
black masculinity: in black conservatism 153; and sport 125; stereotypes of 73–4
Black Muslims *see* Nation of Islam
Black Panther Party 75–6, 89n48
black power: and black is beautiful discourse 81; and framing of 1968 Olympic protests 75–76
black press *see* African American press
black public sphere 8, 96, 133, 158–9, 166, 170–4; *see also* public sphere and African American press
Black racism *see* reverse racism
Blackwell, Joyce 59, 64n39
Blanco, Kathleen 143
Booth, Michael 125
Boston, Ralph 80
Boucher, Geoff 147
Braxton, Greg 95
Broder, David S. 101
Brown, Al 132–3
Brown, Earl 35–8
Brown, James 81
Brown, Michael *see* FEMA
Brown v. Board of Education 45
Brundage, Avery 80
Bush Administration *see* George W. Bush
Bush, Barbara 157
Bush, George H. W. 91, 105, 109
Bush, George W. 140–4, 146, 151; *Decision Points* 140
Byrd, Robert 98

Caramanica, Joe 159–60
Carsley, William 78
Carlos, John 13, 67, 99, 108, 120–1, 126, 149–50; in African American press 78–86, 158, 167; backlash against 69, 121–2; celebrity of 70; in mainstream press 70–8, 84–6, 158, 166–8; and Olympic Project for Human Rights 67–9

celebrity *see* black celebrity
Chang, Jeff 145
Chicago Defender 14, 178; coverage of Eartha Kitt 56–9; coverage of 1968 Olympic dissent 80–4; coverage of Paul Robeson at Peekskill 33–8; coverage of Kanye West 152–4, 156; unique critiques of black celebrity in 33, 57, 81, 153
Chicago Tribune 14, 178; coverage of Eartha Kitt 48, 52–3, coverage of 1968 Olympic dissent 71–3, 75–8, coverage of Paul Robeson at Peekskill 26–7, 31–3; coverage of Kanye West 148–50
Christian, Margena 154, 156
Chuck D *see* Public Enemy
CIA (Central Intelligence Agency) 22, 62
citizenship: and Mahmoud Abdul-Rauf 120, 127–8, 131, 168; and Muhammad Ali 10; and Eartha Kitt 59–60; and race 2, 77, 169; and Paul Robeson 40, 134; and Tommie Smith and John Carlos 77, 126
Civil Rights Act 45, 61, 69, 128
Civil Rights Congress 22, 28, 41n16
civil rights generation 95, 145
civil rights movement 12, 45, 49; media framing of 45–6, 48
Clay, Cassius *see* Muhammad Ali
Cleaver, Jim 107
Clemmons, Montoya 129–30
Clinton, Bill: campaign strategy of 100–2, 105–6, 109; and Jesse Jackson 100–2, 104–5, 108; and Sister Souljah 93–9, 103–7, 109
Cockburn, Alexander 102
Cohen, Richard 96–8, 102
Cold War 13, 21, 73
colorblind ideology *see* enlightened racism and neoliberalism
Color of Change 144
Communism 21–2, 24, 76; framing of 27–31; and racial politics 21–3, 27–9, 37; anti-Communist sentiment *see* McCarthyism
Communist Party *see* Communism
Condon, David 76
Congress of World Partisans for Peace 20
constitutional rights: as frame for understanding dissent 24–5, 59,

123, 134; freedom of assembly 25; freedom of expression 58–9, 126–9, 132–3; religious freedom 123, 126–8, 132
The Cosby Show 91
Cossell, Howard 11, 69
counterpublics *see* public sphere
Cuba 73
culture wars 94, 144

Daley, Arthur 72, 74, 76
Davis, Jr., Benjamin J. 23
Davis, George R. 54
Deford, Frank 123
Democratic Party 100–2, 105; 1968 Democratic National Convention protests 69
Denver Post 14, 178; and Mahmoud Abdul-Rauf 118–19, 121–6
Denver Urban Spectrum 129
Dewey, Thomas E. 25, 30, 38
Diamos, Jason 120
disaster capitalism 150; *see also* neoliberalism
dissent: contemporary retellings of 11, 62, 67, 86, 109, 120–2; frames of 3, 134, 158; and space/location 12–13, 49, 58, 61–2, 70, 151, 165, 168; and technology 172; *see also* Facebook, Twitter, and YouTube
Dixiecrats 21
Dorinson, Joseph 22, 40
Duberman, Martin 23
Dukakis, Michael S. 101
Duke, David 93, 107
Dyson, Michael Eric 154

Ebony 14; and avoidance of racial controversy 19n56
Edsall, Thomas B. 101
Edwards, Harry 67–8
Ellis, LaPhonso 130
Emmy Awards 148
enlightened racism 4, 5, 13, 77, 91, 99, 109, 120–1, 124, 144; *see also* neoliberalism as racial ideology
ESPN 86
Essence 14
Evans, Lee 67–8, 73, 76, 80

Facebook 172
Fanelli, George M. 30, 38
Farrakhan, Louis 119, 132; *see also* Nation of Islam
Fast, Howard 23, 36
FBI (Federal Bureau of Investigation) 62
FEMA (Federal Emergency Management Agency) 143
First Amendment *see* constitutional rights
Fitzgerald, Ella 53
Foreman, George 76
framing 1–3, 8; of 1968 Olympic Protests 69, 70–85; of Mahmoud Abdul-Rauf 122–33; of Hurricane Katrina 142–4; of Eartha Kitt 50–9; and ideology 2, 5, 9; of inequality 85, 122–4, 132, 143–4, 146, 149–51, 156–7, 159, 166–7, 170; of Islam 119–20, 127–8, 129–31, 133; and journalism 2, 165; of Peekskill riots 27–33, 35–9; and politics 2, 8, 100–2; and public sphere(s) 7–8; and race 3, 5, 165–6; of Sister Souljah 96–108; and trends regarding black celebrity dissent 166–71; of Kanye West 142, 147–58
Freedman's Bureau 156
Freedom's Journal 7, 83, 170
Freeman, Ron 80
Frei, Terry 121, 125
Fresh, Doug E. 94
Fulwood III, Sam 100

Gamoudi, Mohammed 81
Garvey, Marcus 132
George, Nelson 91
Gilliam, Dorothy 102
Gordon, Bruce 156
Gray, Herman 9
Great Depression 156
Greene, Charlie 80
Griffin, Booker 78, 80
Griffin, John G. 80
Gulf War 119

Haber, Joyce 53
Habermas, Jürgen: and public sphere theory 6
Haggins, Bambi 60
Hall, John 9, 76, 78
Hall, Stuart 2; conjectural analysis 16
Hancock, Dean Gordon B. 37
Hartmann, Douglas 72
Heisler, Mark 128
Helem, John A. 82–3
Hilburn, Robert 147

Hill, Urla 75, 78
Hine, Jim 80
hip hop 13, 94–6, 108, 144; commodification of 144–5, 147, 154, 158–9; community-based debates about 95–6; as dissent/counterdiscourse 95–6, 145, 154–6, 159; evolution of narratives about 144–6, 159; mainstream framing of 95, 99, 108–9, 159; sampling in 148
hip hop generation 94, 95, 145, 169
historical amnesia 11, 120–22
Hitler, Adolf: comparisons of black dissent to 10, 75
Hoberman, John 4, 125
Hochman, Steve 147–8
Hodges, Jim 119, 121
Horton, Willie 91, 109
HUAC (House Un-American Activities Committee) 21, 28
Hughes, Elizabeth 52, 61
Hughes, Langston 34, 36
Hurricane Katrina 13, 118, 140–1; criticisms of response to 142–3; media framing of 143–4

Ice Cube 111n19
Ice-T 102, 107, 111n19
inequality 45, 61, 140; coverage of in African American press frames 132, 156–7, 166–7, 170; coverage of in mainstream press frames 85, 122–3 124, 143–4, 146, 149–51, 159; evolution of 4; links to unrest 45, 61; in sports 82–3
Ifill, Gwen 101
internationalism 21, 70, 80–1
IOC (International Olympic Committee) 68, 72, 85
Iraq War 142, 144
Ishiwata, Eric 157
Islam: and Mahmoud Abdul-Rauf 116, 119–20, 125, 129–31; racialization of 119
Islamophobia 118–20, 127–8, 133; and Mahmoud Abdul-Rauf 118

Jackson, Chris Wayne *see* Mahmoud Abdul-Rauf
Jackson, Jesse 93, 96, 104–6, 169; and Democratic Politics 100–2
Jackson, Ronald 4
Jacobs, Ronald 8, 92

James, Larry 80
James, LeBron 171
Jet (magazine) 14, 178; coverage of Sister Souljah 105; coverage of Kanye West 154–6
Johnson, Cedric 142
Johnson, John H. 19n56
Johnson, Lady Bird 46, 50–3, 57, 61
Johnson, Lyndon B. 46–7, 61
Johnson, Robert (D.A.) 132
Jones, David R. 106
Jordan, Michael 91, 171
journalism *see* African American press and mainstream press
Juvenile (rapper) 155

Kennedy, Jr. John F. 63n8
Kennedy, Robert F. 11, 69–70, 87n13
Kerner Commission 46
Kimmel, Jimmy 160
King, Jr., Martin Luther 11, 13, 28, 48–9, 63n19, 132; assassination of 69–70; mainstream framing of 42n35, 48–9, 121; and Olympic Project for Human Rights 68
King, Rodney 13, 92, 95, 98, 100, 102, 108
Kish, Zenia 155
Kiszla, Mark 121, 123, 124, 127
Kitt, Eartha 13, 46, 82, 108, 146, 150; in African American press 55–9, 60–2, 158, 167; African American skepticism toward 56; backlash against 48, 62; as Catwoman 49; celebrity status of 49–50, 56–7; civil rights work 55, 65n50; gendering of 49–55, 59, 62, 168; in mainstream press 50–4, 59–61, 167–8; and multiracial identity 49, 53, 60; relationships 50
Klein, Joe 101
Kramer, Michael 102
Ku Klux Klan 29, 35–6, 133, 156; comparisons of black dissent to 10, 75, 93, 98–9

LAPD (Los Angeles Police Department) 92
Lauer, Matt 140
Lauter, David 101
Legendary K.O. 147, 148–9
Life (magazine) 72
Lipsitz, George 98

Lipsyte, Robert: sympathetic coverage of black dissent 11, 71, 78, 121, 128
Live 8 155
Los Angeles Sentinel 14, 178; coverage of Mahmoud Abdul-Rauf 130–2; coverage of Eartha Kitt 56–8, 61; coverage of 1968 Olympic dissent 77, 78–81, 86; coverage of Paul Robeson at Peekskill 35–7; coverage of Sister Souljah 103–7; coverage of Kanye West 153, 156–7
Los Angeles Times 14, 178; coverage of Mahmoud Abdul-Rauf 119, 121, 123–5, 127, 128–9; coverage of Eartha Kitt 51, 53; coverage of 1968 Olympic dissent 71–8; coverage of Paul Robeson at Peekskill 27–8, 31–32, 39; coverage of Sister Souljah 95, 97–102; coverage of Kanye West 147–8, 150–1
Love, David Andrew 132
Lucas, Bob 57
lynching 28, 33, 95, 99; African American narratives of 26, 37, 156; symbolic 4

Maher, Charles 71, 74
mainstream press 1, 7; conventions of 26, 54, 71, 92, 94, 109, 122–3, 147–8, 158; coverage of inequality in 85, 122–3 124, 143–4, 146, 149–51, 159; framing trends re black celebrity dissent 166–71; history of 7–8; integration of 71, 85, 109, 115n104, 170; inclusion of alternative narratives 8, 71, 122, 128–9, 134–5; paternalism in 122
Malamud, Allan 123
Marable, Manning 40, 91
Martel, Ned 150
Martin, Trayvon 171–2
McCain, John 175n10
McCarthy, Coleman 97
McCarthyism 21, 22, 28, 40
McGrory, Mary 101
McVeigh, Timothy 119
Metcalfe, Ralph 73
Mexico City Olympic Games *see* Tommie Smith and John Carlos
Meyers, Mike 141

Million Man March 119
Milloy, Courtland 95
Mills, David: interview with Sister Souljah 92–3, 95
modern racism *see* enlightened racism
Mondale, Walter S. 101
Muhammad, James 152, 156
multiracial identity 49–50; *see also* Eartha Kitt
Murray, Jim 74–5
Muslims *see* Islam
MTV 145, 148

NAACP (National Association for the Advancement of Colored People) 71, 156; Image Awards 172–3
National Newspaper Publishers Association 104–5, 114n77
The Nation 62
Nation of Islam 10, 119
Nazism: African American narratives of 37, 107; comparisons of black dissent to 75
NBA (National Basketball Association) 116–17, 121–3; rules of 117, 128
NBC 140–1, 145, 150, 173
Neal, Mark Anthony 91, 159
Nelly (rapper) 148
Negro Digest 14
Nelson, Jack 97
neoliberalism 123, 140, 142–3, 149–51, 157; in the African American press 153, 158; and economics 126, 143, 150–1; in the mainstream press 123–6, 158; as racial ideology 124, 144–7, 149–50, 160
Newkirk, Pamela 7, 115n104
Newmar, Julie 63n22
Newsweek (magazine) 27, 178; coverage of Mahmoud Abdul Rauf 123; coverage of Eartha Kitt 53; coverage of 1968 Olympic dissent 73–4; coverage of Sister Souljah 101; coverage of Kanye West 146
New York Amsterdam News 14, 178; coverage of Mahmoud Abdul-Rauf 131; coverage of Eartha Kitt 56–8, 61; coverage of 1968 Olympic dissent 80–3, 86; coverage of Paul Robeson at Peekskill 24–6, 34–8; coverage

204 *Index*

of Sister Souljah 93, 102–8; coverage of Kanye West 154–5
The New York Times 14, 178; coverage of Mahmoud Abdul-Rauf 119–21, 123, 127–9; coverage of Muhammad Ali 11, coverage of Eartha Kitt 52, 54; coverage of 1968 Olympic dissent 71–2, 74, 76, 78; coverage of Paul Robeson at Peekskill 24–7, 30–1; coverage of Sister Souljah 96–9, 101–2; coverage of Kanye West 148, 150, 159
NFL 141, 150
Nichols, John 62
Nigatu, Heben 159
Norman, Peter 73, 75, 88n31
NSA (National Security Agency) 62

Obama, Barack 109, 171; celebrity status of 175n10; Obama Era 14, 171
Ogden, David C. 86
Oklahoma City bombing 119
Olajuwan, Hakeem 120
Olympic Project for Human Rights 67–8, 73, 76; boycott movement 68, 72
Olympics, 1936 72
Olympics, 1968 *see* Tommie Smith and John Carlos
Omi, Michael 3
Operation Save Us 153
Owens, Jesse 72–3

Paige, Woody 122–3, 125–6
Pareles, John 96, 102
Paris (rapper) 94
Payne, Ethel L. 56
Peabody, Alvin 104
Peden, Katherine: criticism of Eartha Kitt 54; work on Kerner Commission 46
Peekskill Evening Star 22
Peekskill, NY *see* Paul Robeson
Pencak, William 22, 40
Perry, Imani 144
Phillips, Joseph C. 153
Pittsburgh Courier 14, 178; coverage of Eartha Kitt 55–7, 61
political ideologies: and charity 149–52, 158; and framing 2, 165–6; and race 4, 14, 22, 69, 91–2, 100, 102–3, 105–6, 109, 165–6; and sport 71–4, 83, 158, 166
Poitier, Sidney 53
police brutality 47, 92, 107; and 1968 Democratic National Convention 69; and Peekskill riots 23, 37–8; and post-Hurricane Katrina 142–3; 160n5
Pound, Ezra 36
President's Commission on Civil Disorders *see* Kerner Commission
press *see* African American press and mainstream press
protest *see* dissent
Pryce, Vinette 103–4
Public Enemy (rap group) 94, 163n62
public sphere 6; and celebrities 8–9, 165; and counterpublics 6–8, 169–70; and media 6; and technology 172; in twenty-first century 170–1
Pye, Brad Jr. 81

Quayle, Dan 102, 107, 111n19
Questlove (musician) *see* Ahmir Thompson
Quindlen, Anna 96

racial belief systems: contemporary narratives 122–3; and framing 3, 165–6; and gender 49–50, 53, 60, 81, 90n79; and inequality 4; public attitudes 3–5, 20, 28, 36 45, 69, 86, 91–2, 109, 151; and religion 118–20, 123, 133; and sport 4, 71–4, 82–3, 124–5, 166; stereotypes of 3–4, 21 49–50, 74, 91, 124, 1; and victimhood 27, 33, 51, 92, 99, 143–4, 154; and violence 24, 26, 28–9, 35–7, 92, 95, 99, 143; 43; and World War II 4, 5, 21–3, 28, 37, 44n81; *see also* enlightened racism
Rainbow Coalition 93, 101, 104–6; Rebuild America initiative 107
rap music *see* Hip hop
Reagan, Ronald 105, 109; Reaganism 91, 158
Reese, Stephen 2
Reverend Run *see* Joseph Simmons

reverse racism: and colorblind rhetoric 99, 109; as a frame for black dissent 75–6, 85, 97–100
Reyes, Damaso 154–5
Rhodes, Jane 9, 76
Rivera, Dennis 104
Robeson, Paul 13, 20, 59, 70, 109, 120, 132; in African American press 33–9, 158, 167; backlash against 21–3, 40, 45; and Harry Belafonte 173; celebrity status of 20–1, 40; and Communism 22, 24, 27–31, 45; intertextuality of 20; and labor 21; in mainstream press 24–33, 39 166–7; and Peekskill riots 22–39; politics of 20–1, 34; relationships 21
Robertson, Linda 143
Robinson, Jackie 33
Rolark, Calvin 105
Roosevelt, Eleanor 30
Rosen, Joel Nathan 86
Rosen, Mike 123
Rosenthal, A.M. 98
Run-DMC 148
Rush, Bobby 156
Rutgers University 20
Rutten, Tim 100

Samad, A. Asadullah 153–4, 156
Sanchez, Robert 118
San Jose State University 67, 86
Schmalz, Jeffrey 99
Seagren, Bob 77
Seeger, Pete 23
Sengstacke, John H. 81
September 11 (2001) 133, 136n21
sexism: in African American press 55, 90n79, 108; in mainstream press 50–4, 108
Shakespeare 20
Sharpton, Al 154
Simmons, Joseph 148
Simmons, Russell 148, 155, 169
Simpson, Kevin 125, 126
Sinclair, Abiola 102–3, 106
slavery 4; legacy of 125, 129, 132
Slate, Allin 86
Smith, Tommie 13, 67, 99, 108, 120–1, 126, 149–50; in African American press 78–86, 158, 167; backlash against 69, 121–2; celebrity of 70; in mainstream press 70–78, 84–86, 158, 166–7; and Olympic Project for Human Rights 67–9
Souljah, Sister 13, 92, 134; activism of 96, 103; in African American press 102–8; celebrity of 94–6, 108; and gender 108; in mainstream press 96–102, 108, 158, 166; usage of "Sister Souljah moment" 109; and *Washington Post* interview 92–5
South Africa: contention over inclusion in 1968 Olympics 68, 73, 80
Southern Christian Leadership Conference 49
Soviet Union 21, 34, 73
Squires, Catherine 7, 11n28, 164n77
Stammer, Larry B. 119, 121
Star-Spangled Banner: and Mahmoud Abdul Rauf 116
Steinfels, Peter 128
Stevens, Thaddeus 23
Stewart, Jeffery C. 20
Streeter, Caroline A. 49

Temu, Neftali 81
Tenner, Jack 80, 83, 86
Terrorism: Oklahoma City bombing 119; September 11, 2001 133, 136n21
Thompson, Ahmir 172
Time (magazine) 14, 178; coverage of 1968 Olympic dissent 73; coverage of Paul Robeson at Peekskill 27–8; coverage of Sister Souljah 98, 101–2; coverage of Kanye West 141, 144, 149
Tonkovich, Andrew 129
tragic mullata *see* Eartha Kitt and multiracial identity
Tubman, Harriet 23
Twitter 172
Tyus, Wyomia 80, 90n71

Usher (singer) 148
USOC (United States Olympic Committee): press critiques of 72, 85; segregation in 68; statements re 1968 Olympic dissent

Vietnam War: dissent against 10–11, 13, 47–48, 59 69–70, 121
VISTA 46, 63n8

Walker Esther 103
Walwik, Joseph 26
War on Drugs 91
War on Poverty 61
Washington Informer 14, 178; coverage of Sister Souljah 103–4, 107
The Washington Post 14, 178; coverage of Eartha Kitt 54, 60; coverage of Sister Souljah 92, 94–8, 101–2; For and About Women section 51–2
Waters, Maxine (congresswoman) 154
Welles, Orson 50
We Shall Not Be Moved (song) 27–28
West, Cornel 155
West, Kanye 13, 140; in African American press 152–7, 167; and George W. Bush 140, 142; celebrity of 140–1, 144–6, 159–60; censoring of 145, 150; *The College Dropout* 145; A Concert for Hurricane Relief 141, 145; and Hurricane Katrina 140–3; *Late Registration* 140, 145; in mainstream press 146–52, 159, 166–9; support from other celebrities 148
welfare: conservative narratives of 109, 153, 158

White, Jack 98
white supremacy 92, 132, 134,
Wiggins, Lillian 103, 107
Wilkins, Roy 71, 85
Williamson, Lisa *see* Sister Souljah
Wilson, Jr. Clint 77, 78–9
Wilson, Gertrude 81, 83, 86
Winant, Howard 3–5, 91
Wolde, Mamo 81
womanhood: racialization of 50, 53, 60, 168
Women's International League of Peace and Freedom 47
Wright, Jeremiah 109
Wright, Stan 71, 73, 85
WWI 28
WWII 28; and Double-V campaign 44n81; and racial ideology 4, 19n65

X, Malcolm 132

Yoshino, Kenji: covering 127
Young, John 121, 126
YouTube 148, 175n18

Zibart, Eve 95, 98